CRITIQUE

Review of the
U.S. Department of State's
Country Reports on
Human Rights Practices
for 1995

Lawyers Committee for Human Rights
July 1996

Lawyers Committee for Human Rights

Since 1978 the Lawyers Committee for Human Rights has worked to promote international human rights and refugee law and legal procedures in the United States and abroad. The Chairman of the Lawyers Committee is Norman Dorsen; Michael H. Posner is its Executive Director. Stefanie Grant is Director of Program and Policy. George Black is Research and Editorial Director.

Copies of this report are available from:

Lawyers Committee for Human Rights
330 Seventh Avenue
New York, New York 10001 USA
tel: (212) 629-6170
fax: (212) 967-0916
e-mail: comm@lchr.org

100 Maryland Avenue, NE
Suite 502
Washington, D.C. 20002
tel: (202) 547-5692
fax: (202) 543-5999
e-mail: wdc@lchr.org

ISBN: 0-934143-82-X

Distributed by the University of Pennsylvania Press

Table of Contents

Acknowledgments

This report is a critique of the U.S. State Department's *Country Reports on Human Rights Practices for 1995*. We have selected to review reports on 27 countries and territories that our staff and volunteers monitored closely throughout the year. The absence of a country from this volume does not imply that it had no human rights problems during 1995, or that the State Department's description of those problems was flawless. This is the seventeenth year that the Lawyers Committee has prepared a critique of the *Country Reports.*

This year's *Critique* was prepared by the Committee's staff and volunteers. The volunteers included: Dr. Khaled Abou el Fadl, Adrian Armanini, Suzanne Berman, Joseph P. Berra, Mark Bromley, Michael C. Davis, Elliott Dawes, Joseph J. Dyer, Matt Easton, K.S. Venkat Eswaran, Tracey K. Friedlander, Maria Estela Garcia, Sarah Graham-Brown, Lisa Halustick, Angela Hegarty, Peter Juviler, Elizabeth B. Lin, Joseph E. Lowry, Jessica Montell, Mark Muschenheim, Therese Nelson, David Rivela, Raúl M. Sanchez, Monica Schurtman, Adam Shayne, Kathryn R. Stokes, Tamara L. Tompkins, Eric Tuchmann, Greg Tzeutschler, Peter Verney, Jonathan Werther and Betsy Witten.

Other expert assistance in this effort was provided by Mike Amitay, Nikola Barović, Fanny Benedetti, Barbara Davis, Martin Flaherty, Jean Herskovits, Sidney Jones, Richard Knight, Leah Leatherbee, David Lubitz, Joyce Mends Cole, Saša Milošević, D. Paul O'Brien, Anselm Chidi Odinkalu, Charlotte Oldham-Moore, Srdja Popovic, Joe Stork and Daniel Woubishet.

Preparation of the *Critique* would not have been possible without information produced by other human rights and legal organizations and law firms, both international and locally-based. These groups include:

- The Africa Fund
- Amnesty International
- al-Haq
- American Association for the Advancement of Science
- Andean Commission of Jurists (Peru)
- Antiwar Campaign of Croatia
- Arab Association for Human Rights (Israel)
- Article 19
- Association of the Bar of the City of New York
- Ballard Spahr Andrews & Ingersoll

Critique 1995

- Belarusian League for Human Rights
- Catholic Justice and Peace Commission (Liberia)
- CEJIL
- Center for Antiwar Action (Belgrade)
- Center for Human Rights Legal Aid (Egypt)
- Centro de Derechos Humanos "Fray Bartolomé de las Casas" (CDH-FBLC)
- Centro de Derechos Humanos Miguel Agustín Pro Juárez A.C.
- Centro de Estudios Fronterizo para la Promocion de Derechos Humanos
- Civil Liberties Organisation (Nigeria)
- Colombia Support Network
- Colombian Commission of Jurists (Colombia)
- Commission for Justice and Peace (Haiti)
- Committee on the Administration of Justice (Northern Ireland)
- Committee for the Defense of Human Rights (Nigeria)
- Committee to Protect Journalists
- Constitutional Rights Project (Nigeria)
- Croatian Helsinki Committee
- Croatian Law Center
- Dewey Ballantine
- Egyptian Organization for Human Rights
- Guatemala Human Rights Commission/USA
- Helsinki Commission
- Humanitarian Law Center (Belgrade)
- Human Rights Association (Turkey)
- Human Rights Committee (South Africa)
- Human Rights Foundation of Turkey
- Human Rights in China
- the Human Rights Office of the Archdiocese of Guatemala
- Human Rights Watch
- Immigration and Human Rights Clinic of St. Mary's University School of Law
- Indonesian Human Rights Campaign
- Institute of Legal Defense (Peru)
- Inter-American Legal Studies Program, St. Mary's University School of Law
- International Commission of Jurists
- The International Commission of Free Trade Unions
- International Federation of Human Rights
- International Forum on Indonesian Development (INFID)
- International Gay and Lesbian Human Rights Commission
- International Helsinki Federation (Vienna)
- International Human Rights Law Group
- International PEN
- Israeli Information Center for Human Rights in the Occupied Territories (B'Tselem)
- Kenya Human Rights Commission
- Legal Aid Institute of Indonesia

Acknowledgments

- Legal Research and Resource Center for Human Rights (Egypt)
- Legal Resources Center (South Africa)
- Milbank, Tweed, Hadley & McCloy
- Minnesota Advocates for Human Rights
- National Association of Democratic Lawyers (Nigeria)
- National Coalition for Haitian Rights
- National Land Committee (South Africa)
- National Network of Non-Governmental Human Rights Organizations (Mexico)
- Palestinian Center for Human Rights
- Physicians for Human Rights
- Russian Lawyers Committee in Defence of Human Rights
- Serbian Democratic Forum
- Serbian Helsinki Committee
- Seyfarth, Shaw, Fairweather & Geraldson
- Sudan Human Rights Organization (Cairo and London)
- Sudan Update
- Union of Indigenous Communities of the Northern Zone of the Isthmus - UCIZONI (Mexico)
- Washington Office on Latin America
- U.S. Committee for Refugees
- Weil Gotshal & Manges LLP
- World Organization Against Torture

We are grateful to them all.

Responsibility for all facts and opinions stated in this *Critique* is solely the Lawyers Committee's.

Lawyers Committee staff members who contributed to this effort were Patricia Armstrong, Stefanie Grant, Mireille Hector, Neil Hicks, Antti Korkeakivi, Emma Naughton, Jelena Pejic, Michael Posner, Elissa Steglich and Robert O. Weiner. Leslie Conner acted as the principal liaison with outside volunteers, provided extensive editorial assistance and oversaw production.

The *Critique* was edited by George Black, research and editorial director of the Lawyers Committee.

Lawyers Committee for Human Rights
July 1996
New York, New York

iii

Introduction

Since the Lawyers Committee began publication of its annual *Critique* of the State Department's *Country Reports on Human Rights Practices*, those reports have become a progressively more thorough and reliable guide to human rights conditions throughout the world. The reports aim to provide what the State Department calls "a resource for shaping policy, conducting diplomacy, and making assistance, training, and other resource allocations." In many respects they do that job admirably. At the same time, they have become an ever more useful resource to the international non-governmental human rights community.

While the publication of the *Country Reports* is mandated by Congress, their content is dictated by a detailed and formal set of State Department instructions, annually updated and revised and sent to all U.S. embassies. The good news about the 1995 *Country Reports* is that this year's instructions have incorporated a number of valuable revisions, many of which are directly responsive to criticisms made in previous editions of the *Critique*; the bad news is that many of the reports continue to neglect what the instructions say.

In the introduction to the 1994 edition of the *Critique*, we noted with some frustration that the State Department's *Country Reports*, despite years of steady improvement, appeared to have "hit a ceiling, dogged by persistent shortcomings that prevent them from realizing their full potential as a policy resource."

Unfortunately, the 1995 *Country Reports* exhibit many of the same nagging weaknesses as their predecessors. In acknowledgment of the generally improved quality of the reports, the *Critique*, now in its 17th year of publication, has steadily narrowed its focus to a smaller list (27 this year) of countries that raise particular concerns. This list is deliberately heterogeneous: it is made up of countries where serious human rights violations are occurring; of significant international powers whose conduct is of particular interest; of key U.S. allies where ulterior political considerations may compromise the integrity of the human rights reporting; and of others where past deficiencies in the *Country Reports* suggest that continued scrutiny is useful. Between them, we believe that these 27 countries are a representative sampling of the *Country Reports*, and are sufficient to allow us to arrive at valid general conclusions about the reports' strengths and weaknesses.

The strengths, we repeat, are very considerable. The State Department's Bureau of Democracy, Human Rights and Labor (DRL) takes its mandate very seriously. The overt political biases that marred much of the State Department's reporting on human rights in the 1980s have largely disappeared along with the bipolar conflict that engendered them. Much of the information contained in the *Country Reports* is admirably detailed. The sources employed by the drafters are visibly more diverse with each new edition of the *Country Reports*. In particular, the reports show welcome evidence that embassy officers are conferring closely with local independent human rights monitors and taking their findings seriously.

Yet a number of stubborn problems remain. And they remain despite further revisions to the instructions which the DRL circulates to embassies each summer to shape the following year's *Country Reports*. The latest revisions are nowhere near as substantive as those which emerged from the comprehensive review of State Department procedures initiated by Secretary of State Warren Christopher in 1993. Those revisions made a number of sweeping, and largely positive, changes to the scope of the *Country Reports*, including an entire new section on discrimination based on race, sex, religion, disability, language and social status, and a demand that drafters should take into account the views and standing of local human rights monitors. But the latest round of revisions, while more modest, continues to make the reporting requirements both more explicit and more exigent.

These new instructions are a generally successful exercise in reconciling two different and at times contradictory agendas. On one hand, they reflect the DRL's continued effort to oblige embassies to provide accurate and detailed reporting; on the other, they seek to reduce the workload of beleaguered diplomatic posts and to respond to the intense pressure from the legislative branch to cut back on State Department resources. The clear, practical instructions that have emerged from this process contain many improvements. For example, there is now an explicit requirement for each thematic section of the

Introduction

reports to open with a summary statement of the extent of the legal and constitutional protections for the right under discussion, accompanied by a statement of whether these statutory guarantees are respected in practice. There is also a consistent encouragement of standard language to characterize the U.S. government's position on particular categories of abuses. This approach is helpful in discouraging evasiveness and encouraging the kind of categorical statements that have sometimes been lacking in the past

The new reporting instructions show a welcome and consistent emphasis on government accountability and enforcement mechanisms, and on the proactive as well as the remedial measures needed to make paper rights a reality. They also require the drafters of the *Country Reports* to tackle head-on the problem of impunity, which continues to bedevil a number of societies emerging from one-party or military governments that were characterized by massive human rights violations. Other positive improvements in the reporting instructions deal with:

- The need to monitor progress in ongoing investigations into past extrajudicial executions;
- The circumstances of prisoners held in pre-trial and incommunicado detention;
- Governmental attitudes toward human rights investigations by international as well as national non-governmental organizations (NGOs);
- Tougher new affirmative requirements, in discussing discrimination, for reporting on incitement of violence by non-governmental actors and "societal violence against gay men" (although only men);
- New requirements on enforcement in cases of domestic violence; governmental programs and other initiatives to ensure women's legal rights; and the activities of organized women's groups;
- The need to detect patterns of gender-based violations such as the rape and physical abuse of women in detention, or of refugee women; and

- More precise and comprehensive language on indigenous rights and the rights of religious minorities.

The overall effect of these changes is very positive. At the same time, by significantly raising the standards for drafters, and by explicitly removing some of the loopholes and imprecisions that they have sometimes been able to exploit, the instructions have also raised the threshold expectations of this *Critique*. However, despite the rigor of these instructions, and their manifestly good intentions, the results continue to fall short in key areas.

A number of the Lawyers Committee's concerns about the quality of the *Country Reports* echo those we have stated in previous years. Specifically:

1. The Country Reports remain unwilling at times to hold "friendly" governments overtly responsible for human rights violations. This deficiency takes a number of forms: in some cases reports decline to offer opinions about official culpability in the State Department's own voice, even where the factual evidence is inescapable; in other cases they cloud the issue of state responsibility by ascribing violations to individual members or "rogue elements" of the security forces, as if these entities were not accountable to the government as a whole.

The instructions could not be more explicit on the need for violations to be condemned in the State Department's own voice, stressing that: "We have an obligation to render an opinion on whether reports of a pattern of abuse are credible and who appears to be responsible. Thus, it is not/not sufficient to say 'human rights monitors claim that security forces have been involved in political killings' or 'there are occasional reports of police abuse of detainees or prisoners.' Wherever possible, we must state whether we believe such abuses occurred and, if so, who was responsible."

However, the language of many of the reports continues to be muted by the use of the passive voice, and many governments are still shielded from the full force of criticism by the reports' reluctance to offer a clear opinion on the credibility of findings by NGOs. The reports on Indonesia

Introduction

and Egypt, for example, through a pattern of understatement, omission and misleading language, give a more favorable impression of the human rights records of those governments than the facts warrant.

Meanwhile, as in past years, the report on the Israeli Occupied Territories declines to say directly that the Israeli government is responsible for torture — even though all the available facts support that conclusion. Regrettably, the report is no less forthright in its discussion of deaths in custody under the Palestinian Authority (PA), where there has also been clear evidence of torture. In discussing the conduct of the PA's State Security Court, the report again conceals its own views, preferring to cite the criticisms of local and international human rights groups that this court violates international norms of fair trial and judicial independence. Indeed, the United States has specifically encouraged the PA in these unfair proceedings, with Vice President Al Gore praising the State Security Court and the sentences it has imposed on violent opponents of the peace process. These weaknesses in the report on the Israeli Occupied Territories suggest that international human rights norms can be compromised when larger political goals are at stake.

A number of reports continue to be plagued by the tendency to ascribe responsibility for violations to individual members of the security forces. Thus, "some members of the security forces committed serious human rights abuses" in Egypt; "despite protective efforts by the Government, Indians were frequently the victims of violence throughout the year by the government security forces"; "Russian military forces" were responsible for human rights violations in Chechnya, with no mention of the role of President Boris Yeltsin and his inner circle of "power ministers." This perennial defect can only be rectified if the State Department instructs its embassies unequivocally that there is no distinction between violations committed by the state and those committed by the security forces, and that obfuscation of this point is unacceptable in any of the *Country Reports*.

2. Governments and non-governmental entities are not held to a single universal standard of conduct, nor are conclusions about their responsibility for violations subjected to the same burden of proof.

Critique 1995

Here again, the State Department's explicit instructions to drafters of the *Country Reports* are frequently ignored. The instructions say that: "Obviously, the standard of evidence applied should be consistent. For example, we must not apply a standard of 'proof beyond a reasonable doubt' when evaluating allegations of abuses by friendly governments and at the same time apply a more lenient prima facie test to allegations of abuse committed by guerrilla or other opposition forces." Yet this is precisely what continues to happen.

As in past years, the portion of the report on the United Kingdom dealing with Northern Ireland provides a classic illustration of the problem. Violations by paramilitaries are invariably presented as hard fact; violations by the (friendly) state are presented as "claims," "allegations" or "reports." The same holds true for Colombia, Egypt and a number of other countries engaged in violent domestic conflicts.

The double standard is especially blatant in reports that must deal with the perennially thorny problem of political Islam. The discussion of political Islam in Saudi Arabia, for example, a strategic military ally, entangles itself in a web of double standards. Here and in other Middle Eastern countries, the treatment of human rights abuses by and against Islamic governments and political movements appears to be heavily colored by their attitude toward the Middle East peace process. Thus, just as Palestinian courts are applauded by the Clinton Administration for abandoning due process guarantees in trying Islamist radicals, so the report on Saudi Arabia explicitly invokes the opposition to the peace process of the Committee for the Defense of Legitimate Rights (CDLR), the country's first independent human rights organization — as if this somehow justified the Saudi government's abuses against the group. The report resorts to invective and innuendo to attack the CDLR for its alleged extremism, while using much more neutral language to describe the Saudi government, which commits a wide range of serious human rights violations, including torture, arbitrary arrest and wholesale discrimination against women, in the name of Islam. The principal distinction between these two forms of conservative Islam appears to be that one supports U.S. foreign policy goals in the Middle East and the other does not.

Introduction

While our criticisms in the two areas discussed above remain essentially constant from year to year, and have often been raised in this *Critique*, in other respects the quality of the 1995 *Country Reports* seems actually to have declined. Among the areas to which the State Department needs to give special attention in 1996 are the following:

3. Drafters of the Country Reports should make a much more energetic effort to reflect the findings of the U.N. treaty bodies and other U.N. mechanisms, and generally should be more attentive to governments' international human rights treaty obligations.

The State Department instructions require drafters to "pay special attention to reports by the various U.N. human rights mechanisms," although it adds, somewhat gratuitously, that these "may not be of uniform quality." Compliance with this instruction has always been spotty, and the 1995 *Country Reports* are particularly slipshod in this regard. To cite just a few examples:

- The State Department should pay closer attention to the findings of UN treaty bodies. For example, the report on Hong Kong should have paid attention to the U.N. Human Rights Committee's serious expressions of concern in 1995 about the continued application of the International Covenant on Civil and Political Rights (ICCPR) to Hong Kong after the transfer of sovereignty in 1997; and the report on Guatemala should have discussed the highly critical findings of the U.N. Committee on the Elimination of Racial Discrimination.
- In a number of cases, the reports neglect important developments related to Special Rapporteurs appointed by the U.N. Human Rights Commission. The reports ignore, for example, India's continued refusal to allow visits by the Special Rapporteurs on Extrajudicial Executions and Torture; requests by High Commissioner for Human Rights José Ayala Lasso for the

Indonesian government to implement the recommendations of the same two Special Rapporteurs; and the refusal of the Saudi Arabian government to cooperate with the Special Rapporteur on Torture who found that certain forms of corporal punishment allowed under Saudi law amounted to torture. A discussion of the Saudi case would also have allowed the State Department to shed light on that government's refusal to acknowledge universally applicable human rights standards.

- The *Country Reports* continue to neglect the central importance of treaty obligations in assessing a country's human rights performance. The report on Indonesia ignores the campaign by NGOs and others to have the Indonesian government ratify the Convention Against Torture and Other Cruel, Inhuman or Degrading Treatment or Punishment, which it signed some years ago. Similarly, the report on South Africa ignores that country's obligations under the Convention on the Elimination of All Forms of Discrimination Against Women (CEDAW) and the Convention on the Rights of the Child.

In general, it might be helpful for the State Department to strengthen its instructions on U.N. mechanisms, removing the reference to their "uneven quality" and instead reminding drafters that a country's treaty obligations are the fundamental yardstick by which its human rights conduct should be judged, and that U.N. mechanisms — especially the treaty bodies — are a primary, rather than an optional, reference point. In addition, it is important to remember that the treaty bodies have no enforcement powers, and that by highlighting their findings the State Department's *Country Reports* can offer an added means of bringing pressure to bear on governments who fail to comply with their treaty obligations. This insistence on treaty obligations, and the bodies that monitor them, will also have the salutary effect of further sensitizing the U.S. government to the importance of compliance with international norms that are binding on the conduct of the United States as well as the foreign governments on which it passes judgment.

Introduction

4. The section of the Country Reports dealing with the right to a fair trial is not sufficient as it stands to deal with the independence of the judiciary and attacks on the legal profession. Either a separate category or sharper reporting instructions is desirable if the Country Reports are to deal comprehensively with these issues.

Although many of the *Country Reports* offer valuable discussions of due process concerns, they often neglect both larger structural problems related to judicial independence and specific violations directed against judges, prosecutors and defense counsel. The report on Egypt, for example, fails to provide a serious discussion of the escalating trend of harassment and persecution of lawyers, especially those involved in the defense of politically unpopular clients. The report on Guatemala does not see fit to comment on MINUGUA's finding that an average of four prosecutors and 23 judges receive death threats each month — not only a further indication of how the *Country Reports* neglect the work of U.N. bodies, but also a striking illustration of the problem of impunity, which the reports are instructed to examine. And the format of the *Country Reports* does not appear to allow for any discussion of the Sino-British agreement on the constitution of Hong Kong's future Court of Final Appeal, which has been criticized both by the U.N. Human Rights Committee and NGOs including the Lawyers Committee.

5. While the recent focus on governments' conduct toward human rights NGOs is welcome, future reports should deal much more systematically with the law and practice governing freedom of association, especially as it relates to the ability of human rights defenders to operate free of impediments.

The State Department should be applauded for recognizing the growing importance of national human rights NGOs, not merely as a source of factual information but as a key barometer of the general health of a society. The instructions to drafters of the *Country Reports* appropriately call for full discussion of the legal and de facto restrictions that governments impose on associations, including human rights NGOs. Yet the reports' treatment of freedom of association is generally sketchy, perhaps reflecting the fact that this vital right is not yet widely understood and has been the subject of little commentary and jurisprudence.

In many of the reports, crucial violations of the rights of NGOs are either underplayed or omitted. For instance, the report on Belarus limits itself to stating that the Belarusian Constitution provides for freedom of association; it says nothing about the manifold legal and practical obstacles that the government has placed in the way of the Belarusian League for Human Rights and other NGOs seeking legal registration. Similarly, the reports on Croatia and Egypt, to take just two of many examples, paint an inappropriately benign picture of the environment in which human rights NGOs must operate, and fail to describe the many forms of official harassment with which NGOs have to contend in their day-to-day operations.

6. Once again, the rigid thematic composition of the report presents information in an atomized way that obscures the connections between different categories of human rights abuse, and in the process tends in many instances to obscure the degree of governmental complicity and responsibility.

The 1993 and 1994 editions of the *Critique* discussed at some length the structural impediments imposed by the reports' rigid issue-by-issue format, and suggested that the atomized and disjointed presentation of factual data in so many of the reports could only be corrected by allowing their drafters greater latitude to "join up the dots." In particular, we have suggested the need for a broader narrative essay to serve as the introduction for each country report. This would illuminate the interconnected character of abuses otherwise reported in discrete categories, and would be particularly helpful in uncovering patterns of state responsibility.

Most of the 1995 reports continue to display this weakness, and the most conspicuous offenders — such as Colombia — remain the same as in previous years. The 1995 revisions to the State Department's reporting instructions are not helpful in this regard. True, they encourage clear summary statements of opinion which have often been lacking. But more importantly, they continue to insist on a strict 500-word limit for the introduction to each chapter ("in all but a handful of the most complex reports"), thereby inhibiting the reports' ability to "tell a story."

Ironically, the introduction to one of the 1995 chapters illustrates dramatically how much more effective the *Country Reports* could be if this artificial limit were removed. We refer to the report on Bosnia, which is prefaced by a sweeping synthesis of the main developments of the year, running to some five times the recommended length. This essay sets forth and knits together the principal themes and events that are then echoed and expanded upon in the sections that follow. While an extended introduction of this sort may not be necessary in all cases, the drafting instructions should be revised to encourage such writing as a more general practice rather than a grudging exception.

Although the *Critique* is not competent to comment on the specifics of the editing process, it is hard to dissociate the lengthy and eloquent introduction to the Bosnia report from the strong public stance taken by Assistant Secretary of State Shattuck during the negotiation of the Dayton accords on the need for human rights violators — particularly leading Bosnian Serbs — to be held accountable for their crimes. Here indeed is a case where the report has managed to "join up the dots," and it graces the entire volume.

The lesson that it carries may be a larger one — and one which, despite this example, is much more negative than positive. That is the degree to which, no matter what the reporting instructions may say, the bottom line is defined by political considerations. Clearly the *Country Reports* are not produced in a policy vacuum. After being drafted in the embassy, they pass through a variety of editorial hands within the State Department and are subject to a variety of pressures and competing policy agendas. The results are all too apparent when one reads reports which are internally contradictory, or which shy away from conclusions about government culpability that the evidence compels, or which wilfully ignore the findings of other reputable monitors.

Critique 1995

In the case of Bosnia, human rights considerations were paramount both in the drafting of the Dayton agreements and in the writing of the introduction to the country report. But only the introduction: elsewhere, the Bosnia report shows how other political considerations can intrude. In discussing the attacks on Srebrenica and other "safe havens," for example, the report gives a strikingly accurate and detailed account of Bosnian Serb violations, which precisely mirrors the accounts given by both international human rights NGOs and the U.N. Special Rapporteur. However, on the action or inaction of the international community which was charged with protecting these areas, the report maintains a studied silence — even though the NGOs and the Special Rapporteur were equally eloquent (and accurate) on this point.

The report on Serbia is another notable balancing act, where the politically constraining influence of the Dayton accords is apparent in a different way — this time soft-pedaling direct criticism of President Slobodan Milosevic and distancing his government from abuses committed in Serbia-Montenegro and other parts of the former Yugoslavia. As noted above, the fixation on the parties' fidelity to the "peace process" prevents the *Country Reports* from speaking candidly about the serious human rights violations being committed by both Israel and the Palestinian Authority. And in the case of Turkey, the presence of different authorial voices is apparent, with the editorial cut-and-paste scarcely concealed.

The 1994 edition of the *Critique* made a similar criticism of that year's report on China, and we remarked last year that "the presence of discordant voices" had "come through the editing process intact." The 1995 report on China is a welcome contrast, and shows that the *Country Reports*, to be true to their mandate, need not necessarily conform to the policy considerations of other agencies. However, the thorough, accurate and internally consistent report on China makes the chapter on Hong Kong all the more bewildering. Yet again, with the transfer of sovereignty only a year away, the report inexplicably shies away from any serious discussion of China's negative influence on human rights in the territory. This suggests that the State Department has adopted a conscious, and extremely troubling, "hands off" approach to its human rights reporting obligations in Hong Kong.

There appears to be only one solution to these inconsistencies, and that is to insulate the *Country Reports* from extraneous political pressures. While it would be naive to hope for a purist foreign policy that took into account nothing but a country's human rights performance, it is entirely reasonable to expect that the DRL, the section of the State Department charged with reporting on human rights conditions, should be allowed to do its job free of interference. An objective and unvarnished record of human rights conditions, grounded in a clear understanding of the applicable international law, is of enormous intrinsic value. In the subsequent debates that lead to the formulation of policy, that record must of course contend with other agendas and other interests. But these should come into play when the larger policy discussion begins — and not during the editorial process that produces the *Country Reports*.

The mandate of the *Country Reports* is rooted in the Universal Declaration of Human Rights and in the array of treaties which define specific rights and to which governments have chosen to adhere. Those treaties set forth objective standards, and they call for an objective response. That is precisely what the State Department's rigorous annual instructions to embassies demand. They are, after all, instructions — not informal guidelines or suggestions. The body of international human rights and humanitarian law provides the yardstick by which the State Department can measure and assess a country's compliance with objective norms, much as the Defense Department can measure a country's military expenditures, or the Department of Commerce can assess a country's growth rate or its budget deficit. The message needs to be reinforced at the highest levels of the U.S. administration that compliance with international human rights and humanitarian law is not a negotiable matter. Only then will the State Department's *Country Reports* fulfill the promise that remains tantalizingly out of reach.

BELARUS

The State Department's 1995 report correctly underscores the significant deterioration of the human rights situation in Belarus during the last year. This deterioration is attributable to the authoritarian practices of Belarusian President, Aleksandr Lukashenko, who has exploited the strong powers granted to the executive branch by the Constitution to rule by presidential decree. The tendency of the report, however, to place responsibility for many of the abuses on President Lukashenko without a discussion of the overall social, legal and political environment, obscures the more systemic causes for human rights violations: a Constitution which grants too much power to the executive, a legal system which does not yet provide an appropriate check against abuses of power, vaguely drafted legislation which creates loopholes for abuses, and the fragility of democratic institutions in Belarus.

While the report notes that President Lukashenko "repeatedly ignored limits on the authority of the executive branch," it fails adequately to convey the magnitude and scope of the president's ongoing confrontation with the legislative and judicial branches of government. In 1995, the Constitutional Court ruled several presidential decrees unconstitutional. These included decrees suspending trade unions, eliminating parliamentary immunity for deputies and recalling diplomatic and official passports. Accusing the Constitutional Court of "political intrigues," President Lukashenko declared that he would ignore its decisions and issued formal instructions to executive branch agencies that all presidential decrees must be obeyed. One of the decrees struck down by the Constitutional Court vested the president with the power to determine the salary of the court's chairman. In December 1995, the director of the president's office advised the Chairman of the Constitutional Court, Valerii Tikhinia, to resign voluntarily from his position or face a direct call by the president for his removal. Such external pressure on the Constitutional Court is expressly prohibited by Article 126 of the Belarusian Constitution, and, in response, approximately 125 members of parliament signed a letter to the president protesting his attempt to interfere with the work of the court. In a country lacking a tradition of judicial independence, the president's blatant refusal to submit to the rulings of the nation's highest court for constitutional matters does little to develop respect for the courts among Belarusian citizens and does not bode well for achieving a state based on the rule of law.

President Lukashenko's protracted conflict with the parliament has led to political paralysis and stalled political and economic reforms. However, because the report's description of actions taken by the executive branch against the parliament are scattered throughout its various sections, the report fails to portray the full extent of the president's assault against the legislative branch.

President Lukashenko discouraged voters from participating in the May parliamentary elections, denigrating parliament, and using his domination of the state-owned media to campaign for several referendum questions that were placed before voters at the same time as the elections. The 600,000 Belarusian rubles (about $50) allotted by the government to each candidate for campaign expenses was woefully inadequate. The elections were also put at risk because the government was slow in releasing funds. Aleksandr Abramovich, head of the Central Electoral Commission, appealed publicly to the president several times to release funds so that workers verifying candidates's signatures could be paid. A total of 20 billion Belarusian rubles (about $1.67 million) had been budgeted for the parliamentary elections, while 100 billion Belarusian rubles (about $8.33 million) were spent on World War II victory celebrations that took place just before the elections. In March 1995, President Lukashenko signed a decree calling on local authorities to prevent unauthorized rallies. The decree prevented parties and individuals from organizing large campaign rallies, and the Committee for State Security (KDB) reportedly intimidated candidates and interfered with the elections. President Lukashenko lobbied for a referendum question to be put to the electorate that would have given him the power to dissolve parliament if it "systematically or seriously violates the constitution." On April 11, President Lukashenko put the referendum issue before parliament. In protest, a group of eighteen deputies held a hunger strike the next day on the floor of parliament. As the report notes, Lukashenko ordered the striking deputies removed by the police.

2

Parliament then agreed to put the referendum on the ballot, but as a non-binding one. Later in an interview President Lukashenko defended his actions against the striking deputies, stating that he would act in the same way should the situation be repeated.

The two rounds of voting held on May 14 and May 28 failed to fill two-thirds of the seats necessary to form a new parliament. President Lukashenko refused to work with the old parliament, declaring it illegitimate because it had exceeded its five-year term, despite a ruling by the Constitutional Court that the existing parliament remain the highest legislative body until a new parliament was elected. In the meantime, the president issued a number of decrees aimed at intimidating deputies and interfering with the functioning of the parliament. These included decrees eliminating parliamentary immunity for deputies; recalling diplomatic and official passports; abolishing privileges of all deputies and government officials; amending the state budget (which would reduce funding to the parliament); giving the President the power to set the salaries of senior parliamentary officials (the Law on the Parliament sets the chairman's salary at 95% of the president's); and finally, governing rules on elections to fill the seats left empty in the May elections. The report fails to mention a number of these decrees.

On the eve of the repeat parliamentary elections, which were held in December 1995, President Lukashenko vowed to dissolve the parliament and rule by decree if voter turnout was less than the 50% required by law to make the election valid. As he cast his vote, the president said, "This is the last parliamentary vote in the country for the next five years," adding, "I am not going to waste any more billions of the people's money for some stupid elections ignored by the people." Although the report notes that the December 1995 elections were not held under optimal conditions, it fails to mention that there were instances of intimidation of candidates, including some beatings. However, despite the efforts of the Lukashenko government to disrupt the elections, sufficient voters turned out to seat a new parliament at the beginning of 1996.

The report accurately describes the abusive practices prevailing in Belarusian detention centers and prisons. However, it fails to mention that, according to the Belarusian League for Human Rights, prisoners are often sent to serve their sentences in areas contaminated by the Chernobyl nuclear accident. The report also should have provided some specific examples of police brutality. It could have noted, for example, the beating of member of parliament Vladimir Nester while in police custody in connection with his participation in an unsanctioned Independence Day procession in Minsk on July 27. The report does an accurate job of describing the instances of exceedingly long pre-trial detention (in some cases more than two years) and restrictions on the ability of detainees to consult freely with lawyers.

As in 1994, the 1995 report unfortunately omits any focussed discussion of the Belarusian police and security forces. Belarus is one of the few former Soviet republics which did not liquidate its secret police agency, the KDB. In 1994, President Lukashenko transferred the supervision of the KDB and the Ministry of Internal Affairs from the parliament to his own office. This alarming reorganization has given President Lukashenko a free hand in using the two agencies' forces to suppress internal dissent. In 1995, in an effort to appease the Ministry of Internal Affairs, the president reinstated privileges previously granted to its employees (such as rent subsidies) that had been abolished by an earlier presidential decree.

The report provides a satisfactory account of the government's crackdown on the activities of Belarusian trade unions, although it leaves out some important facts. During the August 21 Minsk metro strike, special police forces not only dispersed strikers but also beat them. In addition to Gennady Bykov and Sergei Antonchik, two other trade union leaders, Nikolai Kanakh and Vladimir Makarchiuk, were also arrested by the police and held incommunicado. Kanakh was sentenced to 10 days administrative arrest, and Makarchiuk to 15. Moreover, in the wake of the Minsk metro strike, government harassment and surveillance of trade unions increased. For example, in early September 1995, the bank account of the Belarusian Independent Trade Union of Miners in the city of Soligorsk, Minsk region, was blocked by the authorities without any explanation. Other trade union activists in the same city were "invited for a talk" at the local KDB offices.

Belarus

In a glaring omission, the report does not discuss the government's restrictions placed upon freedom of association in Belarus, stating only that "the Constitution provides for freedom of association." In October 1994, the parliament passed the Law on Public Associations (*obshchenstvennye organizatsii*) which requires, among other things, that all public associations register with the government. The parliament also adopted a resolution "On Implementing the Law on Public Associations," which mandated that public associations previously registered undergo re-registration with the Ministry of Justice before April 1, 1995. While the language of the resolution would appear to require that the ministry automatically issue new registration certificates to all currently registered public associations, in practice it is using the resolution as an opportunity to disband certain public associations. The ministry is requiring certain public associations to repeat the formalities of holding an organizational meeting, adopting a charter and electing officers before their applications for re-registration will be considered. According to the Belarusian League for Human Rights, as a result of the re-registration requirement, the number of officially registered public associations in Belarus has declined from 700 to 400.

The re-registration procedures mandated by the parliamentary resolution have caused difficulties for the Belarusian League for Human Rights, a non-governmental organization founded in 1992. The League had encountered obstacles when it initially registered with the Ministry of Justice, having to submit its application six times before it was finally accepted. The ministry is now requiring that the League's executive committee adopt a resolution liquidating itself and requesting its removal from the state register. Only then will the ministry accept the League's application to re-register. Furthermore, the ministry has demanded that the League delete a provision of its charter authorizing its members to disseminate information on human rights abuses in Belarus.

While the report does briefly discuss the government's attitude toward non-governmental investigation of alleged violations of human rights, it completely ignores the more fundamental issue of the ability of NGOs to become legally established. This is surprising since the State Department's instructions specifically direct the drafters of the report to address the ease with which public associations may organize and, if required by law, register.

On January 4, 1996, President Lukashenko issued a similar instruction mandating re-registration of all branches of the media, which included all state-owned and independent periodicals published in Belarus and all television and radio companies. This action followed more than a year of harassment of the media and suppression of opposing views by the Lukashenko government. For the most part, the report accurately details the government's interference with the print and broadcast media. As it notes, following a common practice in the former Soviet republics, the government has in place a defamation law which applies identical standards of liability for public and private persons, and uses it to harass and intimidate the media with litigation and the imposition of fines. The participants in the first Belarusian Conference of Publishers of the Independent Press held in March 1996 called for amendments to the existing law on the press and other mass media to protect journalists from a succession of defamation lawsuits brought by government prosecutors on behalf of public officials.

The report states that in December 1994, the Lukashenko government ordered the state printing house to cancel contracts with three leading independent newspapers — *Belorusskaia Delovaia Gazeta*, *Imia* and *Svaboda*. In fact, at least five and perhaps as many as ten newspapers had their printing contracts canceled. Some of these newspapers are now forced to print in neighboring Lithuania. As the report notes, President Lukashenko issued decrees replacing the editors of four leading state-owned newspapers following their attempts to publish excerpts of a speech delivered in parliament on government corruption. According to the Committee to Protect Journalists, Iosif Seredich, the editor of *Narodnaia Gazeta* and a member of parliament, was dismissed by order of President Lukashenko for publishing a letter criticizing the government's pro-Russian policies. The president's decree stated that the letter "incited violence and civil unrest."

In its discussion of press freedom, the report fails to mention a Presidential Decree of October 1995 obliging ministries and other state bodies to disseminate information only through BelTA, the Belarusian state information agency, thereby depriving non-BelTA journalists from obtaining and disseminating information directly from official government sources.

In both the May and December 1995 parliamentary elections, the Lukashenko government virtually eliminated access to the media by opposition candidates. The report states rather vaguely that "[i]n November President Lukashenko attempted to halt broadcasting of television programs featuring candidates for the upcoming parliamentary elections. The candidate [sic] made efforts to obtain air time on other television channels. Some succeeded." According to the Belarusian League for Human Rights, however, no independent candidate was given any broadcast time on television or radio channels of the state-owned Belarusian Television and Radio Company, even though by law the company must provide each candidate access free of charge. At the same time, the state-owned television stations carried programs directed against candidates who opposed Lukashenko's policies. The Chairman of the Parliament, Mechaslav Grib, was forced to resort to the foreign media in order to address Belarusian citizens. Grib's appeal to the public to take part in the parliamentary elections was broadcast by the Belarusian service of both Radio Liberty/Radio Free Europe and the Russian Television and Radio Company. On December 8, a Radio Russia correspondent and one of the candidates, Professor Shushkevich, were denied access to the Belarusian State Radio Complex Studio for an interview with Radio Russia which leases space in the building. Such infringements on access to the media should have been included in the report.

The report also fails to add that the government has interfered with the ability of Belarusian journalists to travel abroad. On December 8, four Belarusian journalists, Pavel Zhuk of *Svaboda*, Nikolai Aleksandrov of *Brestskiy Kurer*, and Alexander Valvachov and Aleksandr Mikhakchuk of *Belorusskaya Gazeta*, were not permitted to leave Belarus to attend an international conference in Prague.

President Lukashenko attempted to extend censorship to the academic sphere by issuing an instruction to the Ministry of Education that it return to using Soviet-era textbooks in Belarusian schools.

(Lukashenko, whose policies are oriented toward reintegration with Russia, has said he believes that the post-Soviet textbooks treated Belarus as "too separate" from Russia). The report states only that Lukashenko "reportedly" signed the instruction. However, after he had denied issuing the instruction, an opposition newspaper published a copy bearing the president's signature.

The report does not provide a complete picture of the status of freedom of religion in Belarus, particularly with respect to the government's policy toward the Roman Catholic Church. Nevertheless, the 1995 report is an improvement over its immediate predecessor, which asserted there was no interference in the practice of Roman Catholicism. Belarus has a significant Roman Catholic population, residing primarily in the western part of the country. In the post-Soviet period, the Roman Catholic Church has relied on an influx of Polish priests to assist in serving reopened parishes. Some government officials are concerned that the Church is being used to promote Polish political and cultural influence among Belarusians. During the last five years, the number of Roman Catholic parishes in Belarus has grown from 103 to 350, but the present government-imposed quota for Roman Catholic priests from Poland is only 50. It is common practice for state-owned newspapers to carry articles complaining about the presence of too many foreign clergy in Belarus. Relations between the Polish Catholic priests and state authorities worsened during 1995, and officials have attempted to expel such priests from Belarus. In one case, a Catholic priest, Father Edward Loeck, who serves in the Shereshevsky parish of the Brest region, was summoned to the official Regional Religious Council and accused of organizing an illegal religious procession because he had failed to get special permission from the local authorities. Father Loeck was threatened with deportation. The incident was resolved only after members of the parish and the procurator's office intervened on the priest's behalf. In December 1995, without explanation, officials of the Belarusian Television and Radio Company shut down the radio broadcast of "Voice of the Soul," a weekly program prepared by Father Vladiislav Zavalnyuk, a Roman Catholic priest.

Belarus

In general, the 1995 State Department report describes many significant events affecting human rights in Belarus. However, it does not provide sufficient analysis of these events that would allow the reader to come away with a fuller understanding of the overall human rights situation. The report's treatment of certain categories of human rights such as freedom of association and freedom of religion is clearly inadequate. Also, the report should have looked more carefully at domestic legislation which has a negative impact on human rights.

BOSNIA AND HERZEGOVINA

In many ways, the State Department's 1995 report on Bosnia and Herzegovina stands out as the best of the four annual reports issued so far on that country. It provides a refreshing example of the potential of the *Country Reports* in general to present a forthright, compelling and well conceived account of the human rights situation in a particular country. The report has three main strengths. First and most important, it is much more tightly organized and better written than the 1994 report. The introduction sets forth key themes and events which the following subsections consistently echo and illustrate. The overall tone and use of language is also much more powerful and evocative, with the result that the Bosnia report almost succeeds in overcoming the perennial problem, common to all the State Department reports, of reading like a disjointed laundry list of unrelated facts. The 1995 Bosnia report actually manages to convey a "story." The themes of that story are brutal and the details are horrific, but that is the sad truth in this devastated piece of the former Yugoslavia, and the drafters of the 1995 report were generally bold and effective in telling it.

A second strength of the report stems from its comprehensiveness. The report identifies most of the important issues and events of 1995 in Bosnia and presents closely detailed accounts of the year's more high-profile military campaigns, such as those waged in Srebrenica in the summer and Banja Luka/Prijedor in the fall. It also presents a more coherent discussion of the phenomenon of ethnic cleansing in its various forms and recognizes several categories of human rights violations which have become more prevalent as the war has gone on. These improvements are directly responsive to criticisms made in last year's *Critique*.

The report's third strength stems from the inclusion of facts and details which suggest that the drafters have read and drawn upon the findings of the United Nations Special Rapporteur and non-governmental human rights organizations. This is a very welcome development, and responds both to specific criticisms made in the Bosnia chapter of the 1994 *Critique* and to a longstanding complaint about the *Country Reports* generally.

In other respects, however, the 1995 report is disappointing. First, it fails to discuss the situation in Mostar in any detail. To note that it is "tense" as it does in the introduction, is to understate the problem, for Mostar is still a completely divided city. Throughout 1995, freedom of movement across the dividing line which separates East and West Mostar was minimal at best. In July 1995, the U.N. Special Rapporteur noted that only 250 people per day were able to cross from one side to the other and that no progress had been made on the establishment of a police force. As a result, levels of criminality in the city remained high and the general security of all citizens was diminished. The U.N. Special Rapporteur also noted that minority groups suffered discrimination in terms of inequitable distribution of humanitarian aid by local agencies, Serbian Bosnians being most affected since they do not have a humanitarian organization of their own. Reports also suggested that Serbs and Muslims in Mostar received notice to enlist in the Croatian Defense Council (HVO - the army of the Bosnian Croats), which forced them to go into hiding to avoid such forced conscription. As one human rights observer noted, "the Croatian entity of Herzeg-Bosna is still very much there and is unlikely to go away, despite what Dayton says, and should not be referred to in the past tense" as the report does.

The report also avoids controversial aspects of several key issues and events. One of these was the total failure of the United Nations Protection Force (UNPROFOR) and, by extension, the entire international community, to protect the Bosnian Muslims living in the safe areas of Srebrenica and Zepa from being overrun and slaughtered by Bosnian Serb forces in early July. Another is the continuing reluctance of the NATO Implementation Force (IFOR) to engage in activities necessary to support the work of the International Criminal Tribunal for the Former Yugoslavia. This includes the unwillingness of IFOR troops to prevent Serbian forces from destroying the sites of mass graves throughout the fall of 1995 or to assist the tribunal in locating and detaining indicted war criminals.

This unwillingness to address the controversial subject of IFOR's proper role prevents the report from reaching the obvious, but politically unpalatable, conclusion about the prospects for peace in Bosnia under the

Bosnia and Herzegovina

Dayton agreement. The key to ending the bloodshed and genocide in the Balkans lies in ending the cycles of violent retaliation; a goal that cannot possibly be realized without more substantial intervention by IFOR and the international community. The report observes that by "punishing the individuals responsible for the atrocities, victims will feel less need to take revenge in their own hands and attack innocent members of other ethnic groups" and recognizes that the war crimes tribunal must play an important role in that process. But at no point does the report explain how the tribunal can mete out such punishments in light of the destruction of evidence by the perpetrators of violations and the fact that indicted war criminals continue to hold positions of power.

As noted above, the report's most notable strengths stem from its tight organization, bold writing and comprehensive scope. These strengths are established in the introduction which, in a welcome departure from the State Department's instructions, is fairly lengthy and makes an admirable attempt to anticipate and synthesize what follows. The introduction opens with a brief summary of the history of the Balkan conflict, then moves smoothly into a recapitulation of the main events and players in 1995. The overall behavior of each of the Bosnian factions is concisely — and for the most part accurately — summarized in bold and evocative assertions which are consistently supported in the ensuing subsections.

Addressing the overall conduct of Serbian factions for example, the report notes that:

> The Serbs continued to lay siege to cities, deliberately shell civilian areas and hospitals, withhold food deliveries, and cut off utilities. They also continued to execute non-combatants and run detention camps in which they executed some prisoners and tortured others. They employed rape as a tool of war, forced large numbers of civilians to flee to other regions, razed villages to prevent the return of displaced persons, and blockaded international relief efforts, including attacks on relief personnel.

Critique 1995

The drafters bluntly describe the Serb assault on the "safe area" of Srebrenica in July as "one of the worst single reported incidents of genocidal mass killing of members of an ethnic or religious group in Europe since World War II"; as "the most massive and savage single act of ethnic cleansing in the four-year history of the war"; and as a major catalyst for the NATO military intervention which led eventually to the Dayton peace talks. The seizure of Srebrenica is recounted at length with a level of detail which closely resembles the findings of both the U.N. Special Rapporteur and international human rights monitors, strongly suggesting that the drafters drew on the work of these invaluable resources in preparing the report. The introduction also highlights the Bosnian Serb attack on the "safe area" of Zepa in July and the continued ethnic cleansing of areas under Bosnian Serb control. Detailed descriptions of the human rights violations which accompanied each of the foregoing events are then set forth in the appropriate subsections.

However, the report maintains a resolute silence on the subject of why or how these "safe areas" were so easily overrun. It refrains from drawing the conclusions that were apparent to non-governmental monitors such as Human Rights Watch, which commented:

> The fall of Srebrenica and its environs to Bosnian Serb forces in early July 1995 made a mockery of the international community's professed commitment to safeguard regions it declared to be "safe areas" and placed under United Nations protection in 1993. Senior United Nations peacekeeping officials were unwilling to heed requests for support from their own forces stationed within the Srebrenica enclave, thus allowing Bosnian Serb forces to overrun it easily and — without interference from UN soldiers — carry out systematic, mass execution of hundreds, possibly thousands, of civilian men and boys and to terrorize, rape, beat, execute, rob or otherwise abuse civilians being deported from the area . . . . The international community grievously failed the thousands of Bosnians who trusted its promise of safety.

14

Bosnia and Herzegovina

The mainly Muslim inhabitants of Srebrenica and neighboring areas such as Zepa were victims of the worst war crimes since the beginning of the Balkan conflict because UNPROFOR was understaffed, undersupplied and undersupported. The magnitude of the failure of this U.N. mission led U.N. Special Rapporteur Tadeusz Mazowiecki to resign in frustration and disgust. In an unusually candid letter of resignation submitted in August 1995, Mazowiecki bemoaned the international community's passivity in the face of Serbian aggression, noting:

> One cannot speak about the protection of human rights with credibility when one is confronted with the lack of consistency and courage displayed by the international community and its leaders . . . . Crimes have been committed with swiftness and brutality and in contrast the response of the international community has been slow and ineffectual . . . . The present critical moment forces us to realize the true character of those crimes and the responsibility of Europe and the international community for their own hopelessness in addressing them.

In discussing the conduct of the Bosnian Army (a multi-ethnic fighting force comprised predominantly of Bosnian Muslims), the report observes that they demonstrated "general respect" for human rights, although "some violations" were committed. This assertion is consistently supported by discussions in the body of the report and generally concurs with the observations made throughout the year by the Special Rapporteur and international human rights monitors. Where the Bosnian Army is responsible for violations, the report describes these forthrightly. For example, on several occasions it cites reports of Bosnian Army forces, assisted by the Croatian military, harassing and murdering followers of the Bosnian Muslim renegade Fikret Abdic who were sheltered in a Croatian refugee camp. Similarly, it notes that government forces seized over 100 Serbian males from Hrasnica, an area outside Sarajevo, for forced labor on the front lines, and that the majority were killed in the line of fire.

Critique 1995

Regarding Croatian factions based in Bosnia, in the so-called Herzeg-Bosna area, the report alludes to decisive military campaigns such as the Croatian recapture of Western Slavonia in May, and observes that the HVO "was credibly accused of human rights abuses against Bosniaks and Serbs and . . . on occasion killed civilians and shelled civilian areas." The report is also forthright in noting that the HVO "appears to be directly under the command of the army of Croatia" and in questioning the degree of independence which the Bosnian Croatian political party (the Bosnian branch of the Croatian Democratic Union — HDZ), maintains from Croatia. Again, discussions in several of the report's subsections give details which generally support these observations, although the extent of atrocities committed by Croatian factions against Serbs during the recapture of Western Slavonia and later of the Krajina region has not yet been satisfactorily documented and is probably understated.

As noted above, throughout the various discussions of human rights abuses committed by all three factions, the report recognizes and highlights forms of human rights abuses which have grown more prevalent as the war has gone on. Many of these have become the latest tools of ethnic cleansing and it is gratifying to see the report acknowledge this fact. For example, the report repeatedly describes incidents in which Serbian forces deliberately shelled civilian areas (particularly hospitals) and interfered with humanitarian aid and the flow of supplies. The report also identifies the Serbian propensity for strangling cities by cutting off water and utility supplies, and describes reports of "grotesque cruelty" to non-Serbs such as slitting the throats of victims, beating prisoners to death, forcing captives to walk across minefields and denying prisoners access to medical treatment. The report properly notes that all sides to the conflict arbitrarily seized civilians who were then used in exchanges for prisoners of war, a blatant violation of the Geneva Conventions. It is also gratifying to see the 1995 report give more thorough attention to the plight of children, addressing particularly the long-term effects that four years of war and loss will undoubtedly have on young children. The report also expands its discussion of the human rights violations inflicted on women in Bosnia in 1995, and correctly recognizes the continuing

16

widespread use of rape as a tactic of terrorization and ethnic cleansing, mostly by Serb forces.

However, while the report generally offers a well organized and well illustrated synthesis of most of the important issues and events of 1995, it entirely misses the opportunity to draw a clear link between the atrocities committed during the various military campaigns and the cycles of retaliation which ensued. For example, the Croatian recapture of Western Slavonia in May caused an estimated 10,000 to 15,000 Serbs to flee for Bosnian Serb-held regions, particularly the Banja Luka area, where, according to officials from the United Nations High Commissioner for Refugees (UNHCR), they retaliated by attacking and destroying Catholic churches and monasteries and beating, robbing and murdering Croats. This same flood of Serb refugees into northeastern Bosnia also incited Bosnian Serb forces to retaliate by slaughtering Muslims supposedly sheltered from harm in the "safe areas" of Srebrenica and Zepa in July. In August, the Croatian and Bosnian armies and the Bosnian Croat militia counter-retaliated against rebel Serb-held areas in the Krajina region in an offensive that displaced some 200,000 Serbs. Bosnian Serb factions responded throughout the fall of 1995 with a campaign of terror against Bosnian Muslims and Croats in northwestern Bosnian cities such as Banja Luka, Prijedor and Sanski Most, leaving a bloody trail of civilian corpses and a slew of disappearances. None of these operations occurred in a vacuum; each laid the seeds for the next round of retaliation. If the drafters of the report comprehend this truth, they fail to state it.

More importantly however, the report fails to link these cycles of violence to the larger issue of the success of the Dayton peace agreement. The report gives a clear and concise summary of the terms of the Dayton agreement, the structure and functions of IFOR and the role of the Yugoslav War Crimes Tribunal. It also observes that "respect for human rights is a fundamental part of the Dayton agreement and a key to the reconciliation process," and, as noted above, recognizes that the work of the tribunal is central to mitigating the drive for revenge. Yet the report fails entirely to recognize that the tribunal cannot successfully prosecute war criminals in absentia or when the evidence of their atrocities is being systematically destroyed. Throughout the fall of 1995 and into 1996, European Union monitors and Bosnian war crimes investigators identified six mass graves in northwestern Bosnia containing approximately 240 bodies of persons suspected to be victims of ethnic cleansing by Serbian forces in 1992; during this same time period, reliable reports began to emerge indicating that Bosnian Serb forces were exhuming these mass graves, thereby destroying this crucial evidence of genocide. Despite such reports, NATO commanders refused to intervene. As one commander put it, "Our job is to separate forces, not look for mass graves . . . . It would be a diversion of soldiers from our main goal." IFOR's refusal to become more pro-active has sent the message to war criminals that there are no repercussions for the slaughter of innocent civilians. This message only encourages the various Bosnian factions to seek retribution themselves by perpetuating the cycles of revenge and violence which have fueled the current conflict from the beginning.

In sum, the State Department's 1995 report on Bosnia presents a forthright, compelling and well conceived account of the human rights situation in that war-torn country. It is tightly organized, well written and employs powerful and evocative language which conveys a "story" of a group of people rather than a fragmented series of facts. It is also more comprehensive than previous reports and draws more heavily on the findings of U.N. mechanisms and other international human rights monitors. Its principal faults are threefold: first, it entirely avoids politically controversial subjects; second, it fails to identify the powerful cyclical character of the violence; and third, it declines to recognize that peace remains a pipe dream until these cycles are broken — something that will only happen once those responsible for the atrocities of the past five years are removed from power and held accountable for their crimes.

CAMBODIA

The State Department's 1995 report on human rights in Cambodia accurately catalogues the basic human rights violations affecting Cambodians during 1995. It acknowledges that the general human rights situation worsened in several respects, and does a good job of detailing the individual incidents that occurred. It also does a fairly good job of recognizing the work done by NGOs in ameliorating and documenting human rights abuses. However, the report does not present a cohesive picture either of the increasing use of intimidation and violence by the Cambodian government and military toward their critics, or of the judiciary's inability to serve as a check on the other branches of government due to its corruption, weakness and lack of resources. As the report notes in its introduction, Cambodia is heavily dependent on foreign aid as a source of national income. In establishing this context for the discussion of human rights that follows, it would have been helpful for the report also to note that Cambodia was actively seeking Most Favored Nation trading status with the United States in 1995, and that in a climate of sweeping reductions in U.S. foreign assistance programs, Cambodia has been largely spared.

The Royal Cambodian Government (RCG) is comprised of a tenuous coalition brought to power by the United Nations-sponsored elections in May 1993. The ruling parties are the Royalist party, the United National Front for an Independent, Neutral, Peaceful and Cooperative Cambodia (FUNCINPEC), the Cambodian People's Party (CPP) and the Buddhist Liberal Democratic Party (BLDP). Instability has been evident in the reluctance of factions within both FUNCINPEC and the BLDP to cooperate with the CPP, which they regard as corrupt.

The general political instability in Cambodia, and the resulting governmental efforts to stifle opposition and criticism are of great concern. While the report gives examples of human rights abuses committed by the executive and the military, it fails to conclude or even indicate that these abuses are all symptomatic of the same fragile and insecure political system. While a complete analysis of the political landscape, or a thorough prognosis are beyond the scope of the report, the failure to interweave the sources of the abuses with the descriptions of the abuses themselves is a troubling omission. The structure of the report dilutes the impact of its evidence by chopping up the incidents and putting them under discrete headings.

In June, the National Assembly expelled Sam Rainsy, a member of the originally elected Constitutional Assembly from Siem Reap, without allowing for any debate. An outspoken critic of the government on a number of issues, Rainsy had recently been expelled from his party, FUNCINPEC. He had also been victimized by threats against his life, and the lives of his family, apparently from the members of the RCG. The National Assembly clearly violated Article 95 of the Constitution, which provides grounds for the removal of an elected official — the loss of party membership is not one of these. While the expulsion seems a clear indication of the willingness of the RCG to violate the rule of law in order to enforce conformity of opinion, the report simply called Rainsy's ousting "an indication that the governing coalition was unwilling to tolerate dissent among members of the parties in the coalition."

The report fails to connect Rainsy's expulsion with the arrest and beating of his bodyguards in July, which are discussed under different headings. The four men reported that 30 to 40 soldiers detained them at a Ministry of Defense base. The soldiers beat and interrogated the guards for 16 hours, and demanded that they identify Rainsy as linked with the Khmer Rouge. They were told, according to one report by Amnesty International, that they had been arrested "for the political crime of involvement with the Khmer Rouge."

There was further evidence of political repression. As the report mentions, FUNCINPEC Secretary General Norodom Sirivudh was arrested for "his alleged involvement in an assassination plot against Second Prime Minister Hun Sen," but was allowed to depart for France in December in a deal brokered by King Norodom Sihanouk. In addition, there was a grenade attack in September on BDLP headquarters, after the party was denied permission to hold a congress in Phenom Penh stadium.

The report states that there was "one reported case of a killing by government agents for political reasons." Two men in Mong Russei district, Battambang province, were arrested and detained at gunpoint by about 30 members of the Royal Cambodian Armed Forces (RCAF). No reasons were given and no arrest warrant was produced. The men were subsequently killed. Local authorities were unwilling to investigate the killings, stating that the men were alleged to be members of the Khmer Rouge. While the report states that the two men killed were "suspected Khmer Rouge members," Amnesty International reports that the villagers and relatives insist that the members were Royalist FUNCINPEC party members, and that this was the reason for their killing.

In an indication of the difficulties involved in bringing the military to justice, the two local militia men arrested for the murders were later released. The State Department notes that there were reports that the military had pressured the court to release the suspects. Political expression in Cambodia is increasingly limited by the military and the executive. The report describes the detention of six people for the peaceful expression of political views. Four of the six were arrested and detained on August 5, 1995 while tying copies of leaflets to balloons in advance of the visit of U.S. Secretary of State Warren Christopher. The leaflets contained political statements critical of the RCG and FUNCINPEC, but in no way advocated violence. The fifth and sixth detainees were the author of the leaflet and another man allegedly involved in its distribution.

As evidenced by these examples, the accusation of Khmer Rouge membership is a common excuse for arrest, detention, and intimidation. It is important that such accusations, without further evidence, do not give the military, the police and the executive carte blanche to act against individuals with impunity. This trend, which is not mentioned in the 1995 report, should be the subject of careful scrutiny in future reports.

The Cambodian press came under attack in 1995, with the RCG using a variety of means to silence criticism. The report states that "the government sometimes limits press freedom in practice," but does not develop a full, clear picture of the pressure the government is exerting, nor of its effect. An ominous new press law went into effect in September, whose impact the report underemphasizes. The report states that human rights groups and journalists criticized the law, but does not fully explore how threatening it is. The new press law allows for criminal sanctions for publication of material that "may affect the national security or political stability of the country." The government has refused to provide a definition of "national security," which has an intimidating and stifling effect. The threat is real, when viewed in the context of the government suspension of publication of newspapers, confiscation of their property and jailing of journalists. Criminal convictions of editors were widespread, and those affected included the editor of *Samrek Reask Khmer* (Cry of Khmer People), the editor of *Voice of Khmer You*, the editor of *Khmer Ideal*, the editor of *Sereipheap Thmei* (New Liberty News), and the editor of *Odom K'tek Khmer* (Khmer Conscience). In addition, three journalists — all critical of the RCG — have died in suspicious circumstances since 1994, and the government has not successfully identified or convicted those responsible in any of these cases.

Intimidation of the press has taken other forms, too. Printers for the English-language *Cambodia Daily* refused to print one issue of the paper after Second Prime Minister Hun Sen questioned whether the paper could legally operate since it did not have the necessary government approval. The *Daily* was forced to find another printer. In a separate incident, Hun Sen told the inhabitants of the village of Kraingyov that their attack on a newspaper critical of a development project overseen by Hun Sen was justified. In this case, the printer for the newspaper (*New Liberty News*) refused to print any further issues of the paper or any other opposition papers.

Widespread and severe institutional shortcomings in the Cambodian legal system continued to frustrate its ability to protect human rights. The report accurately describes the court system in Cambodia, and does so in far greater detail than in 1994. It acknowledges that there is "widespread corruption among judges who do not receive a living wage"; verdicts and the pre-trial custody status of criminal defendants are often determined by bribes; trials last an average of one hour; statements from witnesses and the accused are often the result of threats or beatings; and judicial independence is additionally hampered by the CPP's refusal to allow non-CPP-affiliated judicial candidates to be appointed to the bench. The report also properly acknowledges that the system is flawed due to the shortage of attorneys (Cambodia's first graduating class of lawyers in over 20 years will graduate from law school in 1997), and that the situation

Cambodia

has been ameliorated by NGO-trained defenders and NGO defense lawyers. However, it fails to note that the shortage of defense attorneys will continue to plague the system because the government has limited the practice of NGO-trained defenders to the end of 1997. It also fails to note that the Cambodian Bar Association has severely limited admission of these defenders — Cambodian nationals trained under U.S. AID auspices — to its ranks.

The proper and fair functioning of the judiciary is further undermined by the lack of clear law and procedures in Cambodia. The Penal Code drafted by UNTAC remains in effect, as does the Criminal Procedure Law, which dates from the State of Cambodia period (1979-1991). The report states that "the Government frequently ignored these provisions." This is a remarkable understatement. The report also properly states that the judges often do not have copies of the laws, effectively denying them even a chance of complying with them. In addition, the majority of judges lack formal training and therefore do not understand basic legal concepts such as the presumption of innocence, making for uneven decision-making."

The judiciary is further impeded in its attempts to thwart human rights abuses because, as the report acknowledges, "civilian courts are often unable to try members of the military." Once again, however, the report understates its point: in effect, the military refuses to be tried by civilian courts. While the report indicates that the military court system suffers from the same problems as its civilian counterpart, the military court is additionally weakened because its jurisdiction is not made clear by law, and because it is located in Phnom Penh, making it difficult to try military personnel in the provinces.

Detainees are often held for lengthy periods of time before being charged, and while detained, are often severely beaten. As the report indicates, this occurs "particularly during interrogation." The report does not state that beatings and torture appear to be more common in cases where the defendant is alleged to be a member of the Khmer Rouge, or where the victim is a police officer or someone with ties to high-level government officials.

Critique 1995

The report properly describes the conditions of prisons in Cambodia, which have improved in certain respects, and deteriorated in others. The report typically distances itself from its own evidence by quoting human rights workers as reporting a resumption in the use of shackles and the holding of prisoners in small, dark cells. The report also describes increased overcrowding, food and water shortages, and poor security. The *Phnom Penh Post* published an article about the prison in Kampong Speu, where prisoners were reportedly starving to death. Many of the prison commandants have responded by severely limiting access to prisons and prisoners by human rights monitors. The report also adds that "[t]here were unconfirmed reports of the existence of small, illegal detention facilities in several provinces."

In Kompong Cham the United Nations reported that fear of escape by prisoners had caused the prison commandant to require that prisoners be locked in cells 23 hours a day. The U.N. also reported — though the State Department did not — that prisoners generally lacked medical treatment, and that they lacked access to NGO defenders and to bail unless their families took the initiative.

Prostitution, and especially child prostitution, is an increasingly serious problem in Cambodia. The Cambodian Women's Development Association estimates that the number of commercial sex workers has burgeoned to 17,000. The report estimates that roughly one third are girls aged 12-17. The U.N. reports that there are increasing reports of kidnapping and trafficking in virgin children sold by poor families in provincial districts.

The Vietnamese in Cambodia continue to suffer from discrimination. Here again, the State Department fails to note what the U.N. has reported: that certain provincial and municipal authorities have been directed to register, detain and expel "illegal aliens." It does note that because there is no nationality law, it is difficult to determine who is an alien.

Overall, the State Department's report on Cambodia for 1995 is fair and accurate. Its weakness lies not in its compilation of egregious human rights violations, but in its failure to provide an overall picture of the political drama that is unfolding in Cambodia, and the context within which systematic rather than isolated human rights abuses continue to occur.

China

In December 1995, a Chinese court sentenced Wei Jingsheng, China's most prominent dissident, to 14 years in prison for the peaceful expression of his political beliefs. In many ways, Wei's latest odyssey — from protracted incommunicado detention to a courtroom closed to foreign observers — epitomizes the state of human rights in China today. Wei's warrantless arrest in 1994, his 20 months of detention without charge, and his hasty trial for conspiracy to overthrow the government reflect the deficiencies of Chinese legal process. His harsh sentence symbolizes the government's continued intolerance of internal dissent and its resistance to international human rights scrutiny.

In describing the plight of Wei Jingsheng and other Chinese citizens, the State Department's 1995 report on China accurately and critically captures the deplorable human rights situation in the PRC. As the report correctly observes, by the end of 1995 "almost all public dissent against the central authorities was silenced by intimidation, exile, or imposition of prison terms or administrative detention." Overall, the report gives a well rounded portrayal of the variety of human rights abuses in China, and the ineffectiveness of the Chinese legal system as a means of controlling those abuses. Compared to the previous year's report, the 1995 report takes a big step forward in expressly recognizing the emptiness of the Clinton administration's premise that "constructive engagement" with the Chinese government to encourage economic liberalization will naturally lead to an improvement in the human rights situation in China. The report comments:

> The experience of China in the past few years demonstrates that while economic growth, trade and social mobility create an improved standard of living, they cannot by themselves bring about greater respect for human rights in the absence of a willingness by political authorities to abide by the fundamental international norms.

While the 1994 report strained to characterize China's human rights record as "diverse," the 1995 report clearly indicates that the scope of ongoing political, social and religious repression in China far outweighs the few points of progress made over the last year.

A particularly strong part of the 1995 report is the section on arbitrary arrest, detention or exile. This section benefits from the State Department's new policy of beginning each section with a summary of applicable laws. Rather than recite information about individual cases, the section does an excellent job of recognizing recent patterns of arbitrary arrest and detention on pretexts of parole or criminal violations or under the pretense of compulsory "vacations." This section might have been made even stronger, however. In discussing how officials kept Chinese dissidents away from the September 1995 Beijing Women's Conference by detaining them under questionable charges, the report should have clarified that the brief list of individuals named in the report was not exhaustive. Others not mentioned in the report — including activists Xu Shuiliang, Qi Zhiyong and Jiang Qisheng — were also detained for questioning for the duration of the conference.

In addition, this section in the 1995 report fails to correct one of the oversights noted in the 1994 edition of the *Critique* with regard to detention under "supervised residence." The report should have noted that the provision for "supervised residence" in Article 38 of the Criminal Procedure Law seems to justify house arrest only at the defendant's own home. This article states that: "A defendant under surveillance on his residence cannot leave the designated area. The order to impose surveillance on the defendant's residence shall be carried out by the local public security station, or by an entrusted people's commune, or by the unit to which the defendant belongs." The fact that the Code envisions surveillance by local officials or work unit colleagues demonstrates that the provision was originally intended to authorize house arrest at the defendant's own place of residence. Moreover, Article 38 poses a clear distinction between taking a defendant "into custody," and imposing surveillance on his residence. Therefore, recent instances in which the police have purported to use "supervised residence" orders to arrest and remove dissidents like Wei Jingsheng or Liu Xiaobo to undisclosed locations appear to exceed the proper scope of the provision. (Liu Xiaobo was released in January 1996 after nine months of detention).

28

China

With respect to the lack of due process in capital cases, too, this year's report repeats an oversight alluded to in last year's *Critique.* The report fails to link the exceptional speed with which various death sentences have been imposed, reviewed and carried out, to 1983 regulations that accelerate the adjudication of certain serious criminal cases. A cross-reference to these regulations would have clarified the legal pretext for several cases mentioned in the report in which defendants were convicted and executed within a matter of days.

In other areas, however, the 1995 report successfully incorporates changes suggested by last year's edition of the *Critique.* Most importantly, it clarifies the way in which January 1994 regulations on church group registration have enabled the Chinese authorities to tighten state control over unofficial religious activity. The 1995 report also acknowledges that the Chinese government has imposed an outright ban on at least one unauthorized religious sect, the Shouters. On the topic of eugenics, this year's report clarifies that the current Maternal and Child Health Care Law not only recommends but actually mandates abortion or sterilization for persons suffering from certain hereditary, contagious or mental disorders. Finally, the 1995 report makes another welcome change in incorporating a description of relevant International Labour Organisation (ILO) actions into its discussion of worker rights. The ILO proceedings may provide a much-needed window into the status of worker rights in China, particularly given the crackdown on independent union organizers in recent years. Next year's report should continue to make greater use of China-related findings by the ILO and other intergovernmental bodies.

One of the most fundamental weaknesses in the 1995 report is its frequent failure to illuminate the connections between different categories of violations. A principal example of this weakness is the report's treatment of freedom of movement and worker rights. Specifically, the report fails to relate the government's restrictions on freedom of movement to the inability of unauthorized migrant laborers to enforce their rights as workers. The inadequate enforcement of labor regulations is not just a result of occasional corruption or inadequate inspection regimes, as the report implies. On the contrary, China's household registration requirements systematically condemn a large part of the labor pool to illegal work status when rural residents or minors (who are too young to be eligible for the identification cards and residence permits that would allow them to work) migrate without government permission in search of work in more developed areas. Because they lack the proper registration, these migrant laborers fall outside the protections of the All-China Federation of Trade Unions, China's new Labor Law and local minimum wage standards. As a result, they have no legal recourse against abusive employers or corrupt officials. In some cases, the work situations of undocumented migrant laborers may be so coercive as to amount to forced labor. Future reports should take this possibility into account in their discussion of compulsory labor.

Another example of thematic disjunction is the report's failure to discuss the link between the government's repression of independent religious activity and its crackdown on political dissent. While the report makes the connection between religious and political dissent in the contexts of Tibetan and Muslim unrest, its analysis of abuses in Han-dominated areas treats the authorities' infringements of religious freedom and free speech as unrelated phenomena. As a result, the report fails to recognize the overlap between the dissident religious and political communities. Furthermore, it artificially separates related elements in the government's campaign against all dissident expression, especially that which the government suspects of exhibiting subversive foreign influence. This artificial separation plays into the government's interest in atomizing dissident activists to prevent them from making common cause.

Another recurrent weakness in the report is that it cites a number of ostensibly progressive laws or regulations without providing information about the effectiveness of those provisions. For example, the report mentions favorably the passage of implementing regulations for the State Compensation Law which came into force January 1, 1995, allowing citizens to sue government actors for malfeasance and recover damages. The report does not speak to the actual use of the law, however. Even assuming that no data is yet available on the implementation of the law, the report could have discussed potential practical constraints on the effective use of the new law, in the same way that it points out systemic barriers to the effective use of the 1990 Administrative Procedure Law permitting detainees to challenge the legality of their detentions. Similarly, substantive information about enforcement of the December 1994 prison law, which the report mentions, would be helpful in assessing whether the extensively documented human rights abuses in Chinese prisons occur in an atmosphere of impunity. On this topic, the 1995 report might have noted that prison officials at the Hewan Labor Camp took no corrective action after political detainee Tong Yi reported her January 16 beating at the hands of fellow inmates who had been designated by prison officials as camp "trustees."

In many areas, the State Department's 1995 revisions to its instructions to those drafting the *Country Reports* has raised the standard of reporting. The result is that coverage that might have been considered adequate in the past is no longer satisfactory. For example, the report's fairly detailed coverage of the status of women does not meet the new requirements for reporting on this topic. According to the 1995 instructions, the section on women's rights should describe the nature and effectiveness of the government's programs to redress problems of economic and social inequality. In accordance with these guidelines, the report should have discussed in greater detail the Chinese government's failure to combat effectively employment discrimination against women. In particular, the report could have underscored the absence of proactive government programs to redress the disparate impact of economic reforms upon working women; the government's own unequal treatment of female and male employees through "protective" legislation for female workers; and the ways in which government registration requirements constrain the formation of independent women's advocacy groups and unions.

Problems of violence against women also merit greater coverage. In accordance with State Department guidelines concerning the problem of trafficking in women, the report should have described China's 1991 legislation against the abduction and sale of women. As the *Critique* noted last year, discussion of the 1991 anti-trafficking provisions should take into account the failure to criminalize the intentional purchase of women generally, without regard to whether the buyer knows that the woman has been abducted or whether he agrees to release her within a certain period of time. Future reports should also address government action against domestic violence. While the report notes that volunteers in Beijing have established a telephone hotline for victims of domestic violence and that domestic violence can be grounds for criminal prosecution, a more meaningful portrayal of the government's response needs to include specific information about preventive programs, support for abused women, and the nature of the criminal or administrative enforcement regime (including whether Chinese law imposes the same penalties for domestic violence as for violence against strangers).

On the question of political representation, the 1995 report satisfies the State Department's requirements with respect to women's participation, but fails to include any information about the representation of China's ethnic minorities in the government. Next year's report should rectify this omission.

The report's coverage of children's rights and welfare does a good job of noting the variety of abuses raised over the last year, such as sex-selective abortion, female infanticide, trafficking in children and conditions in orphanages. The report's overview of child welfare legislation is also satisfactory. In order to satisfy the revised guidelines, however, next year's report should also discuss sex discrimination in the government's provision of education and health care services to children.

While the report's coverage of extrajudicial killings in 1995 is adequate, the revised State Department guidelines also require updates of cases outstanding from previous years.   To this effect, the report should have noted developments (or the absence thereof) in several cases reported in 1994 from Tibet, Fujian and Guangdong, where the outcome of investigations or prosecutions was unclear.   In addition, State Department guidelines specify that the rubric of arbitrary or summary executions includes the imposition of capital punishment "where the accused is not allowed to present a defense or is denied basic due process rights." Under this definition, the Chinese authorities' custom of holding mass public rallies where multiple defendants may be tried, sentenced and executed in one combined ceremony might qualify as summary executions.   For example, Amnesty International reported that on February 14, 1995, Yunnan officials announced death sentences for 26 accused drug traffickers, then had them executed immediately afterward

— apparently with no chance to appeal. On May 16, simultaneous drug sentencing rallies held throughout Guangdong province resulted in the immediate execution of 51 people, with another 219 individuals given suspended death sentences or fixed prison terms. In the past, the U.N. Special Rapporteur on Extrajudicial, Summary or Arbitrary Executions has expressed concern about China's use of the death penalty after summary trial proceedings. Future reports should incorporate any relevant findings of the Special Rapporteur on this subject.

On the question of the integrity of the Chinese judiciary, the report correctly observes that political pressure, corruption and conflicts of interest may contaminate judicial decisionmaking. The report might have further highlighted these problems by noting the lack of judicial independence in the introduction to the report, as required by the State Department's revised reporting instructions. In addition, next year's report should address the effects of 1995 legislation designed to professionalize the judiciary and law enforcement bureaus.

In its discussion of government interference with privacy and family rights, the report should have noted the Chinese government's plan to force the resettlement of over one million people to accommodate construction of the Three Gorges Dam. Next year's report should note new developments in this area.

In a number of areas, the report satisfies the letter of State Department guidelines but omits mention of key cases. For example, the report accurately states that the government intensified its control over the expression of unauthorized views in 1995. As an example, the report might have noted an October incident in which a peaceful park demonstration by the immediate family of imprisoned pro-democracy activist Chen Ziming ended in the detention and questioning of his wife Wang Zhihong, three Hong Kong journalists and a CNN cameraman who had covered the protest. The report should also have discussed a 1995 crackdown on television stations and producers. As the Committee to Protect Journalists reports, in November 1995 the Ministry of Radio, Film and Television moved to shut down stations in Hunan and Yunnan provinces for broadcasting "pornographic or politically sensitive" programs. In the course of the same campaign, the ministry fined at least four other stations across the country and barred them from broadcasting locally produced programs in the future. In December, the Ministry announced a series of new regulations targeting independent television producers. Designed to censor programs deemed "crude, excessive or detrimental to society," the regulations limit the establishment of new television production firms and require all producers to apply for licenses and submit annual production plans for government approval.

As with the section on freedom of the press, the report's depiction of religious repression and persecution omits significant information. It notes a number of incidents of official persecution of Chinese Christians, then concludes with the statement that: "Elsewhere, authorities tolerate the existence of unofficial Catholic and Protestant churches as long as they remain small and discreet." This statement misleadingly suggests that the report catalogues all the Chinese government's most egregious actions against unofficial churches. In fact, the report omits any mention of the government's Easter raids on unofficial "house churches" across the country. For example, Amnesty International reported the Easter arrests of between 30 and 40 Roman Catholics at Yijiashan in Jiangxi province. Many of the detainees sustained police beatings during their detentions. According to Amnesty, two of the women detained, Gao Shuyun and Huang Guanghua, were so badly beaten they later needed help in feeding themselves. Another major incident omitted from the report was an April 18 raid in Hubei, reported by Human Rights Watch/Asia, in which security officials armed with electric batons broke up a training class for new pastors and arrested at least 67 Chinese and three foreign Protestants. The report should also have noted government persecution of Roman Catholics in Hebei where, among other incidents, police reportedly detained for six months and severely beat the priest Chi Huitian for refusing to cancel an unofficial Easter Mass. In light of the March 1995 arrests of 11 Beiliwang sect leaders in Guangdong for "cheating people out of their property" and "sexual promiscuity," future reports should take note of whether the police step up their use of common criminal charges to intimidate religious leaders, as they have tried to do with political dissidents in recent years. Finally, future reports should also be alert to the government's attempts to curtail public worship by physically restricting the size of church accommodations, as was done in June 1995 in Xinjiang; or by demolishing churches, as was done in Gang diocese, Guizhou, in July, and in Baoding diocese, Hebei, in November.

The report is basically fair and accurate in its depiction of abuses in Tibet in 1995. Strong points in this section include the acknowledgment of widespread employment discrimination against Tibetans and a discussion of government efforts to control the growth and operation of Tibetan monasteries. As an example of the latter, the report should have mentioned that China has begun expelling monks from their monasteries for "political reasons." According to Amnesty International, the March 1995 expulsion of an abbot and teacher from Yamure monastery in Medro Gongkar county was the first such expulsion in recent years. In a crackdown on demonstrating monks at the Nalanda monastery in Penpo Lundrup county, 64 monks were reportedly expelled by a "reeducation team" of Chinese authorities.

In addition, the report fails to mention some key cases that would have bolstered its assertion that the Chinese government continued to be responsible for widespread human rights abuses in Tibet during 1995, including torture and intensified controls on freedom of speech. While the report relates the case of Gyaltsen Kelsang, a young Tibetan nun and political prisoner who reportedly suffered from prison beatings and hard labor, and died shortly after her medical release from prison, it should also have cited the similar case of Sherab Wangpo. According to the Dalai Lama's government-in-exile in Dharamsala, India, the 18-year-old novice nun died in April soon after her medical release from a three-year political sentence. She was reportedly tortured and severely beaten during her detention in Drapchi Prison.

Similarly, the inclusion of more information about police beatings of detainees would have substantiated the report's general statement about the lack of safeguards for prisoners in Tibet. For example, Amnesty International reported that two monks from Lhasa's Jokhang Temple were arrested without explanation, detained for three days, and severely beaten by police at the Gutsa Detention Center in Lhasa in January. The police reportedly threatened the monks with further punishment if they told anyone what had happened. The report might also have included mention of other specific instances of police violence and extortion throughout the year, such as the incident reported from Gyab-drag nunnery in which police officials demanded that the families of 13 nuns detained for protest pay 2,000 yuan to secure the release of each one.

Despite the specific weaknesses detailed above, the 1995 report is a generally accurate and hard-hitting portrayal of the decline in the human rights situation in China over the last year. The 1996 report should continue this year's critical focus, while doing more to recognize the connections between different categories of rights violations and while making an even greater effort to raise its reporting level to meet the State Department's elevated standards for dealing with issues such as women's rights, discrimination and governmental impunity. Even as the Chinese government continues to try to preempt international scrutiny of its human rights record, the continued emergence of China as an economic and political superpower demands that careful attention be paid to its record of compliance with international norms of behavior.

COLOMBIA

In 1995, Colombia did little to improve its dismal human rights record. Despite President Ernesto Samper's repeated affirmations of his nation's commitment to the respect of human rights and his well-publicized increase in Colombia's already enormous governmental human rights bureaucracy, the right to personal safety and humane treatment in Colombia remained seriously imperiled. The impunity which pervades all aspects of Colombia's human rights situation remained institutionalized, and the efforts of the Samper administration to bolster the Colombian government's sagging public image failed to curb the pattern of chronic human rights abuses.

Like previous State Department reports, the 1995 report assigns disproportionate responsibility for human rights violations to guerrillas, narcotics traffickers and paramilitary groups, and fails to implicate the state sufficiently for its active role in such abuses. The State Department's choice of words and phrasing throughout the report blinks at the voluminous information linking the government to widespread abuses, and fails even to acknowledge the evidence linking the head of the country with some of the world's most violent and dangerous drug traffickers — and, by implication, the violence associated with them.

The report is not lacking in hard information about the human rights abuses that took place in 1995, and in some places offers a provocative analysis of the human rights situation. Yet the overall tone is almost schizophrenic, and the report departs from reality in several spots in an apparent effort to limit institutional criticism of the government and the armed forces. At times, the report sets forth facts and circumstances that all but compel a conclusion which is contradictory to that which it states or implies. For instance, the report takes note of the more than 2,000 murdered members of the leftist Patriotic Union party (*Unión Patriótica*, UP) but characterizes this situation as "what the UP perceives as a campaign of assassination waged against its leadership." What the State Department perceives of this state of affairs is never stated, but where the facts are so overwhelmingly clear, the State Department should have affirmed the UP's own conclusion or offered some explanation for its diffidence.

Other examples reflect the apparent tension between the State Department's desire to mute its criticism and its knowledge of the very ugly nature of the human rights situation in Colombia. For example, the report states that "Colombia does not imprison citizens for political beliefs or expressions of political convictions," but adds: "[H]owever, the [International Committee of the Red Cross] reported that it monitored 1,800 cases of citizens imprisoned under accusations of rebellion or aiding and abetting the insurgency, which are punishable under law." Many of these prisoners were non-combatants who in some cases were held for months before formal charges were filed.

Aside from the fact that the situation concerning those accused of "political" offenses is significantly worse than the report acknowledges, the State Department does not attempt to reconcile or explain the outcome of these apparently contradictory statements. Equally hard to fathom is the report's assertion that "[t]he Government generally did not interfere with the work of human rights NGOs." In fact, such organizations, the report notes, "were often threatened and intimidated" by the guerrillas, paramilitary forces or individual members of the police and military forces. In addition to inverting the proper order of those most likely to harass and intimidate human rights groups, the report again takes the liberty of implying that soldiers' actions against human rights organizations are somehow not associated with the military's historical institutional hostility toward and violence against the human rights community.

Internal contradictions resonate in several major themes throughout the report, including: (i) implicit acceptance of the notion of separation of government action from the actions of paramilitary groups and the uniformed services; (ii) praise for the Colombian government's repeated attempts to implement initiatives for the protection of human rights; and (iii) sympathy or understanding for the government due to its lack of the necessary resources to combat the paramilitary forces, guerrillas and narcotics traffickers.

Perhaps the most troubling of these are the State Department's repeated attempts to draw an artificial distinction between human rights violations committed by the state and those of the military and national police, as if the latter two were agencies unrelated to the government. One example is the report's statement that "[d]espite protective efforts by the Government, Indians were frequently the victims of violence throughout the year by the government security forces, paramilitary groups . . ., narcotics traffickers, and guerrillas." And as noted earlier, the discussion of attacks on NGOs attempts to make an artificial distinction between the government and the army, and between individual soldiers and their institution. The report contends that the government respects the rights of peaceful assembly and association in practice, though in 1995, the national police periodically shot, arrested, harassed and used excessive force against peasant protesters.

The report's portrayal of the state, military, security forces and national police as individual parts without any relation to a whole, allows the State Department to praise the government for its human rights efforts while pointing a finger at the uniformed forces. The report has liberal praise for the government for, among other things, acknowledging state responsibility for the 1989-1990 Trujillo massacres; announcing the formation of special task forces to combat paramilitary violence; appointing an anti-kidnapping czar; opening special human rights units; and attempting to negotiate with guerilla organizations. When the report proceeds to point out that, in spite of such efforts by the government, the police and the armed forces were responsible for "widespread human rights abuses"; that the military continued to cooperate with violent paramilitary groups; and that such groups engaged in social cleansing, it also distances the perpetrators from the government.

In many instances, the report cites only half-year statistics, inevitably making the pattern of human rights violations appear less extensive than when viewed as a whole. For example, the figures for murders, complaints of threats and forced disappearances, and "social cleansing" victims were cited for January through June only, despite the abundance of full year statistics offered by NGOs. The report's March 1996 publication date should permit the Department of State to obtain data and information for the full calendar year of 1995.

As in the past, the report fails to condemn human rights abuses in its own voice or to criticize the perpetrators directly. Rather, it often speaks only of "allegations" or "claims" by others, even where such claims are demonstrably credible.

The report also omits relevant examples of the government's serious violations of human rights. The most notable include the murders by paramilitary forces of 11 civilians directly in front of a local police station (without any police response) in Apartadó on May 14, 1995, and an attack by military helicopters and planes on the village of Puerto Trujillo, Meta, killing and injuring women and children. The army claimed there were guerrillas in the latter village, despite the fact that there was no return fire. The matter-of-fact reporting style diminishes the actual horror and extent of such abuses.

The report is also quick to state that there were arrests of individual officers but rarely acknowledges that there was generally no subsequent prosecution or conviction. The mere statement that an investigation "resulted in the arrest of an army major who commanded the army base"; or that as the result of the formation of a special task force, "several paramilitary leaders were arrested"; or that following massacres in Meta, the government established a special commission to seek a solution to the violence, gives the false impression that the government is moving forward with respect to prosecuting the perpetrators. The State Department is well aware that in less than one percent of such cases is a soldier successfully prosecuted.

Set against this record of impunity were those government measures which actively stripped Colombians of fundamental rights, such as the due process guarantees recognized by the Colombian Constitution. Such measures include the continued and widespread use of the "public order" or "regional" justice system and the imposition, on two occasions in 1995, of states of exception.

The report observes that in 1995, "[h]uman rights groups continued to charge that [the regional justice] system violated basic legal norms and procedural rights," but makes few critical judgments of its own about the regional courts and generally fails to give such allegations the attention they merit. The report obscures the fact that many of the regional courts' particular attributes — closed proceedings; secret evidence; anonymous witnesses, prosecutors and judges; and the widespread use of the military for police functions — have failed to achieve their stated purpose. And even if these courts were to succeed in their own terms, this still evades the fundamental question of whether this "success" would justify such systematic abuses. As the Lawyers Committee has indicated elsewhere:

> [T]he well-known procedural deficiencies of the judgment phase, including the anonymity of judges, prosecutors and witnesses, are nearly overshadowed by one central fact: in large areas of the country, the Government has effectively handed police powers to the military, which now arrests and detains suspects based on evidence to which the defense can rarely even gain access . . . . With prosecutors failing to exercise appropriate control over the military's arrest and detention practices, and judicial review so decimated that Colombia's Supreme Court considered it unconstitutional for a judge to scrutinize an order of pre-trial detention, the justice system is in reality distorted beyond reasonable recognition.

The report's short section on torture refers to individual incidents but does not capture the pervasiveness of torture throughout the country, or the state's role in fostering the environment in which it flourishes. To do so, the report might have added, for example, that the Colombian Commission of Jurists (formerly known as the Andean Commission of Jurists) notes that a person is tortured every 48 hours in Colombia, and "[a]ll available information indicates that military and police agents, in addition to their paramilitary allies, are the principal parties responsible for acts of torture in Colombia." One NGO case study concluded that 93% of persons detained by the police or armed forces were subjected to physical and/or psychological torture before being formally charged or released. In essence, the information available regarding the use of systematic torture paints a much different portrait of the level and pervasiveness of such atrocities in Colombia than does the report.

It would also have been useful for the report to discuss how torture is connected to other forms of abuse. For example, during the period between October 1994 and September 1995, Colombian human rights

NGOs counted 418 extrajudicial executions preceded by torture. The victims of such executions displayed various wounds, ranging from burns to mutilations, and many of the women had been raped. A discussion of the rampant impunity enjoyed by perpetrators of such offenses also would have been informative.

In short, although the report makes an effort to catalogue the wide variety of human rights abuses that remained unabated in Colombia in 1995, as in 1994, the report fails to come to terms with the complex ways in which these various abuses are interconnected. A more comprehensive approach would have documented the pivotal role the government has played in perpetuating the human rights disaster which Colombia has become. The State Department's instructions for the drafting of the *Country Reports* note that "[i]t is important . . . to make a conscientious effort to report what the available evidence shows and, where it is ambiguous, to report that." The report has failed to follow this guideline.

Although the report accurately acknowledges that certain actions taken by the Samper administration were likely to condone human rights abuses, it generally oversells the government's measures to confront Colombia's human rights crisis. For example, the government "took steps to reduce human rights violations," such as acknowledging responsibility for the 1989-90 massacres in Trujillo. The government's admission is welcome. However, the acknowledgment, however unprecedented, by a president who was not head of state during the period in question is no substitute for actions designed to curb current and future abuses, particularly when President Samper later publicly denies that such abuses continue. When the Colombian government began to study reforms for the military justice system in 1995, one set of such proposed reforms suggested major systematic changes to better protect human rights, while the other set maintained the current military characteristics (including the power to handle cases involving extrajudicial execution, forced disappearance and torture). President Samper supported the latter proposal, continuing, in the words of one human rights organization, the Colombian government's tradition of "winking at impunity." The president compounded matters in an October 1995 speech, stating that allegations that security forces committed human rights violations were "without foundation, presented by their enemies," and vowing to defend military jurisdiction.

Rather than exposing the failure of the Colombian judicial system to address abuses, the State Department comes close to appearing to justify them. More than once, the report notes that the judiciary and police have insufficient resources, especially funds, to properly investigate most killings; suggests that the judicial system has "continued to experience growing pains as the various courts, prosecutor's offices, and ministries attempted to define their roles and streamline their operations" following the 1991 judicial reorganization; and maintains that the judiciary remained "overburdened and in a state of chaos, staggering under a backlog of over [one] million cases." These are accurate statements, and in the case of court backlogs, one of the greatest reasons for due process violations. However, they are both a predictable result of other governmental policies, such as widespread arbitrary detentions, and to a large extent, irrelevant to the problem of impunity in military tribunals.

In the areas of arbitrary detention, the right of citizens to change their government and freedom of political association, the report tends to focus on the laws on the books rather than on day-to-day practices. With respect to detention, the report notes that the Colombian Constitution prohibits illegal detention, and that those detained have the right to be brought before a judge within 36 hours of arrest, as well as the right to petition for habeas corpus, which petition must be acted upon within 36 hours. Taking understatement to misleading extremes, the report simply states that "instances of arbitrary detention continued."

The report offers a straightforward treatment of the imposition in 1995 of two states of exception by the Colombian government. As it notes, these resulted in widespread violations of human rights, including what would otherwise constitute illegal detentions and searches, while the government apparently ignored the impact which its declaration of a state of emergency would have on "a judicial system that could not even address the needs of citizens under normal circumstances."

In addition, when discussing prison conditions in Colombia, the report accurately assesses these as "harsh," especially for those prisoners with "reduced means of support," and notes that "overcrowding and dangerous sanitary and health conditions remained serious problems."

The *Country Reports'* tradition of atomizing human rights issues that are interconnected continues in the 1995 report. Thus, the report separates its discussions of freedom of speech and press, freedom of peaceful assembly and association and "respect for political rights: the rights of citizens to change their government." While categories of this nature may be useful, the rigid structure has in fact, kept the report from providing the rounded, contextualized picture of the human rights situation that would allow policy makers to make genuinely informed decisions. Taken as a whole, these violations constitute a pattern of mutually reinforcing official activities rather than a large collection of isolated acts. Greater interplay between the narrow thematic discussions would better illuminate the overall situation.

The report's discussion of individual issues is also too narrowly focused in some spots. For instance, the section on freedom of speech and press never extends beyond the media — though this discussion, as far as it goes, is notably more subtle and probing than other portions of the report. This narrow focus ignores the many situations in which people seek to exercise freedom of speech in the context of political marches and meetings. The report distorts the truth by stating that "[t]he authorities do not normally interfere with public meetings and demonstrations," when in reality, in 1995, there were several instances in which the government did not merely interfere, but violently repressed public gatherings. In August 1995, approximately 800 farmers were stopped by the army on their way to participate in demonstrations, and were told they could proceed no further because guerrillas were killing peasant farmers in the direction they were headed. The peasants sat down in the road and demanded to meet with the department's governor, whereupon the soldiers proceeded to beat and tear-gas the peasants, which included minors. One of the protesters fainted on a bridge as a result of the tear gas, and a peasant farmer who came to her aid was attacked by members of the police and thrown off the bridge. Several other protesters have not been seen since. Law student Humberto Peña Taylor, who had been shot and seriously injured during a 1993 student demonstration, was shot and killed in June 1995 in a law faculty cafeteria by two men presumed by students to be working with members of state security forces.

The third subsection on political rights, dealing with the right of citizens to change their government, emphasizes the set of formal constitutional guarantees such as those providing for elections and secret ballots. An emphasis on the formal provisions, however, comes at the expense of a detailed account of the actual extent to which such formal guarantees are available to citizens. The report's claim that "all parties operate freely without government interference" is demonstrably misleading, if not false.

In fact, the government is, at best, complacent about activities that repress basic democratic rights. A Colombian government study has concluded that members of the security forces have been among the main perpetrators of violence against Patriotic Union activists, discussed above. Further, as Amnesty International has noted, although political parties and independent organizations technically are free to operate in Colombia, "members of all political parties have been victims of human rights violations including illegal detention, torture, 'disappearance' and extrajudicial execution because of their political views and activism."

Under its section on respect for political rights, the report notes that "critics" assert that vote-buying is a regular feature of elections in some regions, but makes no attempt to assess the accuracy of such a claim, instead stating that citizens exercise the right to vote in regular, secret ballot elections that have "historically been considered fair and open." Again, Amnesty International takes a different view, reporting that "[d]uring election campaigns paramilitary forces have been reported to threaten local people with death if they fail to vote for the traditional parties most closely associated to powerful economic sectors."

The report's section on women, children and indigenous groups does a better job of evaluating actual practice in its discussion of formal legal provisions. The report acknowledges that rape and other acts of violence against women are pervasive, and that the law provides relatively mild sentences and does not penalize marital rape or other forms of marital abuse. It also notes that discrimination against women "persists."

Critique 1995

As in the section on women, the report should be commended for distinguishing between the lofty set of formal rights accorded children in Colombia and the reality of day-to-day life for a significant number who suffer grave human rights abuses, as well as for recognizing state involvement in such crimes. As the *Washington Post* noted in January 1995, Colombian children are — on paper — the country's most protected citizens, while in practice, they are more likely to be murdered than children in any other country in the world. Some startling figures portray the gravity of human rights conditions for Colombian children. A child dies violently, on the average, every four hours in Colombia, and the annual total of 2,219 children killed each year now outstrips Brazil's notorious level of violent deaths for children by nearly 50%. An estimated 5,000 to 10,000 street children are in Bogotá where they are often abused, beaten and raped by police. Nationwide, an estimated 30,000 children were abandoned or placed in situations of risk as of October 1995. There are 45,000 annually documented cases of child abuse in Colombia. Some 600,000 children of grade-school age do not attend classes because there is no space available.

The report notes that vigilante gangs, often linked to the police, murdered children in several major cities as part of "social-cleansing" measures; that merchants and citizens' groups often allegedly hire off-duty police agents and contract killers to rid neighborhoods of children suspected to be beggars and thieves (although the report fails to attempt to verify such "allegations"); and that the Office of the Defender of the People reported "clear complicity by police officers in some of these killings."

The same section also notes the deaths of children in conflict zones caught in the crossfire between security forces, paramilitary groups and guerrillas; the deadly "leg breaker" land mines laid by guerrillas that have killed or mutilated many children; and the recruitment of minors for guerrilla groups despite national and international condemnation. The report does note that an estimated 800,000 children between the ages of 12 and 17 work — often under substandard conditions — in agriculture or in the informal sector as street vendors, in the leather tanning industry and in small, family-operated mines. Despite this acknowledgment, the report does not criticize the lack of government attempts to curb underage employment, but rather chooses to praise a government media outreach campaign designed to inform child laborers of their rights and where to turn for help (although the report does not discuss the mechanics of this program or how the government expected young workers to gain access to such information).

The Colombian government is well-known for its capacity to publicize its numerous initiatives to address widespread human rights abuses. The official human rights bureaucracy in Colombia is extensive, and is designed to create the impression that while abuses may occur, they are not a matter of official intent. The unfortunate truth is that the history of abuse and official complicity is too long to sustain this relatively benign portrait. The 1995 State Department report fails to dispel the illusion, and in some areas perpetuates it. Confronted with a high volume of reported abuse and the government's trademark flurry of ostensibly responsive activity, the State Department's critical faculties appear to have been muted, making its report as a whole less than the sum of its many parts.

CROATIA

The year 1995 was characterized by a significant increase in human rights violations in Croatia. This increase is largely attributable to the two Croatian police/military offensives to regain Serb-held territories. On May 1, Croatian forces regained control of Western Slavonia in operation "Flash," which violated the ceasefire agreement of March 29, 1994. On August 4, the Croatian Army launched operation "Storm," a major military offensive to recapture the Krajina region from the rebel Serbs who had occupied it since 1991. These offensives were carried out despite international concern over the likely repercussions for the Serb majorities in these areas. Reports from numerous dependable sources confirm claims that the Croatian Army, Special Police units and Civil Police were directly responsible for serious violations of human rights and humanitarian law both during and after the two offensives. These violations continued through the end of 1995. As a result, almost 200,000 Serb civilians, representing most of the Serb population from the territories they had previously occupied, fled from Western Slavonia and Krajina to Serbia and neighboring Bosnian Serb-controlled parts of Bosnia. This mass exodus constituted one of the largest displacements of civilians since the war began in 1991. Additionally, thousands of Serb homes and religious edifices have been looted and destroyed in what appears to be an attempt to erase all signs of Serbs ever having lived there.

The increase in war-related human rights violations was matched by a simultaneous increase in human rights violations not directly related to the military campaigns. Illegal and forced evictions continued to occur despite years of efforts by human rights groups to put a stop to them. In Split, local human rights groups received reports of new cases of human rights violations every week. Serb and Muslim minorities in the government-controlled parts of Croatia continued to suffer discriminatory treatment in employment, housing, justice and the enjoyment of cultural rights. The Croatian government suspended the constitutional safeguards for minorities which guaranteed the special status of districts which were predominantly populated by national minorities, created separate educational institutions and secured proportional representation in the parliament, government and judiciary. The state also continued to exercise control over the media through a variety of methods.

The 1995 State Department report does a good job of addressing most of the different categories of human rights violations which took place during the year and provides relevant examples to support its claims. However, despite its breadth, closer scrutiny reveals a number of structural faults, omissions and patterns of apparent bias which seriously undermine the report's overall objectivity and integrity.

The report contains a vast amount of information. However, proper analysis of its content is seriously hampered because of the way in which it is organized and presented. Related issues and events are discussed piecemeal and information is repeated in several different places. This may be attributable to the format outlined in the instructions distributed by the State Department to those drafting the *Country Reports*. In any case, the report's organization is confusing and lacks focus. For example, the Croatian government's discrimination against Muslims in the issuance of citizenship papers is discussed under the heading of Freedom of Religion, and again later under the heading of National/Racial/Ethnic Minorities. Also, the report refers to the human rights violations which took place during operations "Flash" and "Storm" throughout the document (and under numerous different subheadings), but the facts surrounding the two military offensives are presented on page 824, while the killings which occurred during and after the offensives are discussed earlier, on page 820 and the mass looting, destruction and burning of property carried out by the Croatian military is discussed on page 823. Killings are mentioned again on page 824 and burning and looting repeated for a second time on page 825. By scattering related information in this way and presenting necessary background information only after discussing the specific cases to which it applies, the report dilutes the significance and magnitude of the implications of the May and August offensives for the Serb population in the formerly occupied territories of Croatia. The report should therefore have focused on the two offensives and then described human rights violations within that context. To address the topic of human rights in Croatia in any other way is to fail to recognize the responsibility of these offensives for the sharp increase in human rights violations in Croatia in 1995. Furthermore, by presenting the information relating to human rights violations in that way the reader would more easily distinguish the forest from the trees. It would become clear that Operations "Flash" and "Storm" constituted an ethnic cleansing campaign — something the report appears deliberately to evade.

The case for the existence of a Croatian ethnic cleansing policy is a strong one, made stronger by statements like this from President Franjo Tudjman on September 4, 1995: "And those from abroad who condemn us for burning Serbian houses on the liberated territories of Croatia, let them remember the biblical principles from the Old Testament — eye for an eye, tooth for a tooth!" Further evidence confirming the existence of a Croatian ethnic cleansing campaign is obtained from the numerous international human rights monitors who witnessed its deadly aftermath. The European Community Monitoring Mission Special Report concluded that the "events in the five weeks following 'Operation Storm' suggest that the first aim of Croatia was to recover her territorial integrity and to re-establish communication routes between continental Croatia and Dalmatia. A second achievement of the operation has been the disappearance of a sizable and unwanted minority." Additionally, an anonymous European Union monitor was quoted in *The New York Times* as saying ". . . now they (the Croats) are carrying out a campaign of ethnic cleansing as effective, and often as brutal, as that carried out by the Serbs. Only the uniforms are different; the behavior is the same."

The argument is further strengthened by the Croatian government's systematic and blatant disregard for human rights and international law witnessed in the Krajinan city of Knin, on which over 2,000 shells rained down from Croatian positions during the first 24 hours of the August offensive, despite the fact that there were no reports of Serb soldiers positioned there. The absence of Serbian military positions within the city suggests that Croatian forces were deliberately targeting the predominantly Serb civilian population. "Knin went from 35,000 people to 500 living and 500 dead," said Colonel Andrew Leslie, chief of staff of the U.N. force based in Knin during the beginning of Operation Storm, in an interview with *Time* magazine. He concluded that "[t]he behavior of the Croatian military was appalling. It had to be government policy."

Despite the overwhelming evidence of a Croatian ethnic cleansing campaign, the report never refers to it as such. It describes the Croatian Army's killing of Serb civilians during and after the military operations, their massive looting and burning of Serb homes, their harassment and ill-treatment of Serbs and the failure to protect those who remained in the formerly Serb-controlled areas, and yet fails to conclude that these actions collectively comprised an ethnic cleansing campaign. The terms "ethnic cleansing" and "genocide" are never used to describe the apparent intentions and results of the campaign by the Croatian armed forces. The report does, however, accurately identify the activities of the army of the so-called Serbian Republic of Krajina and the Serbian Army in Eastern Slavonia as ethnic cleansing campaigns. This apparent double standard and failure to assign equal blame for the same crimes places the report's objectivity in question and suggests a possible bias in favor of the Croatian government.

The report's possible bias is also implied in statements that are tainted with ambiguous or forgiving language. The paragraphs describing the human rights situation in Serb-controlled regions of Croatia are sharply worded, and the authors of the report do not mince words in attributing responsibility for violations. For example, it writes: "The police and military forces continued to use violence, intimidation and displacement against Croats and minorities to settle incoming Serb refugees and achieve their goal of ethnic cleansing in the areas they controlled." Unfortunately, the same candor is not always apparent in describing the actions (or lack thereof) of the Croatian authorities. Statements like: "The Government failed to establish adequate civil authority to control vengeful renegade arsonists, looters, and murderers who still operated with impunity in the reclaimed areas months after the offensive had ended" are misleading in so far as they imply that the Croatian government expended serious efforts in order to protect the property and lives of ethnic Serbs in the formerly Serb-occupied areas. To the contrary, the participation of Croatian active-duty personnel and especially professional "home guard" in the murder of innocent Serb civilians has been amply documented, as has their involvement in other heinous crimes, as described in Section 1 of the report.

The report's failure to recognize the evidence that Croatia's May and August offensives constituted ethnic cleansing is mirrored by its failure to identify the "soft" ethnic cleansing policy which Croatian authorities have employed in the remaining months of 1995. These subtler methods are meant to uphold the results of the ethnic cleansing campaign executed during the offensives and are directly at odds with the Croatian government's numerous verbal commitments to the safe return of those Serbs who fled during the war.

According to the report, by year's end, the Croatian government had charged only 11 individuals in connection with the 2,878 cases of arson that were reported to the United Nations. The report also claims that Croatian authorities have "clarified" 770 out of the 1,054 identified cases of looting (a 73% rate of "clarification") and brought charges against 1,260 people. Although this appears impressive, the ambiguity of what is meant by "clarified" brings into question whether or not justice has truly been served. By mid-1996, there had been no convictions with respect to looting, further weakening the government's claim that it is taking action. Moreover, by mid-1996 there had also been no convictions for killings that took place. Such a dismal record clearly gives grounds for questioning the sincerity of the Croatian government with respect to the apprehension and prosecution of criminals. When displaced Serbs who wish to return to their homes in Croatia learn that Croatian authorities have successfully investigated and charged individuals in so few cases, they will rightly believe that the Croatian government is not seriously concerned with assuring their safety, despite its public assertions that they are welcome to return.

Another form of deterrence is the apathy and passive consent demonstrated by members of Croatia's police force in the field. This trend was noted by the U.N. press officer in Knin who told *The New York Times* on September 30: "Our U.N. patrols are continuing to find bodies, usually of elderly Serbs, killed in their homes." Despite repeated requests by the U.N. to the Croatian authorities to intervene, they appear to make little effort, and usually do nothing. This claim is further supported by the Croatian Helsinki Committee (CHC), whose fact-finding missions have witnessed Croatian police officers ignoring gangs of looters as they drove past in cars filled with plunder. Such reports should come as no surprise in light of the fact that the CHC has also received reports of uniformed Croatian police and military personnel participating in the looting themselves. This passive consent by Croatian authorities with respect to vigilante activity was typical during the two offensives and especially in the months following.

The shortcomings of the judicial system, the passive consent of the police toward criminal elements, the Croatian government's apparent defiance of the War Crimes Tribunal at the Hague, along with the passage of the property law regarding Serb property, the suspension of constitutional safeguards for minorities and the bureaucratic obstacles to obtaining citizenship papers are all methods intended to erode Serb confidence and security, thus deterring them from ever returning to their homes in Croatia. They exacerbate an already difficult situation faced by those ethnic Serbs wishing to return and provide further evidence of the Croatian government's objective of creating an ethnically pure state.

As the report notes, a number of human rights groups operate in Croatia. However, there is no mention made of the Croatian government's attitude toward them. Despite the Croatian government's numerous pledges to cooperate with human rights organizations, it has been known to interfere with their work. For example, the Croatian Helsinki Committee for Human Rights was denied access to Croatian jails in order to investigate conditions — rumored to be dismal — following the death of an inmate under questionable circumstances. Government officials justified this denial of access on the grounds that the investigation would cause too much unrest among the prisoners and prison officials. The report also fails to mention how Croatian forces denied access to international monitors and U.N. troops wanting to investigate reported mass graves. The European Community Monitoring Mission Special Report stated that it is difficult to gain access to areas in order to investigate reports of killings. The mission attempted to investigate a rumor that Croatian army troops were burning corpses at a church in Knin. Their report states that they "were denied access by a large security presence but witnessed an excavator digging inside the cemetery along with medical personnel, two ambulances and a medium size refrigerator truck." The mission also reported that it visited mass graves in Gracac where it counted 71 graves. It stated that burials were continuing and that many Serbs are still missing.

In addition to interfering with the work of human rights organizations by denying them access to important evidence at sites where violations are reported to have occurred, the Croatian government also carried out a program of disinformation about the number of civilian casualties, missing persons, summary executions and the existence of the mass graves, thus further thwarting the efforts of human rights organizations.

The Croatian government continued to exert great pressure on the independent media. In 1995 there were numerous cases of aggressive government censorship, but two examples will suffice to describe accurately the government's attitude toward independent media. The first case involved the seizure and burning of hundreds of copies of *The Feral Tribune* (an independent and analytical newspaper with a satirical approach, critical of the government), by so-called "unidentified individuals" in various cities across Croatia. These supposedly unrelated incidents occurred simultaneously and the fact that reporters and cameramen from the government-controlled media were on hand to record the incidents, coupled with the fact that police officers at the scene failed to stop these criminal acts, suggests that the action was premeditated, that government officials were notified ahead of time and that they were not random independent occurrences.

The second incident involved the banning of Radio Labin, an independent radio station known for its critical views of the government. The Croatian government defended this act with arguments that were dubious at best. The government claimed that another group which supported the Bosnian branch of the Croatian Democratic Union (HDZ) should be allocated that particular frequency because of the higher quality of its work — although it had never been on the air and had no equipment. The officially controlled media acted as a conduit for attacks on behalf of the government against individual journalists and the independent media as a whole. Roman Latkovic, a journalist for *Novi*

List, one of Croatia's two independent newspapers, was viciously attacked and categorized as an enemy of Croatia in a lengthy narrated report on the evening news on Croatian national television. This harangue was prompted by an article by Mr. Latkovic in which he encouraged Croatia's citizenry to take any and all democratic steps necessary to remove President Franjo Tudjman from power. The lengthy commentary was a reply by the television station in defense of President Tudjman and featured a picture of Mr. Latkovic for the entire duration of the narrative. Mr. Latkovic received 169 anonymous crank calls and death threats in the 24 hours following the broadcast and as a result was forced to flee the country out of concern for his physical safety. Individuals from NGOs were also the target of government attacks in the officially controlled media. For example, Ivan Zvonimir Cicak, the president of the Croatian Helsinki Committee for Human Rights, is regularly vilified in the state-controlled press and television as an enemy of the state. Like Mr. Latkovic, he has never been given the opportunity to speak in his own defense. This sort of one-sided polemic has unfortunately become the norm on Croatias only national news program, and the Croatian media in general has become a regular medium for ethnically based hate speech.

While some journalists and noteworthy individuals suffered attacks on their reputations via the government-controlled media, others were physically threatened. In what later became a well publicized event, Vice President Borislav Skegro put a gun to the head of Edita Vahovic, a journalist who had sharply criticized him a few days earlier in an article in *Novi List*. Ms. Vahovic pressed charges against Mr. Skegro, but the proceedings were dropped by the government due to his immunity during his tenure as a government official.

Croatia has committed itself to respect human rights in times of armed conflict as outlined in the four Geneva Conventions of 1949 it has ratified as well as in a number of OSCE documents. The Code of Conduct on Politico-Military Aspects of Security adopted as part of the Budapest Document at the OSCE Budapest Review Conference in late 1994 sets forth the standards by which the participating states are to abide in events of armed conflict. Croatia became a fully recognized member of the OSCE in 1994. Although the OSCE commitments are not legally binding, they nevertheless have political authority and constitute sources of obligations for the participating states.

Paragraph 33 of the Budapest Document states that:

[t]he participating States deeply deplore the series of flagrant violations of international humanitarian law that occurred in the OSCE region in the recent years and reaffirm their commitment to respect and ensure respect for general international instruments, including the 1949 Geneva Conventions and their additional protocols, to which they are a party.

Article 36 of the Code of Conduct states that: "Each participating State will ensure that any decision to assign its armed forces to an internal security mission is arrived at in conformity with constitutional procedures. Such decisions will prescribe the armed forces' missions, ensuring that they will be performed under the effective control of constitutionally established authorities and subject to the rule of law. If recourse to force cannot be avoided in performing internal security missions, each participating State will ensure that its use must be commensurate with the needs for enforcement. *The armed forces will take due care to avoid injury to civilians or their property.*" (emphasis added) As the State Department amply documents, the Croatian government's behavior with respect to human rights in 1995 was not at all consistent with these commitments.

According to the November 7 report of the U.N. Special Rapporteur, civilian targets, including residential areas of Knin, were deliberately targeted by the Croatian army. Eyewitnesses reported that fleeing Serbs were shot dead by Croatian army soldiers during both military operations. International human rights groups and U.N. and European monitors have all concluded that killings of civilians during the actual fighting did take place without any military justification. According to the EU Monitoring Mission Special Report with respect to Krajina, "newly killed Serbs were found at the rate of six per day." The most common murder method was shots to the back of the head or slit throats. Moreover, the government has done little or nothing to bring the perpetrators of these crimes to justice.

The Special Rapporteur's reports of July 5 and November 7 stated that serious violations of humanitarian law and human rights law occurred during and after both military operations The EU Monitoring Mission Special Report concluded that grave breaches of international law were committed by the Croatian authorities during and after Operation "Storm." Based on evidence gathered during a fact-finding mission to the Krajina from August 17-19, the International Helsinki Federation for Human Rights and the Croatian Helsinki Committee concluded that "violations of OSCE human dimension commitments and the Code of Conduct on Politico-Military Aspects of Security appear to have been committed during and after Operation Storm. Violations of human rights and humanitarian law have also taken place and many allegations require further investigation."

The State Department report makes no mention of Croatia's human rights commitments under international law or the OSCE commitments it has pledged to uphold. The Croatian government's reluctance to fulfill its obligations is also evidenced by its failure to deliver all indicted war criminals within its borders to the Hague. According to reports, Ivica Rajic, a war criminal indicted by the war crimes tribunal in the Hague, has been living with his family in a government-owned flat at the Motel Dujlovo in Split. Meanwhile, another indicted war criminal, Dario Kordic, is currently traveling without any restrictions throughout Croatia. This blatant disregard for the commitments it agreed to in the Dayton Peace Agreement is perhaps the most flagrant demonstration of the Croatian government's defiance of the international community and its refusal to respect fundamental human rights norms.

Croatian President Franjo Tudjman has expressed his views on the return of the Serbs to Croatia with great clarity. In an interview by Olga Ramljak of *Slobodna Dalmacija*, Tudjman said:

> If you remember, in one of the agreements between myself, Dobrica Cosic [then-president of the Federal Republic of Yugoslavia] and Milosevic in Geneva in 1992, we agreed about

the first steps towards returning to normal living conditions and pointed out that we would enable 'voluntary resettlement.' However, things took another course and what has happened has happened despite these people's personal tragedy, but the result will be positive because the role of the Serbs will be as small as it was during the time of the Turks.

By association, Tudjman's comments also speak volumes about the position of the current Croatian government. The position, in short, is one of ethnic intolerance and the promotion of an ethnically pure state. The persecution of ethnic minorities by civilians and the military and police, the resistance to reintegration, silencing of the media and other repressive measures are evidence of such a position. The omissions and choices of terminology in the State Department's report on Croatia make it appear at best ambivalent and at worse consciously biased. Furthermore, the report also casts a dark shadow over U.S. foreign policy toward Croatia and the former Yugoslavia as a whole, since its failure to recognize and strongly criticize the culpability of the Croatian government with respect to human rights violations could be considered by default an act of consent.

The escalation in the frequency and severity of human rights violations over the course of 1995 does not bode well for the development of a democratic state in Croatia governed by the rule of law. The Croatian government continues to violate the human rights of its citizens in the face of international pressure and condemnation. In addition to the report's weaknesses, which are mentioned above, it does not address the consequences of these actions for the future of pluralist democracy in Croatia, and thus diminishes the impact and significance of its findings.

EGYPT

The human rights situation in Egypt continued to deteriorate in 1995. Security forces operating under the Emergency Laws, which have been in force since 1981, acted with complete impunity and total disregard for any basic human rights. Arbitrary arrests, incommunicado detention, hostage taking, torture, extrajudicial killings, restrictions on freedoms of association and expression and executions after palpably unfair trials have become the norm. The Egyptian government made a mockery out of the People's Assembly elections held in November. A large number of candidates from opposition parties were arrested and widespread fraud and tampering was reported. Furthermore, the escalating pattern of violence continued with a vengeance. As of November 1995, 963 people have been killed in politically related violence in the past five years. Three hundred thirty-three (35%) of them died in the past ten months alone.

As in previous years, the 1995 State Department report is generally accurate and comprehensive. It documents widespread human rights abuses perpetrated by the Egyptian government and rebels. The report is particularly assertive and straightforward in its appraisal of the Egyptian political system. It repeats the often quoted statement that, "The ruling NDP dominates the political scene to such an extent that the people do not have a meaningful ability to change their government." Additionally, it is candid in its discussion of torture, stating that "there were numerous credible reports of mistreatment and torture." Furthermore, the report correctly documents the increasing use of military courts to try political opponents. It states, "The use of military and state security tribunals under the Emergency Law has deprived hundreds of civilian defendants of their constitutional right to be tried by an 'ordinary judge.'" The report admits that "military courts do not guarantee civilian defendants due process before an independent tribunal." However — and again as in previous years — the main problem with the report remains its tone and language. The latter is often mechanical and detached and, at times, equivocal and inconsistent. It does not reflect a sense of urgency about the increasingly abysmal human rights situation in Egypt. In addition, the report occasionally includes inexplicable statements that would only serve to appease the Egyptian government.

According to the State Department instructions for drafting the *Country Reports*, each report should indicate in the introduction what type of system the government claims to exist and the system that actually exists — for example, a republic, a monarchy or an authoritarian regime. The report says that according to its Constitution, Egypt is a social democracy in which Islam is the state religion. It goes on to state, in a matter-of-fact fashion, that Hosni Mubarak was re-elected unopposed to a third six-year term by the People's Assembly in 1993. The report then asserts that the ruling party commands large majorities in the popularly elected People's Assembly, and that the government reported that 50% of registered voters turned out to vote in the November People's Assembly elections. These statements simply reflect what the government claims the system to be without independently appraising the validity of this claim. In fact, the Egyptian political system is an authoritarian one in which there is a huge discrepancy between the enumerated constitutional and legal guarantees and the political practices of the state.

The report affirms that, "The Government generally respects many human rights, but others are restricted by the continuing imposition of the emergency law." This is a shocking statement. Indeed, in light of the numerous human rights violations documented later on in the report, it is close to incomprehensible. One is left guessing as to how or why the report reaches the conclusion that the Egyptian government respects "many human rights." This statement is neither defended nor explained elsewhere in the report.

Earlier, the report states that "some members of the security forces committed serious human rights abuses." According to the instructions to those drafting the *Country Reports*, this language should be used only "in instances in which only a few members of the security forces were culpable." However, just a few paragraphs later the report states that: "In fighting the terrorists, the security forces mistreated and tortured prisoners, held detainees in prolonged pretrial detention, and allegedly committed extrajudicial killings . . . . Aside from the antiterrorist campaign, the local police have abused common criminal suspects."

These statements raise at least two problems. First, the report gives the impression that the security forces commit abuses only in the context of fighting terrorism. This is simply inaccurate and is a gross understatement of the impunity by which the security forces operate. Second, it is not clear whether the report is arguing that only a few members of the security forces were involved in human rights abuses. If in fact this is the report's argument, besides being misleading, the report itself contradicts this assertion on several occasions.

Reflecting the same ambiguity in the section on torture, the report states that "there is convincing evidence that some police and security officers, as well as prison guards, routinely abuse and torture detainees." This statement implies that torture is the result of indiscretions by individual officials rather than a government-sanctioned — and even government-mandated — policy. This is inconsistent with the report's assertion that there are numerous credible reports of mistreatment and torture. In fact, reports of torture by the security forces and police are so widespread that it is fairly clear that torture has become a governmental policy. In 1995, military courts consistently ignored allegations of torture in admitting coerced confessions and handed down draconian sentences. Security forces engaged in house demolitions, destruction of crops, random arrests, hostage-taking and the torture of children to extract confessions from their fathers. Investigations into human rights abuses by security forces are not made public and are woefully inadequate. The report itself admits that the government stated that "it will not disclose further details of individual cases of police abuse for fear of harming the morale of law enforcement officers . . . ." It is quite clear that abuses are not the result of individual indiscretions by "some" members of the security forces. Rather the whole apparatus of the Egyptian government sanctions and promotes policies that do not exhibit the least regard for the citizens of the country.

Confronted by certain egregious governmental violations, the report often fails to use the active voice or to draw conclusions. The State Department instructions to drafters of the *Country Reports* specify that it is not sufficient to state that human rights monitors claim certain violations took place. Rather, the report, whenever possible, has an obligation to render an opinion and draw conclusions in its own voice.

When discussing extrajudicial killings the report states: "There were several credible reports . . . that security forces were involved in what amounted to extrajudicial killings, because they allegedly were issued shoot-to-kill orders in certain antiterrorist operations." When it discusses deaths in custody, the report states that according to the government, 71 prisoners died in custody in 1995 and that the government denies charges of intentional mistreatment. The report additionally states that after a large number of deaths in the New Valley Prison (13) the government ordered that the medical facilities be brought up to standard, and that government investigations in both the Istikbal Torah and Abu Zaabal prisons (where 58 deaths had occurred) concluded that the prisoners there died of natural causes. On the other hand, the report asserts, human rights groups, family members and defense lawyers "alleged" that at least some of the deaths were the result of torture and mistreatment. Furthermore, the report adds, the authorities "reportedly" denied family members permission to view the bodies of relatives.

It is very positive that the State Department finds reports of shoot-to-kill orders to be credible. This is particularly significant in light of the fact that Egyptian Foreign Minister Hassan el-Alfi, in a rather shocking statement, seemed to imply that in certain circumstances the government has a right to conduct summary executions. On May 10, 1995 el-Alfi said: "During the past years, we have been very patient in our fight against terrorism. . . . We could have annihilated the terrorists. . . . We found weapons and got full confessions from the people who are currently in prison, which would have entitled us to kill them on the spot."

Nevertheless, the report's failure to take an equally assertive stand on deaths in custody is a major omission. Amnesty International has documented a large number of cases of death in custody in 1995. Nearly all the cases, whether in New Valley, Istikbal Torah or Abu Zaabal prisons, involved extensive and persistent torture. Families of the dead have not been given copies of any medical and autopsy reports or even death certificates. Some were not even told the cause of death. Although the government claims that it investigates all deaths in custody, the methods of such investigations are questionable and the findings are not made public.

The report is equally inconclusive about the number of political detainees in Egyptian prisons. The government claims that it has imprisoned between 2,500 and 4,000 "suspected terrorists." Unofficial estimates by Egyptian or international NGOs range from 15,000 to 20,000. As the report acknowledges, this estimate does not include the undetermined number of detainees who are held incommunicado without being registered in the prison system. Nevertheless, the report merely reproduces the official and unofficial figures without reaching any conclusion of its own as to the actual number of political detainees.

The pattern of ambiguity is recreated when the report addresses the harassment and detention of lawyers. Last year's edition of the *Critique* called attention to an alarming trend of harassment and persecution of lawyers. This trend continued unabated in 1995. The report states: "Human Rights groups and defense lawyers have claimed that the government has intimidated lawyers representing terrorist suspects by detaining and questioning them on the activities of their clients." It goes on to say, "The Government contends that some defense lawyers are suspected of collaborating in terrorist groups and that therefore the detention is legal." The report gives no sense of how it evaluates these competing claims. This is particularly alarming because in recent years there has been a marked increase in the number of arrests and physical abuse of lawyers defending unpopular causes. As the International Commission of Jurists stated in a recent report, "The right of individuals to a legal defense and the duty of lawyers to accord this defense are threatened by systematic government intimidation, arrest and abuse of lawyers [in Egypt], as well as the administrative detention and torture of their clients."

In a similar fashion the report fails to take a clear and precise stand when assessing governmental attitudes regarding human rights organizations. Although acknowledging that the government has refused to license local human rights groups, the report states that these groups are allowed to operate openly and that at times they enjoy the cooperation of government officials. The report does acknowledge that on at least six occasions the government banned meetings of human rights groups or denied them permits to hold conferences. Additionally, the report states that the Ministry of Justice issued an advisory ruling requiring all human rights organizations registered as private corporations to re-register as NGOs as defined by Law 32 or face punitive actions. Of course, the problem here is that once these organizations attempted to register under Law 32, they would be denied a license by the government, as has been the case with the Egyptian Organization for Human Rights (EOHR) The report then states that human rights organizations have expressed concern over a hostile campaign by the government-controlled press and over verbal attacks by senior government officials. However, the report concludes, the government did not close down any group during the year.

Although the report is factually accurate, all of this is presented in a detached language and the only affirmative conclusion reached is that human rights organizations were not closed down and that they are allowed to operate openly. Nevertheless, the reality of governmental policies is far more problematic. Besides interference with their meetings, as stated above, human rights NGOs withstood a variety of other pressures in 1995. New legislative regulations were introduced aimed at increasing government control over the activities of NGOs. The government introduced plans to create a government-appointed NGO council which would supervise the activities and funding of NGOs. Furthermore, in January the Ministry of Justice and the Foreign Ministry stressed that it is illegal for NGOs to receive funding from any foreign institution or individual. Even more, staff members of human rights organizations were harassed. Security forces pressured 12 EOHR members to resign by threatening them and warning that they belonged to an "illegal" organization. High-ranking government officials, as well as the officially controlled media, impugned the motives and questioned the integrity of local and international human rights groups and activists. For example, Ambassador Adel Safli, Deputy Minister of Foreign Affairs of International Relations, accused EOHR of being a "subversive group." Interior Minister el-Alfi accused Human Rights Watch/Middle East of being clearly biased against Egypt, accused other human rights organizations of relying on terrorists for their sources of information and accused the EOHR of being funded by foreign powers bent on harming Egypt — such as the Lawyers Committee for Human Rights.

The attitude of the Egyptian Government toward its abysmal human rights record has been dishonest and even insolent. Senior government officials characterized last year's *Country Report* on Egypt as "fabrications" and "lies." Interior Minister el-Alfi asserted that the *Country Reports* are biased and based on stories appearing in opposition papers sympathetic to terrorism and on reports of organizations with suspect motives. Furthermore, el-Alfi boasted about Egypt's submission of its periodic report to the U.N. Committee for Combating Torture. Ironically, the Committee deplored the fact that Egypt did not prepare the report in accordance with the Committee's general guidelines and that the information provided was general and not specific.

Last year's edition of the *Critique* noted that the 1994 report should have avoided the impression that the State Department tacitly agrees with the Egyptian government's attitude toward human rights abuses. The Egyptian government seems to grow more obstinate each year, and the Interior Minister's claims more outrageous. The ambiguity and indecisiveness of the 1995 report on several material points can only lend support to the Egyptian government's lack of seriousness about its human rights commitments.

When discussing the opposition's concerns about the guarantees provided for fair elections, el-Alfi exhibited a typically dismissive attitude. In response to a comment that the opposition complains that the guarantees are insufficient, his response was: "Naturally, any oppositionist is bound to make justifications and attacks." In fact, the People's Assembly elections were anything but fair. The elections were marred by a massive amount of manipulation and fraud. The election violations are too extensive to recount here but what follows is a partial list. First, the government arrested over 1,000 representatives of Muslim Brotherhood candidates during the first and second rounds. Candidates from various opposition parties were arrested as well. Second, security forces rigged voting in entire constituencies after expelling candidate representatives or voters from polling stations. Third, the elections were conducted without representatives of opposition candidates being present, either because they were arrested or forced to leave the polling stations. Fourth, fraud was widespread: many photocopies of voting cards were found inside the ballot boxes; the numbers and data on candidates' lists were altered; electoral rolls were forged, with up to 20,000 bogus names being added in some constituencies. Also, election lists were manipulated through the repeated addition of names of relatives of National Democratic Party members. Fifth, sub-polling station chairs, public polling station chairs and police stations refused to receive or record any election violations. Additionally, the Supreme Administrative Court ordered the annulment of elections in 109 constituencies and ordered the suspension of the Minister of the Interior's decree to conduct a second round of voting in these constituencies. The government ignored the ruling and proceeded with the second round of elections anyway. Furthermore, acts of thuggery and violence by government supporters and security forces left 878 wounded and 51 dead. This was the highest number of deaths and injuries in any single election in Egypt's parliamentary history.

The report does not describe this alarming state of affairs. It simply reports that voting was marred by irregularities. However it states many of these irregularities appeared to result from either inadequate crowd control or a breakdown in the oversight system. It asserts that: "Violent incidents, mostly among supporters of competing candidates, resulted in about 20 deaths." Furthermore, the report states: "Critics maintain that the government's campaign of arrests of Muslim Brothers was designed to exclude the Brotherhood from the legislative elections." The report's detached language and, in fact its overall conclusions about the Egyptian elections, defy comprehension. The number of dead stated by the report is the official number. The report does not review any other figures or even mention their existence. Ultimately, the report gives the impression that the irregularities that marred the elections were the result of mismanagement rather than a coordinated and deliberate policy. Human rights observers have consistently documented numerous cases of deliberate ballot box stuffing and other violations. The government detained a total of 1,712 people, most of them candidate representatives.

Egypt

The ruling NDP won 93.93% of all the seats, independents won 3.15% and the opposition parties won 2.92%. Most of the independents applied to join the NDP after winning. These figures and facts are alarming and demand a more affirmative stand by the report.

The Egyptian government implemented several new restrictions on the freedom of association in 1995. The report clearly asserts that "[s]ubstantial restrictions on these freedoms continue," and it competently reviews several of the new limitations. However, the report fails to mention that the Egyptian government amended the regulations governing the chambers of commerce to give the finance minister direct supervisory powers. In addition, the government now appoints the deans of college faculties. Previously, faculty members elected the deans. The University Council is now dominated by government appointees. Previously, it was dominated by elected members. Furthermore, the government abolished elections for the position of village headman. These positions are now filled by government appointees.

In an effort to limit the freedom of press, the government passed Law 93 of 1995 which imposes criminal penalties for acts of speech. The report's coverage of Law 93 and freedom of speech and press issues is generally good. The report states that under the new law the definition of criminal libel is so vague that it "imposes severe limitations on press freedom." In fact, the new law mandates fines and imprisonment for broadly defined offenses such as "publishing false or biased rumours, news and statements or disconcerting propaganda" if such material "offends social peace, arouses panic . . . harms the public interest or shows contempt for state institutions or officials." Under the new law the prosecutor no longer has to prove malicious intent in libel and defamation cases. Furthermore, the new law revoked statutes prohibiting the detention of journalists pending the investigation of press-related offenses.

The report, however, incorporates a passage that makes its position rather ambiguous. It states that under the previous press laws, "penalties [were] so minimal and the judicial process so long and costly that individuals or officials who [were] wrongly defamed [had] no realistic legal recourse. This has given some opposition, and even government-controlled newspapers license to publish rumours." One is left to wonder whether the report believes that the new draconian press laws are somehow justified because of the problems that the previous laws posed. Furthermore, libel and defamation laws in a democracy do not prevent the press from publishing rumours and do not avoid costly and time-consuming litigation. Yet this does not justify the passage of draconian press laws that effectively prohibit criticism of public officials or the discussion of controversial public issues.

The report is far more assertive and comprehensive in condemning the denial of citizens of the right to due process by military and state security tribunals. For the first time since the 1960s the government has tried civilian defendants in military courts on non-violent charges. The report candidly states that "the military courts do not guarantee civilian defendants due process before an independent tribunal." In 1995 military courts were used to silence political opponents for holding opinions the government deemed unacceptable. These trials are such a fundamental denial of due process that they have been called "kangaroo trials." In the trial of Muslim Brotherhood members, 350 lawyers, including Britons, Americans and Germans, walked out of court and withdrew from their cases in protest. As the report notes, the trials are rushed and there is no adequate appeal process. In fact, in 1995, in the re-organization of the *Jihad* case, involving Islamists accused of a variety of terrorist offenses including attacks on tourists and government officials, 42 defendants were tried in 48 days. Two were sentenced to death, 28 to prison and 12 were acquitted. From December 1992 to May 1995, military courts, after woefully unfair trials, sentenced a further 64 defendants to death. Amnesty International has stated that it considers these death sentences to be summary and arbitrary executions. To make matters worse, acquittals before these courts mean very little; of the 158 civilian defendants acquitted in military trials only two have been released.

In summary, as last year's *Critique* noted, the human rights situation in Egypt is deteriorating with each passing year. The year 1995 witnessed new restrictions on civil liberties and new extremes in human rights abuses. Future State Department reports should adopt a much clearer and more assertive tone that conveys a real sense of urgency. Furthermore, future reports should avoid giving the impression that Egypt is receiving preferred coverage because of its close relationship with the United States. As in previous years, the report is generally accurate and comprehensive in its basic presentation of factual material. However, as in previous years, it is often ambiguous and equivocal in tone, as if reluctant to hold the Egyptian Government responsible for its human rights commitments. Ambiguity is not the only problem. At times the report is also disingenuous and openly misleading — as when it asserts that the Egyptian Government respects many human rights.

ETHIOPIA

The 1995 State Department report begins by stating that "Ethiopia's political landscape changed significantly in 1995." Yet the basic terrain it goes on to describe remains remarkably similar to what it has been in recent years. Since its overthrow of Mengistu Haile-Mariam in 1991, the Ethiopian People's Revolutionary Democratic Front (EPRDF) has dominated Ethiopian politics. The EPRDF's record of respecting human rights is significantly better than was that of the Mengistu government. The EPRDF has curbed many of the abuses that were prevalent under Mengistu, and continues to take further measures to ensure respect for basic rights. Nonetheless, serious abuses continue. And the EPRDF's stated commitment to human rights often outstrips its commitment in practice. Against this background, two criticisms can be made of the 1995 State Department report. First, although the report should be commended for its catalog of abuses, its reliance on the EPRDF's stated goals and positions and its dismissal of various credible reports of abuse overstates the progress the EPRDF has made, and understates the seriousness of the current abuses. This is particularly evident in the report's discussion of the May 1995 elections and the issue of press freedom. Second, it fails adequately to address the likely impact that the EPRDF's policy of devolving power to regional government units will have on respect for human rights at the regional level.

National and regional elections were held in May and June to elect a successor to the Transitional Government (TGE), which had governed Ethiopia since the overthrow of Mengistu in 1991. Although dominated since its inception by the EPRDF, the TGE originally included several opposition parties, the most influential of which was the Oromo Liberation Front (OLF), which held 12 of the 87 seats in the TGE Council of Representatives. Following the OLF's boycott of the 1992 elections, the TGE and the EPRDF became essentially the same. Most opposition parties boycotted the May-June elections, as they had in previous years. As expected, the EPRDF won an overwhelming number of seats in the new government of the Federal Democratic Republic of Ethiopia (FDRE). The FDRE is thus, as was the TGE, dominated by the

EPRDF. And Meles Zenawi, the president of the TGE, is now the prime minister of the FDRE.

Although viewed by international observers as generally fair, the elections were marred by being boycotted by most opposition parties. While recognizing the EPRDF's harassment of some opposition parties, the report appears to dismiss the boycott as being based on the opposition parties' "refus[al] to test the TGE's stated willingness to allow opposition participation." In this regard, the report cites, without attribution, a "widespread finding that opposition participation was possible." The report continues on to imply that opposition is limited to "some elites" who are dissatisfied with the EPRDF's policy of ethnic federalism.

All of this is at significant odds with the finding of various observers. Terrence Lyons of the Brookings Institution, in his article "Closing the Transition: the May 1995 Elections in Ethiopia" (*The Journal of Modern African Studies*, 34 (1996), pp. 121-142) for example, found that, in several regions where the EPRDF might have expected significant opposition, EPRDF "intimidation contributed to a political climate in which many potential candidates and their supporters feared repression and arrest," and that a "pattern of [EPRDF] intimidation . . .undoubtedly created a climate of fear that sharply limited the ability or willingness of alternative candidates to compete . . . ." And Mr. Lyons found that opposition was not limited to "elites," but extended also to ethnic-based political parties. The report itself acknowledges that certain groups, including the OLF, are excluded from political participation. Given this, the opposition parties' refusal to test the EPRDF's "stated willingness" to allow opposition participation appears more reasonable than implied in the report.

In this regard, the May-June elections do not represent the landmark step on the road to representative democracy that the report portrays them to be. Nor do they represent a harbinger of future improvements in other areas of human rights. The same persons previously governing the country remain in control. And their commitment to representative democracy and human rights remains questionable.

74

Ethiopia

As with its coverage of the May-June elections, the report significantly understates government restrictions on the press. The report acknowledges that the government often restricts press freedom. In assessing the extent of such restrictions, however, the report refers only to the arrests in May and November of 22 journalists, and the continued detention at year's end of 15 journalists. These numbers are significantly below those reported by human rights monitors. In its annual worldwide survey, *Attacks on the Press*, for example, the Committee to Protect Journalists (CPJ) identified 36 journalists who were arrested in 1995, and found that 31 journalists remained in detention at year's end. CPJ found that, for the third consecutive year, Ethiopia has imprisoned more journalists than any other country in Africa. And Amnesty International stated in its April 1995 report "Accountability Past and Present: Human Rights in Transition" that, since enactment of the Press Law in October 1992, over 100 journalists have been arrested and a score more summoned for interrogation.

The report's understatement of the severity of press restrictions is not limited to statistical coverage. In addition, its choice of language tends to understate, if not to appear to excuse, government restrictions. Thus, the report appears to excuse the government's prosecution of the publication of inaccurate stories and its refusal to speak to the private press, stating that "much of the private press continues to lack professionalism," and that many journalists fall victim to provisions of the Press Law prohibiting the publication of false information. The report fails to note, however, that if government officials refuse to speak to the press, the accuracy of the press's reporting of official events is likely to be impaired. More significantly, the report fails to note that, in practice, prosecutions are limited to articles critical of government policy. There are no reported cases of the government prosecuting the publication of inaccurate articles favorable to the government. Finally, the simple inaccuracy of a report does not in any case justify the criminal prosecution of the journalist.

Along these same lines, the report overstates the government's accommodation of opposition access to the press, stating that the government "made efforts to open the official media [which is controlled by the government] to opposition political views prior to the May elections." The report fails to note, however, that, at the same time, the government imposed what CPJ described as a "crackdown on the independent media." And the report overstates the robustness of the private press in stating that 20 biweekly and weekly papers are in publication, while failing to note that this represents a significant decline from the 65 such publications which were in operation in 1993.

While most pronounced in its discussion of the May-June elections and press freedom, the report's dismissal of credible reports of abuse also underplays the seriousness of human rights violations in other areas as well.

In its discussion of torture, the report may underplay the extent of extrajudicial detention, stating that officials "sometimes" use unmarked houses and military camps for the detention and interrogation of political opponents. Amnesty International in fact pointed to the existence of a parallel detention system, stating that:

> There appear to be two systems for holding government opponents: the official police and prison system and a closed system run by the security service or the military. In the official system there is more openness and prisoners' rights are generally protected, although abuses of human rights still occur. In the closed system prisoners' rights under national law and international law and standards are ignored.

In discussing the detention and trial of former officials of the Mengistu regime and opposition figures, the report appears to disparage the credibility of allegations that some of the detainees are, in fact, political prisoners, attributing such allegations only to opposition groups. In fact, Amnesty International also concluded that some detainees appear to be political prisoners.

In addition to these various understatements of the government's responsibility for human rights violations, the second major criticism of the report is its failure to address the likely impact of the Ethiopian government's policy of devolving power to regional government units on respect for human rights at the regional levels. The government has begun, and is committed to continuing, to devolve judicial and police power down to regional government units. This devolution of power, while intended to bring government closer to the people, is rife with potential for abuse. In this regard, the report notes that the questionable independence of the regional judiciary and its lack of resources operate to deny most citizens the full protections provided for in the Constitution. The report also notes that police procedures, such as warrantless searches, are more lax outside Addis Ababa. And Amnesty International has found that prison conditions outside the Addis Ababa area oftentimes fall below international standards. The State Department report does note that the majority of human rights abuses occur outside Addis Ababa, but should have extrapolated on the significance of this fact by pointing out that fully 85% of Ethiopians live outside the capital.

Finally, the report's discussion of restrictions on the freedom of association of independent human rights monitors should have highlighted the deregistration of the Action Professionals Association for the People (APAP). Although the report correctly notes that 47 Ethiopian and international NGOs had their registration certificates revoked in 1995, it goes on to list APAP as a currently active group. APAP is a highly reputable legal aid and public interest advocacy organization and the only one of its kind in Ethiopia. The Ethiopian government had no valid grounds for its deregistration. At the end of 1995, no human rights monitoring or advocacy organization was registered to operate in Ethiopia. Additionally, the lack of official registration procedures from the Ministry of Justice — which, as the report says, now has primary responsibility for NGOs — means that no new human rights monitoring or advocacy organizations can register and begin their much-needed work.

In sum, the report is generally commendable for its cataloguing of current abuses. It is also to be commended for addressing summary executions and other violations committed by opposition groups. It understates, however, the severity of the current abuses, and overstates the government's recent progress in implementing respect for human rights. Such overstatement may be understandable in comparison with the abuses committed under the prior Mengistu regime. It is not, however, supported by the facts. The year 1995 did not bring any major improvement in respect for human rights by the Ethiopian government. On the contrary, the government appears to accept the status quo. And, depending on the outcome of the government's policy of devolving power to regional units, human rights conditions in Ethiopia are quite as likely to deteriorate as to improve in the future.

GUATEMALA

In its 1995 report, the State Department at last begins to take full measure of the gap between human rights rhetoric and reality in Guatemala. With refreshing candor and, in many instances, admirable detail, the report describes the incidence of violence and the inadequacy of institutional responses, and identifies the responsible parties. Information from independent sources, primarily the United Nations Human Rights Verification Mission (MINUGUA) and several respected NGOs, adds to the report's breadth and depth. Unlike many of the *Country Reports* reviewed in this publication, the report on Guatemala often presents the clear voice of the State Department, evaluating progress, assessing claims and raising important criticisms. The deeply rooted power structures and their long history of wilfully disregarding virtually every right of the country's poorer citizens has imbued Guatemala's human rights crisis with a pervasiveness that is hard to capture within the limits posed by the *Country Reports'* restrictive reporting framework. Nonetheless, this year's report goes a long way toward making the problem clearer.

The most notable improvement in the 1995 report concerns impunity. The revised State Department instructions for drafting the *Country Reports* place greater emphasis on the question of impunity and government accountability for human rights violations. In the particular case of Guatemala, this is an especially well-targeted addition. Throughout the report, the State Department has added language acknowledging the issue of impunity and assigning blame where it is due.

The report is still not without its flaws. The section on international humanitarian law is devoted almost entirely to a discussion of guerrilla violations. As far as it goes, this discussion is informative, yet the virtual silence regarding the Guatemalan Army conveys an impression that the State Department can hardly attempt to maintain: that in the two sides' prosecution of the armed conflict, the army's misdeeds are merely incidental. To offer just one striking example, the October 1995 massacre at Xamán, in which troops killed 11 and wounded at least 30 members of a refugee resettlement, is mentioned in the report's first section on extrajudicial killings, but is omitted from the later discussion of violations of humanitarian law. Even if the State Department does not share the Lawyers Committee's view that killings of non-combatants by army units belong in this section as a matter of principle, the army's claims that its soldiers were reacting to hostile fire in the Xamán incident should have been enough to justify its inclusion here — as well as an examination of whether those claims had any merit.

In addition, the treatment of cases reviewed at length by the U.S. government in 1995 in response to allegations of torture, murder and subsequent cover-up by Guatemalan CIA assets and soldiers under their authority is incomplete. In general, however the criticisms leveled by this *Critique* are relatively minor, and are offered to encourage continued improvement.

Additional detail and texture would have been helpful to readers seeking to understand the motives and mechanisms of violence in Guatemala. For instance, murder victim Abner Esau Avenado is described in the report only as a professor at the San Carlos University (USAC), whereas in fact, Avenado was writing on Guatemala's oppositionist student movement of the 1960s. At the time of his killing, he was researching several abductions believed to be politically motivated. Bartolo Solís Sunin, abducted and beaten during an interrogation by unknown assailants, is identified without stating that he was a member of the Mayan Defense Organization, an important clue to the motive for the attack. Without such information, the presentation of numerous incidents tends to flatten out in the report, diminishing the value of the references.

The discussion of freedom of association would have been strengthened by a more explicit acknowledgment that many of the problems discussed elsewhere in the report are violations of this fundamental right. In a paragraph dominated by a discussion of free assembly, the report points out the "cumbersome and difficult" process required for organizations to obtain legal status. The hostile attitude of the military and the civilian government toward domestic and international human rights organizations, documented later in the report, directly implicates this important right, and illustrates the areas in which the collective exercise of rights is considered most threatening to

Guatemala

Guatemalan authorities. MINUGUA has reported that in the last third of 1995 it received nine complaints of violations of freedom of association, mostly alleging harassment of human rights organizations and trade unions. Several NGO members were shot in 1995. One case involved an activist of the well-established Mutual Support Group (*Grupo de Apoyo Mútuo*: GAM), a group of relatives of the "disappeared" attempting to discover the fate of their family members. After being shot and wounded, the victim was later harassed in the hospital by the National Police assigned to provide her with protection from additional attacks. In March 1995, the union leader at the RCA *maquiladora* was killed after the factory's owners threatened a group of workers who had filed a suit against the company alleging the unjust dismissal of 70 employees.

As in previous years, the report fails to adequately examine the issue of racial discrimination. The section on discrimination against Guatemala's indigenous peoples is identical to that contained in the 1994 report, with a bland statement of the constitutional guarantees afforded to the country's diverse ethnic groups and the same single sentence addressing the general issue of human rights abuses ("Indigenous people suffered most of the serious human rights abuses described throughout this report.") It is true that many of these abuses are mentioned in a number of the issue-specific sections of the report. However, the general character of such discrimination should have been stressed more strongly, especially in view of the rejection by the U.N. Committee on Racial Discrimination of the Guatemalan government's statement that no form of racial discrimination is practiced. The committee concluded in its report dated March 17, 1995 that de facto discrimination persists against indigenous communities and "noted with concern that no legal protection is offered in practice against such discrimination." The committee laid the principal blame on the militarization of indigenous areas.

During 1995, a number of past attacks on U.S. citizens in Guatemala received significant attention because of allegations that individuals paid by the CIA for providing information were linked to the violence or its subsequent cover-up. The report mentions several of the more prominent cases, including that of Michael DeVine, murdered in 1990. The results of a review of CIA links to this case and a criminal investigation by the Justice Department, made public in 1996 by a presidential review board, as well as the efforts by lawyers working for the DeVine family, all go significantly beyond what the State Department reports here.

Although the report indicates that one of the soldiers convicted in the DeVine killing, Francisco Solbal Santay, was unable to identify the exact burial location of others killed in the course of a military cover-up for an exhumation team, a witness at the site says the team made little attempt to exhume or identify the bones located at the site to which Solbay Santay led them. Moreover, the special prosecutor assigned to the case after "the Public Ministry launched a new investigation to try to determine the intellectual authors of the murder" took virtually no action.

The report correctly observes that "it is widely believed that military officials facilitated [the] escape" of Guatemalan Army Captain Hugo Contreras, convicted of ordering the operation that ended in DeVine's murder. In fact, a soldier was found guilty of allowing Contreras to escape, on the day he was convicted, from the military base where he had been held. It is also widely believed that Col. Mario Roberto García Catalán, head of the military base near DeVine's Guatemala home, dispatched the surveillance team of soldiers that killed DeVine. A court dismissed charges against him, however, as the report notes. It does not add however, that García Catalán had been awarded a medal for "professionalism" during the course of the proceedings, apparently reflecting the army's view of the investigation and its implications.

Guatemala's revised criminal procedure code is a step forward, with, as the report highlights, strong provisions for defense rights and a more open manner of proceeding. The Lawyers Committee shares the State Department's observation that the difficulties of implementation have meant that "the commitment to transform a dysfunctional judicial system into an effective one is being seriously tested." Even this is an understatement. The head of the Public Prosecutor's Office reported that during 1995, 750 formal charges had been filed, but only 40 judicial investigations were opened. According to MINUGUA, there are approximately four death threats against prosecutors and 23 against judges every month. The issue of judicial independence deserves greater attention in future State Department reporting; it is, perhaps by definition, the single largest influence on the provision of a fair trial. By incorporating references to the latter in the section on denial of fair public trial, the report implicitly acknowledges this important connection.

The case of anthropologist Myrna Mack, murdered in 1990 by a military death squad, highlights the limits of judicial resolve where the military is concerned. As the report points out, the investigation into the criminal responsibility of three officers accused as intellectual authors of the killing was "paralyzed" for much of 1995 until a new prosecutor was named to the case. Once the Public Ministry began making requests for documents regarding the chain of command between one of Mack's killers, convicted in 1993, and the three superior officers, the military stonewalled, refusing to turn over even organizational charts on grounds of national security. The military judge assigned to the case under the revised criminal procedure took no action, despite a legal requirement that he review such documents in order to assess the validity of the military's contention, and to release appropriate materials. In addition, the judge has made no effort to call the military to account for discrepancies — possibly fabrications — in documents regarding the case which the military has turned over to the prosecutor. The authorities' performances in cases such as Mack's, which have benefited from intense international attention, do not bode particularly well for the thousands of less celebrated matters with which the judiciary must contend. The progress, or lack of it, toward a fair and reliable justice system should be as central to the State Department's reporting as it will be to the prospects for meaningful improvement in Guatemala's human rights situation.

The 1995 report gives reason to anticipate that the State Department's reporting on Guatemala will now begin to meet a higher standard than it has in prior years. Of particular interest in 1996 will be information gleaned from the U.S. government's review of the connection between U.S. intelligence and the Guatemalan security agencies. Guatemala's military intelligence is a pervasive presence, never far removed from the locus of human rights violations. (Claims by former President de León Carpio that he dismantled a notorious military intelligence unit known as the *Archivo*, are undermined by reports that its activities continue, a point which the report misses.) The June 1996 report of the Intelligence Oversight Board (IOB) is one of the first opportunities to evaluate information that sheds light on questionable relationships with inadequate oversight. In fact, one of the IOB's most important findings was that although the CIA's Guatemala station kept its Washington headquarters well-informed, the CIA omitted or glossed over negative developments regarding human rights when reporting to Congress or other executive branch agencies. Now that some of the reasons why the United States may have traditionally muted its human rights criticisms of Guatemala are out in the open, such extraneous factors can be neutralized in the State Department's reporting. This year's effort is a strong start.

HAITI

The State Department's analysis attempts to strike a difficult balance: while noting the dramatic improvement in Haiti's human rights landscape in 1995, the report nonetheless points to several areas of continued concern, including events at the end of the year which suggest that Haiti's past legacy of rampant human rights abuses and systematic impunity continue to undermine attempts by President Aristide, and his successor René Préval, to foster both reconciliation and justice in a bitterly divided society. On the whole, the State Department report is accurate and presents a balanced overview, praising the Aristide government's progress while raising concerns over institutional weaknesses that continue to handicap the new Haitian National Police (HNP) and the moribund judicial system. In a few areas, however, the report skews this balance by glossing over highly politicized issues and dismissing the significance of abuses that are linked to deficiencies in the nation's judicial infrastructure. These inconsistencies in an otherwise detailed account of human rights conditions in Haiti at the end of 1995 seem an inevitable outcome of the politicized nature of current U.S. policy toward Haiti and the approaching presidential campaign in the United States.

Until very recently, the Haitian state was little more than an instrument of extortion. Given this legacy, it is not surprising that in most cases, the state's miserable judicial infrastructure shares much of the blame for the continued existence of human rights abuses. A general lack of standardized legal records, the existence of vague and inconsistent charging procedures and the notable shortage of judges, legal texts and legal representation for most Haitians all help to explain why incidents of prolonged arbitrary detention remain common. "Haitian justice lacks everything: resources, competent personnel, independence, stature and trust," according to the National Coalition for Haitian Rights (NCHR). At the same time, however, this appalling lack of infrastructure provides a convenient excuse — a defense that corrupt or simply uninterested public officials are often eager to exploit as a justification for the continued existence of abuses. The truth is actually more complex: a lack of resources and training explains some, but not all of the abuses.

Improvements in management and infrastructure within the Justice Ministry and the HNP, for example, would clearly alleviate many of the strains which currently provide an opportunity for corrupt individuals to manipulate the system. Nonetheless, improvements in infrastructure alone will not prevent future abuses, and the State Department's failure to acknowledge this point fully is perhaps the most significant deficiency in its 1995 report.

Corrupt elements within the HNP, as well as corrupt and incompetent judicial officials and rogue elements in the new prison agency (National Penitentiary Administration, APENA), must be removed from office and sanctioned. Accountability must become the rule rather than the exception.

As the State Department notes, 1995 marked the first time that Haiti was governed for a full year by a democratically elected president. The presence of democratic institutions, coupled with President Aristide's efforts to dismantle the military and an abusive system of rural warlords, known as section chiefs (*chefs de section*), resulted in a dramatic improvement in human rights conditions early in the year. By September, however, as the fourth anniversary of the 1991 coup which overthrew the democratically elected government of President Aristide approached, Haitian human rights groups began condemning the systematic failure of the justice system to prosecute cases dating back to the coup period. By the end of the year, the government had not successfully prosecuted a single member of the Haitian armed forces. Only a handful of cases from the coup period have gone forward at all, the most famous of which was the case against Gérard Gustave, an attaché known as Zimbabwe, who was sentenced to life at hard labor for participating in the 1993 killing of Antoine Izméry, a prominent Aristide supporter. In other coup-related cases, defendants have been sentenced *in absentia* for participating in the murders of prominent Aristide supporters, a practice which the Lawyers Committee joins other human rights organizations in condemning. Although the State Department mentions the use of *in absentia* hearings, the report fails to express concern at the government's reliance on such proceedings. Moreover, in at least one of the *in absentia* cases, a conviction was obtained with scant evidence and without any meaningful judicial inquiry into the allegations. In another, many observers believed that the accused could have been located, apprehended and brought to face trial had local officials been willing to make a serious effort.

This frustration with the state's failure to address human rights abuses from the coup period has been exacerbated by concerns within the Haitian human rights community regarding the Truth and Justice Commission (*Commission Nationale de Vérité et de Justice*), the body President Aristide created to investigate coup-related abuses and to recommend appropriate mechanisms for compensating victims. Local organizations have criticized the lack of transparency in the commission's work and the atmosphere of secrecy that has surrounded its final report. Unfortunately, the State Department fails to raise these concerns, which, justified or not, are likely to frustrate the government's ability to implement the Truth Commission's final recommendations. Since a number of problems, some self-inflicted, prevented the commission from launching any major field investigations before July, the commission's investigative work was conducted in a remarkably short period of time, and despite the impressive number of cases that the commission ultimately reviewed, the compressed time frame raises questions regarding the comprehensive nature of the report.

Unfortunately, as this publication was going to press in July 1996, the government still had not publicly released the Truth Commission's full report. If the government does, as it has intimated, establish a compensation system based on recommendations contained in the report, compensation must not be limited to those who are named in the report, as many Haitians did not have an opportunity to file a complaint. The commission's records, moreover, should be preserved in a secure location, a concern the State Department fails to raise and one which the Haitian government has failed to consider.

This perception of impunity, coupled with structural weaknesses in both the police and judicial systems, contributed to many of the troubling incidents that occurred throughout the year. The most immediate — and the most deadly — ramification of the common perception that the judicial system is completely incapable of handling even minor cases, let alone the politically charged cases from the coup period, was the alarming number of street lynchings, and other forms of popular justice, that took place throughout the country. The State Department cites 100 instances of mob justice that resulted in death. The frequency of such incidents declined throughout the year (U.N. reports indicate that 45 people were stoned or beaten to death by crowds in March, compared to 18 in July) but the issue remained a major concern.

While the Haitian government condemned instances of popular justice in general terms, President Aristide did not personally intervene in a strong manner to denounce these acts. Moreover, he shares at least some of the responsibility for the instability, and the increase in mob violence, that occurred in November. During a funeral for a slain parliamentarian, Aristide delivered an impassioned eulogy in which he called on citizens to take the law into their own hands and to assist the police in a disarmament campaign. The report takes note of this disturbing incident but fails to emphasize its significance. In contrast, Human Rights Watch and NCHR, in an open letter to President Aristide, noted with great alarm that his speech on November 7 encouraged civilian mobs to discard procedural protections, including the Haitian Constitution's guarantee of a fair trial, and that the president's words led to vigilante killings in at least eight cases. In a report to the U.N. General Assembly, Secretary-General Boutros Boutros-Ghali also noted that the disturbances following Aristide's speech served to highlight the "underlying fragility of the situation" in Haiti.

In a section of the report with the most significant political ramifications for the United States, the State Department concludes that there were more than 20 execution-style murders between February and November 1995 in which robbery did not appear to be a motive. In many, although not all of the cases, the victims were linked to the former military government. One of the exceptions involved the execution of Jean Hubert Feuille, a pro-Aristide member of parliament and cousin of President Aristide. Surprisingly, in that particular case, the report suggests that theft may have been a motive in the slaying, despite credible reports, including statements by another deputy who was also wounded in the attack, that discount robbery as a likely motive.

Haiti

Unfortunately, investigations into all of these killings have been conducted in a politically charged climate, with Republican lawmakers and some Clinton administration officials claiming that the Aristide government has sought to impede the investigations. The report notes, for example, that the Aristide government, after requesting FBI assistance in investigating the murder of Mireille Durocher-Bertin, an advocate of the military regime, sought to impede the operation by failing to cooperate with the FBI. Despite these assertions, no credible evidence links government agents to any of the killings. U.S. officials close to the investigation have in fact said privately that the Haitian investigative team's performance compares favorably with that of the FBI. The U.N./ Organization of American States International Mission in Haiti (MICIVIH) has simply concluded that "[i]t has not been possible to determine links between the different cases other than by profession or business association. Nor have the motives been established. No evidence has emerged so far to link the killings to state agents. Judicial investigations into the killings have made little progress."

The report is similarly reserved in its evaluation of the HNP. It notes that there were at least three incidents involving deadly use of force by members of the HNP. However, between July 1995 and the end of January 1996, MICIVIH reported that members of the HNP were responsible for at least nine killings, 20 non-fatal shootings, seven incidents of cruel, inhumane or degrading treatment, and 27 incidents of abuse of authority. These U.N. figures are also somewhat misleading, however, as the number of fatal shootings by members of the HNP decreased in relative terms throughout the year due to a corresponding increase in the size of the force as successive classes graduated from a U.S.-supported training program. In addition to the excessive use of force, a U.N. report has also noted that repeated breaches of basic disciplinary codes have raised concerns over general discipline within the new force. Common disciplinary breaches that have been attributed to members of the new force include: failure to wear uniforms; failure to identify police vehicles as such; the possession and use of firearms while off duty in violation of regulations; and reliance on inappropriate methods of crowd control.

Critique 1995

In general, the State Department should have presented a more accurate picture of these abuses, many of which have been attributed to lack of experience and the relative youth of the police force. In many respects, the HNP represents the key to stability in Haiti. If the HNP acquires an abusive reputation, particularly in Haiti's volatile slums, such as Cité Soleil, or if corrupt members of the force squander the positive reputation of the new force, instability will quickly replace the relative calm of the past year. By clouding the concerns that have been raised over the performance and the reputation of the force, the report evades an important and useful discussion of pitfalls that could emerge in the coming months.

Unfortunately, the mechanisms that the Aristide government created to allow Haitian citizens to file complaints against members of the HNP also seem weak, and the report's statement that the HNP has already concluded 12 internal disciplinary actions, with 20 more investigations pending, serves to obfuscate the institutional weaknesses that plague the Office of the Inspector General, the department responsible for internal investigations. A U.N. report indicates that disciplinary measures for transgressions by individual police agents have not been forthcoming, warning that "the prosecution system has been slow to respond in establishing individual responsibility for instances of death or serious injury at the hands of the police," and that public confidence in the HNP "has suffered as a result."

The report properly raises concerns over longstanding provisions in Haitian law that serve to limit criminal court sessions for major criminal offenses to two sessions per year and two weeks per session. With such a limited trial calendar, periods of prolonged detention are common in most criminal cases. The report fails to note the true scope of the problem: for instance, in Gonaïves there has not been a single criminal court session since 1991. While deficiencies associated with the administration of justice in Gonaïves may be more exaggerated than in other regions of the country, in general terms, the problems there are sadly emblematic. The first criminal court session in Gonaïves in four years, which, after several postponements, was scheduled to take place in December, had to be postponed due to strikes by local justices of the peace and court clerks (*greffiers*), many of whom had not been paid in months. Unfortunately, as a U.S. survey of Haiti's judicial infrastructure confirmed, this was not an isolated incident; justices of the peace in many regions of the country were not being paid, despite the announcement of a nationwide increase in judicial salaries in an effort to combat corruption. By ignoring this issue, the report seems to dismiss the rather significant impact of the ministry's repeated failure to meet its payroll. Unfortunately, management problems in Port-au-Prince are bringing justice to a halt in areas such as Gonaïves and encouraging corruption — an endemic problem in the Haitian judiciary — throughout most of the rest of the country.

The report accurately notes that the number of arbitrary arrests decreased significantly in 1995. However, such arrests are still far too common. In October, for example, MICIVIH reported that a woman was arrested in place of her 13 year-old son. Fortunately, MICIVIH intervened in this and other similar cases, including one in which MICIVIH observers discovered that no charges were pending against a child in detention. It is not surprising, however, that such arbitrary arrests are still common in a country where the police are generally unable or unwilling to conduct meaningful investigations. Due to the near total lack of police investigations, many arrests are still based entirely on public denunciations (*clameur publique*), a fact the report notes without appropriate alarm. In a detailed report entitled "Human Rights After President Aristide's Return," Human Rights Watch and NCHR note that in July 1995, a murder trial in Mirebalais led to two convictions, both of which were based entirely on public denunciations and statements by the victim's relatives. Neither the police nor the investigating judge in the case presented any information obtained through an independent police investigation. The report highlights another troubling case in which Captain Patrick Bastien and Dieumeitre Lucas were arrested in February for plotting against the state. The warrant authorizing the arrest of the two men contained no specific allegations and no reference to dates or specific acts, and failed to identify the specific section of the penal code which the men were alleged to have violated. The two were released, on a provisional basis in September, seven months after their arrest.

Critique 1995

Declaring October "a month of justice," the public prosecutor in Jacmel organized a number of trials for coup-related offenses that were based on similar public denunciations. In at least four of the trials, complaints filed by civilian parties were similar, accusing former members of the Front for the Advancement and Progress of Haiti (FRAPH), a paramilitary organization that terrorized Haitian citizens with impunity during the coup period, of menacing actions. The four complaints failed to specify exact dates and they lacked even basic descriptions of particularized incidents of intimidation or persecution. Moreover, due to the politicized nature of justice in Jacmel, the public prosecutor, who has since been replaced by the Justice Ministry, regularly traveled with his own private bodyguards, many of whom were routinely outfitted in dark sunglasses, civilian clothes and pistols, in a style reminiscent of Haiti's former attaches.

As the State Department indicates, credible reports of arbitrary detentions decreased in 1995, but pre-trial detention is still being used improperly and legal time-limits for such detention are regularly exceeded. Under Article 26 of the Haitian Constitution, no individual may be incarcerated for more than 48 hours without being brought before a judge for an arraignment. The report accurately notes that "an overburdened, often corrupt, and inadequate judicial system regularly detained suspects well beyond the 48 hours permitted for arraignment." While this statement is clearly accurate, the report fails to note that compliance with this rule continued to improve dramatically throughout the year. By December, it appeared that the 48 hour time-limit was being honored in a majority of cases in Port-au-Prince. A much more significant concern is that following arraignment, those who have been indicted often languish in detention with no indication of when they will be tried. In a report to the U.N. General Assembly, Secretary-General Boutros-Ghali emphasized this significant failing in the system, noting that the vast majority of individuals in detention have not been tried and that many do not understand why they are being held.

The report recognizes that the Ministry of Justice has made a "sincere effort to correct this failure," but that 87% of the inmates in the National Penitentiary were still in pre-trial detention in September. Citing the same survey, the Secretary-General has noted that near the end of the year, 1,504 out of a total of 1,703 detainees were awaiting trial and that sentences had only been handed down in 199 cases. The report goes on to note that the Ministry of Justice has established a project through which law students assist detainees in preparing their cases. Since Haiti lacks a system of public defenders, this is a welcome innovation. The report should have noted, however, that the program, and others like it which are financed by a variety of donors, while praiseworthy, has been operating on too small of a scale to have a significant impact. The director of one of the prison projects estimated that its efforts secured the release of approximately 35 prisoners per week from the National Penitentiary in Port-au-Prince, but that at the same time approximately 135 new prisoners were brought in each week.

These statistics also reveal the significant increase that has occurred in the prison population. U.N. estimates suggest that there was a 40% increase in the nation's prison population between June and November. Worth mention is that one contributing factor in the escalating prison population is the continued detention of Haitians for offenses that are not criminalized under Haitian law, such as indebtedness and, in at least one case, homosexual relations.

The report does a good job of scrutinizing the devastating conditions that exist in prisons throughout the country, noting, for example, that in a two week period at the end of the year, nine prisoners died from malnutrition. What the report fails to note is that prison conditions have actually improved dramatically — which should emphasize how truly critical conditions were at the beginning of the year, rather than suggesting that conditions are now acceptable. Unfortunately, conditions still do not approach the standards outlined in the U.N. Standard Minimum Rules for the Treatment of Prisoners. Nonetheless, as Human Rights Watch and others have noted, wilfully cruel and inhuman treatment of prisoners became the exception rather than the rule in 1995.

In general, the report provides an accurate assessment of the devastating economic conditions in the country. As it recognizes, the minimum wage will generally support a single worker at a subsistence level but "cannot adequately support additional family members." In fact, several studies suggest that the average worker attempts to support four or five additional family members on this salary.

Though abject poverty plagues the vast majority of Haitians, conditions for impoverished women and children are materially worse. The report, while noting discrimination that has long afflicted rural Haitian women, including the *de facto* rationing of jobs and education to the detriment of women, fails to note the consequences of poverty — exacerbated by years of bitter economic and political turmoil — on the health of the nation's women and children. Estimates suggest that 35-40% of all pregnant women have at least one sexually transmitted disease. In cities, between seven and ten percent of pregnant women have tested positive for HIV, and the percentage is estimated to be even higher in slums such as Cité Soleil. Chronic malnutrition and anaemia in women result in low birth rates for children, and up to one-quarter of all children suffer from malnutrition in childhood. Nine women are estimated to die in childbirth for every 2,000 live births, one of the highest rates in the world. A U.N. survey on AIDS in Haiti, moreover, recently found that 29% of female respondents stated that their first sexual encounter had not been consensual.

In addition to omitting these grim statistics, the report fails to note that many women have suffered disproportionately in the aftermath of the coup. During the three years of military rule, men were forced into hiding or killed in greater numbers, and, as a result, many women are now responsible for raising families on their own. In addition, during the military's three years in power, women were subjected by military or paramilitary forces to gross human rights violations, including widespread and systematic incidents of rape. The mental and physical consequences of this systematic campaign — such as a higher incidence of sexually transmitted disease, infection, pregnancy, abortion, HIV infection and social stigmatization — have only recently become apparent. The justice system's failure to prosecute rape cases from this period simply adds to the clearly unjustified perception that rape is in some way a less significant category of human rights violation. Nonetheless, throughout 1995, complaints relating to incidents of rape during the coup period were referred by judicial officials to the Truth Commission or the

Haiti

Ministry of Women's Rights and Status; unfortunately, neither of these agencies is empowered to initiate formal judicial proceedings.

The report also fails to note that women, particularly women who have never had children, are still occasionally accused of witchcraft and subjected to torture and murder at the hands of angry mobs. An incident in Port-au-Prince in December is sadly typical of similar incidents that have occurred throughout the country. On December 7, two women, one aged 69 and the other 23, were beaten and then burned to death, following accusations that the older of the two women had killed a neighborhood child through witchcraft. The child reportedly died from a high fever and vomiting earlier in the day.

The report's failure to raise these issues under the section devoted to the human rights of women raises questions about the State Department's commitment to conducting a thorough, gender-specific examination of rights for each country chapter in its annual survey. The report's pro forma, two-paragraph analysis of the rights of at least one half of Haitian society stands in contrast to the careful attention afforded to nearly every other subject in the report. The State Department must take this section more seriously in the future, as it is a distinctly important element of any review of general human rights conditions in the country.

The section on children, in contrast, is more thorough, although it fails to mention a disturbing riot at the children's detention facility at Fort National on November 28 in which at least 20 minors were subjected to cruel and inhumane treatment, including beatings, by four APENA guards. The report does mention a similar incident that took place at Fort National in June under the heading of "Torture and Other Cruel, Inhuman, or Degrading Treatment or Punishment." The report's discussion of the practice of selling rural children into forced servitude in the cities is well presented and recognizes that the practice has increased in recent years as economic conditions have continued to deteriorate.

Unfortunately, the report does not mention the unaccompanied minors who were forcibly returned to Haiti from the U.S. naval base at Guantánamo Bay in 1995. Disturbing reports indicate that some of these minors, many of whom lost their relatives at sea while fleeing the repressive military government, have been placed with distant relatives in unsatisfactory or abusive homes, and that a number of the children may actually be living on the street. Since informal surveys conducted by MICIVIH suggest that at least 30% of all of the children in detention at Fort National are street children, some of these repatriated minors seem destined to end up in detention. Given the financial and logistical resources at the disposal of the U.S. Embassy, embassy personnel should undertake a survey of the unaccompanied minors who were repatriated from Guantánamo Bay before completing next year's human rights report, since U.S. officials are largely responsible for the placement and welfare of these children.

Haiti presents a difficult challenge for the State Department and other human rights observers. The human rights situation is immeasurably better than it was in prior years. Many of the abuses reflect a legacy that under the best of circumstances will require years to eradicate. The Aristide and Préval governments, despite their missteps, have made great strides toward ensuring respect for human rights, in part due to assistance from the United Nations, the United States, Canada and other donor nations. However, the problems that exist must be confronted squarely, despite the domestic political pitfalls. For the first time in decades, Haiti has a government that is receptive to the notion of institutional improvements in human rights. More complete reporting can only serve to enhance the prospects for meaningful progress at a critical moment in Haiti's history.

INDIA

As in previous years, the State Department's 1995 report provides a fairly balanced and accurate assessment of developments in the area of human rights in India. However, like its predecessors it also suffers from a few shortcomings. These include erroneous and/or misleading statements, significant omissions and a lack of attention to detail in places.

In the introductory section, for instance, the report, while noting that the primary responsibility for maintaining law and order rests with India's 25 state governments, goes on to state that "the Union Ministry for Home Affairs controls the nationwide police service." This is likely to confuse the uninitiated reader into believing that the police force as a whole is unitary in character and is controlled by the Central Government in New Delhi. In fact, the police are organized on state lines, with each state government being responsible for its own force, although recruitment and deployment of senior police officers is carried out through a centralized service.

The report is similarly imprecise when it states, in the section discussing the right of citizens to change their government, that "the President may proclaim a state of emergency *in any state* in the event of war, external aggression or armed rebellion" (emphasis added). In fact, the power of the president to declare a state of emergency extends to any part of the national territory, including *parts* of a state, as well as to the country as a whole.

The report refers, intriguingly, to a Supreme Court judgment of May 1995 in which the government's authority to suspend fundamental rights during an emergency was apparently upheld. Despite extensive inquiries with legal experts, the Lawyers Committee has not been able to identify any such judgment. It may be recalled that the 1994 edition of the *Critique* noted a similarly mysterious reference in last year's report. As the Lawyers Committee pointed out then, the authors of the report would do well, as a matter of good practice, to give appropriate references whenever they cite case law.

In the section on political and other extrajudicial killing, the report rightly refers to terrorist attacks carried out by militant groups in

Kashmir. A significant omission, however, concerns the kidnapping and killing of innocent foreign tourists. The report could have referred to some of these cases, especially to the killing on August 13 of the Norwegian, Hans Christian Ostro, by the Al-Faran organization. These cases could also have been mentioned in the section on violations of humanitarian law, involving as they do contravention of Common Article 3 of the Geneva Conventions.

Similarly, in recording the extrajudicial killings by security force personnel in Kashmir, the report could have cited a widely publicized incident which took place in Gada Kocha, Srinagar, on February 10, in which six civilians were killed in cold blood by members of the Border Security Force (BSF), allegedly in retaliation for an attack made on a BSF bunker by armed militants earlier that day. This incident, in which some 38 bystanders were reportedly beaten up by soldiers when they tried to approach the bodies of those killed, drew widespread condemnation from human rights monitors within and outside the country.

The report rightly refers to the continuing phenomenon of disappearances and unacknowledged arrests, especially in Punjab, and cites two relevant cases. It could have usefully added that, in a number of such cases, police officers have harassed the families of those abducted by demanding money in return for their release. Amnesty International publicized one such case, that of Gurdeep Singh, whose family had to pay the police a bribe of Rs. 20,000 (approximately U.S.$700) after he was picked up and kept in unacknowledged detention. Mr. Singh was subjected to a second abduction on August 13, and his whereabouts remained unknown at the end of the year.

The value of the section on torture by police and paramilitary forces could have been enhanced by the inclusion of a few examples from the hundreds of cases reported in the Indian media during the year. Much concern was expressed, for instance, over the brutal treatment in February of a Kashmiri lawyer, Zahid Ali Lone, who was arrested without explanation by the Special Task Force of the Jammu and Kashmir Police, allegedly on suspicion of links with militants. Mr. Lone was made to stand blindfolded for 34 hours, threatened with extrajudicial execution, hung from the ceiling by his feet and given electric shocks to his genitals.

India

On a positive note, the report could have noted the conviction in June of some 40 Indian soldiers for torture and other human rights abuses committed in Kashmir over a four-year period. Many of them were sentenced to rigorous imprisonment for 10 years and dismissed from the army.

The report correctly notes that the Terrorist and Disruptive Activities (Prevention) Act (TADA) — which it erroneously refers to as Terrorism and Disruptive Activities (Prevention) Act — was allowed to lapse in May and that it had not been reinstated or replaced by the end of the year. It could have usefully added that the government did, however, circulate a draft law, entitled the Criminal Law (Amendment) Bill, to replace TADA. This came in for sharp criticism from human rights monitors on the grounds that many of its provisions were just as inconsistent with international standards as those of TADA.

In the section on the denial of fair public trial, the report rightly refers to the inaccessibility of the legal processes to the poor. It could have underscored this point by mentioning that the arrangements for free legal aid at the state's expense leave much to be desired and fail to meet the frequently expressed concerns in this area.

The report is rather cursory in its treatment of freedom of speech and of the press. It fails to note some prominent examples of attempted censorship by the government, such as the banning in July of a book by an American academic, Paula Newberg, which discussed the insurgency in Kashmir (a ban which was lifted some three weeks later after it was discovered that the book highlighted Pakistan's complicity in fomenting the insurgency); the threat to prevent the Indian launch of the computer software, Windows 95, on the grounds that it contained a map showing the borders of the country incorrectly (a threat which was revoked after the makers of the software apologized and agreed to withdraw the map from its Indian copies); and a similar threat to the importation of a book, *The Moor's Last Sigh*, by Salman Rushdie, which allegedly contained passages that were seen as a parody of a prominent Bombay politician.

The report could also have given a more comprehensive account of the politically motivated attacks on journalists in different parts of the country. It could have referred, for example, to the widely-publicized physical assault on Prakash Swamy, editor of the Madras-based *Junior Vikatan* in April, allegedly at the instance of the state's chief minister, after his paper had published an article critical of her; or to the beatings inflicted on 15 members of the Jammu Journalists Association who were participating in a peaceful demonstration on March 31 to draw attention to threats to journalists in the state. Another attack on press freedom which fails to find mention in the report concerns the treatment of a new magazine, *Outlook*, at the hands of activists belonging to the Bombay-based Shiv Sena party: as well as burning inaugural copies of the magazine, the party's supporters defaced billboards carrying its advertisements and threatened news agents to deter them from distributing it.

On the positive side, the report could have noted a government proposal aired in July to abolish the Board of Film Censors. Based on a survey carried out by the Ministry of Information and Broadcasting in which media professionals and state officials were asked for their views on the continuing relevance of film censorship, the government reportedly concluded that such censorship was being rendered irrelevant by the increasing difficulties in controlling information entering the country via satellite television.

In the report's section on freedom of religion, the statement that "there is no national law to bar proselytising by Indian Christians" is potentially misleading, because such laws do exist in some states and have been used to prosecute missionaries. In January, for instance, a court in Ambikapur in the state of Madhya Pradesh sentenced a Christian priest and a nun to six months' imprisonment each and ordered them to pay fines after finding them guilty of violating a state law which forbade religious conversions through coercion or inducements. The authors of the report would have done well to note relevant cases such as this.

The report runs the risk of presenting too rosy a view of the treatment of refugees. In the first place, it fails to refer to the continued refusal by the Indian government to recognize as refugees tens of thousands of Chins who arrived in northeastern India after fleeing from persecution in Burma. The plight of these people is compounded by the fact that they are not even allowed to seek protection and assistance from UNHCR —

unlike refugees elsewhere in the country — due to the denial of access to UNHCR personnel to the seven northeastern states. The report also fails to note the inhuman conditions of some of the refugee camps in south India where tens of thousands of Sri Lankans are housed. These conditions have been documented extensively by human rights monitors who have expressed grave concern over such matters as the cramped nature of the accommodation, lack of hygiene and sanitation, and inadequate medical facilities. Allegations have also been made of camp officials threatening to withhold rations and monetary stipends from refugees unless they agreed to leave the country.

The report quite properly praises the democratic nature of the Indian polity, with citizens being given the right to freely choose their representatives at periodic elections. It could have usefully added that the smooth conduct of elections has often been marred by instances of vote-rigging and intimidation of voters, leading sometimes to large-scale violence. A particularly egregious example of this phenomenon, which the authors of the report should have noted, occurred in Bihar in March. Just days prior to the state elections, police officers on election duty (chosen from outside the state) were reported to have participated in a systematic campaign of rape, assault and extrajudicial execution of local residents, which led to grave concerns being expressed over the safety of the civilian population generally.

The report pertinently highlights the inconsistent attitude of the Indian government toward the grant of permission for on-site visits by international human rights monitors. It could have usefully referred to the harassment meted out to a young Canadian academic, John Cockel, who was researching the functioning of the National Human Rights Commission while on holiday in the country in August. As part of his research, Mr. Cockel had visited Srinagar, but on his return to Delhi, his passport was confiscated and he was asked to leave the country forthwith. Another significant omission in the report is its failure to note the Indian government's continued refusal to grant the requests of the U.N. Special Rapporteurs on Extrajudicial Executions and Torture permission to undertake visits to the country.

Critique 1995

In the section on discrimination based on race, religion, etc., the report correctly refers to the personal status laws of Muslims which allow a man to have up to four wives. It should have noted an important Supreme Court judgment, delivered in May, in which the court expressed disapproval of the increasingly common practice of Hindu men converting to Islam merely to circumvent the prohibition contained in the ordinary law against polygamy. Significantly, the court criticized the government for not implementing the constitutional mandate to "secure for the citizens a uniform civil code throughout the territory of India." The court also asked the government to file an affidavit by August 1995 outlining the steps it was taking to enact such a civil code. Future reports should be attentive to progress in enacting a uniform civil code applicable to Hindus and Muslims alike, which, as the Supreme Court noted, is necessary "both for the protection of the oppressed and promotion of national unity and solidarity."

INDONESIA

The State Department should be credited with producing a mostly thorough and accurate picture of human rights violations in Indonesia in 1995. The report's introduction clearly identifies important patterns, noting that elements of the armed forces continue to be responsible for the most serious human rights abuses. The introduction also highlights the pattern of increasing violations against dissidents in East Timor, Irian Jaya and Aceh. In several instances, the report draws the important distinction between changes in official policy and actual practice. For example, in its description of the welcome step by the government to lift the "ET" (ex-Tapol) stamp found on the identity cards of former political prisoners, the report notes that there has been no promise that their civil and political rights would be restored.

However, despite its overall quality, the repetition of omissions and weaknesses from previous years' reports is disheartening. These include a reluctance to express criticism in the State Department's own voice, understatement of military involvement, some instances of excessive credence given to government claims or estimates, and understatements or omissions that provide a more favorable impression of the government than the facts warrant. Some important incidents were omitted altogether, perhaps in the attempt to avoid a "laundry list" of violations. The weakest sections of the report concern indigenous peoples, acceptable conditions of work and freedom of religion.

The report continues to mention human rights violations in the context of reports from other sources, rather than using its own voice, especially in the areas of extrajudicial executions, disappearances and torture. This tendency is particularly pronounced in the introduction, even where the report uses its own voice in citing security forces in the relevant section. Where the State Department has numerous sources and reports that it characterizes as knowledgeable, credible and detailed — as it does in discussing the killings of civilians without justification in Aceh and Irian Jaya — it seems reasonable to make an assessment of whether security forces committed these acts. For example, the killings in Irian Jaya were reported by a foreign NGO and then confirmed by investigations by the Catholic Church in that province and by the

Critique 1995

National Commission on Human Rights (*Komisi Nasional Hak Azasi Manusia*, or *Komnas HAM*). Yet these killings are still referred to as having "reportedly" taken place, or as having occurred "according to credible, detailed reports" — language that is repeated throughout. However, elsewhere in the report it notes outright that tensions in that area "led to a crackdown by government security forces, resulting in the deaths of civilians."

The 1994 edition of the *Critique* noted a reluctance to mention military involvement in particular cases, despite general statements that the armed forces are responsible for most human rights violations. That trend continues in 1995, in some cases repeating the same omissions as the previous year's report. In a discussion of the military role in labor disputes, the report makes passing mention of the 1994 conviction of a soldier in the Marsinah murder case, in which a young female labor activist was abducted and murdered in 1993 following a strike at her factory. The report refers only to the fact that a soldier was convicted in the case. It fails to mention either that it was only the court-martial of one low-ranking officer for procedural violations or that, based on a report by the Legal Aid Foundation, there is a strong possibility that Marsinah was killed at the district military command and that responsibility lay with high-ranking military authorities. In its discussion of the military's response to human rights violations, the report's section on extrajudicial killings conflates the issue of excessive force by police with that of politically-motivated extrajudicial killings. Military prosecutions deserve a separate discussion.

Military involvement is again understated in the description of the HKBP case, a complicated case in which two factions — one of them backed by the government — have been fighting for control of the largest Protestant church in Indonesia, the Huria Kristen Batak Protestant. The report mentions only that the authorities have treated violence by the two sides differently, but omits that the military has played an active role in intimidation and violence as well.

The report does mention the activities of the hooded, vigilante "ninja" gangs that stoned and burned homes and attacked residents in Dili, East Timor in February 1995. However, it omits reports that these gangs primarily targeted East Timorese pro-independence activists; allegations that members of the military observed but made no effort to stop some of the gangs' attacks; and that security forces reportedly hired these gangs to intimidate activists. Amnesty International has also raised concerns that the "ninja attacks," and retaliations against them, were used not only to intimidate but also as a pretext for subsequent arrests of those opposed to Indonesia's presence in East Timor. In addition, while noting the waves of arbitrary arrest and detention in January, and again in October and November 1995, it omits the round-up of 30 East Timorese in March, supposedly for pro-independence activities, and the refusal of authorities to release information about their detention for several days. The mention of only certain waves of arbitrary arrests and the omission of the security forces' likely involvement in the "ninja" attacks prevents the report from adequately characterizing the nearly constant climate of fear for dissidents in East Timor in 1995.

In addition, the report contains instances of understatement, overstatement, incomplete reporting and omission. While many of these inaccuracies are subtle, it is a cause of concern that they are consistently favorable to the government at the expense of dissidents, indicating either an incomplete grasp of the facts or a general unwillingness to criticize the government. The level of caution in accepting claims by non-government sources is not applied in all cases to government claims and estimates.

For example, the discussion of the treatment of labor activists is understated, with no references to two arrests of members of the independent labor union SBSI and continued inadequate attention to labor activists not associated with SBSI. Neti, an SBSI activist, was arrested in November with four others after attending a political trial in Jakarta, while Roliati Harefa, SBSI Vice Chair of Binjai (North Sumatra) Branch, was arrested at Binjai police station on December 30. She had gone to the police station to complain that her supervisor had assaulted her twice after she protested that she had been unfairly dismissed. While the report mentions the SBSI members tried and sentenced in connection with the labor demonstrations in Medan in 1994, it fails, as it did last year, to mention labor activists operating outside SBSI. Three activists were sentenced in Medan in 1994 and served out their sentences in 1995. These are significant as indications of the government's general attitude toward any labor activity, and not just that of SBSI, and because local activists unaffiliated with a national organization are less visible nationally and internationally and may be more vulnerable to harassment and unfair trials.

In the section on freedom of religion, the report echoes language from previous years, despite evidence of growing religious intolerance by the government, which, for example, is increasingly using blasphemy charges against perceived opponents. The government-sponsored Association of Muslim Intellectuals (ICMI), headed by Suharto protégé B.J. Habibie, deserves mention as an example of the government's increasing promotion of Islam as an instrument in maintaining power. It is likely that the creation of ICMI facilitated the Islamic backlash noted in the report.

The section on indigenous peoples, an extremely important issue in Indonesia, is inadequate. While there is a reference to the problems faced by indigenous inhabitants in the area of the Freeport McMoRan mine, the larger context of land tenure is not addressed. Lacking individual titles, the ancestral lands of indigenous peoples, such as the Dayak of Kalimantan, and the many ethno-linguistic groups in Irian Jaya, are considered state land, and are frequently expropriated for both private and public projects. These include mining, logging, plantation agriculture and the transmigration of settlers from other islands. These in turn lead to conflicts between settlers and indigenous inhabitants of the affected areas, and to human rights abuses such as intimidation, harassment and arbitrary arrest by security forces. These problems are only likely to increase in coming years. Also, a crucial explanation in the 1994 report has been deleted; it noted that according to some reports in Irian Jaya, workers were forced into debt and then indentured to companies. Without that explanation, the report's comment that workers are "being separated from their traditional economy" no longer seems so serious.

The discussion of freedom of the press is good but omits several instances of violence directed at journalists, and understates the importance of government moves to control journalists. For example, in January a journalist from the weekly *Genta* in Pekanbaru, Riau, was beaten unconscious by unknown assailants after writing a story about timber thefts involving businessmen and Department of Forestry officials. In August, Ricky Pitoy Tafuama, a reporter for the leading daily *Kompas*, was beaten by police in Bandung while reporting on a land dispute. The report notes that the government-controlled Association of Indonesian Journalists (PWI) expelled 13 members of the Alliance of Independent Journalists (*Aliansi Jurnalis Independen*: AJI) which had been formed by journalists after press bans in 1994, and also notes that the government threatened publishers with sanctions if they employed journalists not associated with PWI. While perhaps implied, the report should have stated outright that expelled journalists lost their jobs. The Committee to Protect Journalists estimates that some 80 journalists have lost their jobs as a result of sanctions and press closings, undoubtedly an important means of increasing self-censorship.

According to the report, the government allowed the International Committee of the Red Cross (ICRC) access to prisoners in various parts of Indonesia, including Aceh and East Timor. The report's section on NGOs in Indonesia mentions only vaguely that the ICRC experienced difficulties in East Timor. It makes no mention of the government's refusals and delays in allowing prisoner visits by the ICRC, including visits to Martinho Pereira, the alleged ringleader of the Jakarta embassy protests by East Timorese in December 1995. This practice of haphazard denial of ICRC visits has continued into the early months of 1996, with the denial of ICRC access to 15 East Timorese arrested in Jakarta on January 12. In addition, the report fails to mention that, according to Amnesty International, ICRC visits in East Timor are ineffective at stopping torture before or after the visits, and that officials sometimes pressure a detainee not to describe their treatment to the ICRC or even to accept ICRC visits at all.

At the same time as the report understates the degree of repression, it overstates some measures of progress. While noting some of its limitations, the report seems to overstate the increasing independence of the National Commission on Human Rights, and its willingness to criticize the government. *Komnas HAM* continues to act with greater independence than was predicted for the government-sponsored commission and has become an important tool for protecting human rights. However, it is still constrained by its weak legal standing, unclear mandate and occasional interference from the military. While it did, as noted in the report, question the military and charge it with abuses in the killings of six civilians in Liquisa, East Timor, *Komnas HAM* did not issue its report on the killings to the public, except in the form of a three-page press release. Although *Komnas HAM* found that the soldiers responsible for the Liquisa killings had also tortured their victims, the court-martial that tried the soldiers did not charge them with torture, indicating the limited effect of a body with no enforcement powers.

The report accurately recognizes some signs of nascent judicial independence, particularly in the successful suit brought by the employees of the banned periodical *Tempo* against the Minister of Information for revoking its publication license. But the limits of that decision and the overall context of a year of political trials indicates that the judicial branch is still far from independent. While a Jakarta administrative court found that both the banning of *Tempo* and the 1984 press law on which it was based was unlawful, the administrative court has little actual influence.

Regarding evidence of continued judicial improprieties, the report does not note the unfairness of the trial of two AJI members and an office assistant for charges relating to criticisms of the government. Unfair aspects included the inadequacy of the evidence, the inappropriateness of the charges, the intimidating military and intelligence presence in the courtroom, and the violations of criminal procedure. The findings for *Tempo* (which was reversed in any event by the Supreme Court in June 1996) and against the AJI in the same year show that despite the positive indications of an independent judiciary, there has been little genuine progress in strengthening the judiciary's independence on sensitive press issues. Similarly, the investigation of parliamentarian Sri Bintang Pamungkas following demonstrations against Suharto in Germany was marked by serious violations of criminal procedure.

The tendency toward overstatement or excessive credence in government claims is well exemplified by the discussion of labor. The report provides a thorough and fairly accurate description that nonetheless goes too far in accepting government claims and neglects the issue of working conditions. The discussion on labor also deserves special attention due to its relevance to the decision by the office of the U.S. Trade Representative regarding the continuation of Generalized System of Preferences (GSP) trade status for Indonesia, a decision that has been suspended but not resolved.

The 1994 State Department report noted that following a change in regulations that year to allow the formation of plant-level unions that could carry out collective bargaining agreements, 192 such associations had formed by the end of the year, although only one had concluded a collective bargaining agreement with management. The 1995 report accepts uncritically the figure that 900 plant-level unions had been formed by December, a figure that some labor organizations find unlikely. The fact that only 24 collective bargaining agreements were reached belies the claim of such a large number of plant-level unions. In addition, many of those that have been formed are thought to be unions on paper only, "yellow unions" set up by the Ministry of Manpower and management with little or no worker participation. The report should include a strong caveat that the credibility of these unions is dubious.

Likewise, the observation that the government-sponsored union SPSI has carried out a process of decentralization into 13 independent unions should have put the word "independent" in quotation marks, and the government role in these official unions should be made more explicit. For example, the sectoral unions were to have the power to collect membership dues directly; instead all dues go to the Ministry of Manpower for distribution, so the 13 so-called independent unions are in reality totally dependent on the government. While the report accurately details the role of government functionaries in the SPSI leadership, the statement that the government has "a great deal of influence" is an understatement. In fact, the government controls SPSI.

The capacity for and understanding of collective bargaining in Indonesia may be overstated as well, putting the statistics cited into question. Instructions for those drafting the *Country Reports* note that for "genuine collective bargaining to exist the most directly affected workers should be able to participate in the negotiations or to ratify/reject agreements." However, these conditions are most likely not present in many of the collective bargaining agreements cited by government figures. The report also notes a decrease in labor unrest and assumes that it was due to an increased level and enforcement of the minimum wage. In fact, strikes continued to be frequent, and government efforts may have increased rather than decreased unrest in the short term due to growing worker awareness and confidence in demanding a fair wage.

The report notes incorrectly that military intervention in labor matters has been prohibited; rather only one of the two regulations authorizing such intervention has been revoked. The other regulation, authorizing intervention in labor disputes in the name of internal security, remains on the books. The non-governmental Legal Aid Foundation documented some 150 instances of such intervention in 1995.

The report also gives inadequate attention to working conditions. Compulsory overtime and mistreatment of the largely female work force employed in the manufacture of light exports, such as garments and footwear, are common. In addition, employers often respond to increases in the minimum wage by reducing benefits such as insurance and allowances for food and transport. The worst conditions continue to be in light export manufacturing, extractive industries and plantation agriculture — all of which merit special attention in the 1996 State Department report.

As in previous years, the report contains references to the restrictions placed on citizens formerly associated with communist organizations, but fails to describe the continued use of the supposed communist threat to justify the government's "security approach." Despite the welcome release of three long-term prisoners and the removal of the ET stamp from identification cards, government officials have shown that they have no wish to abandon the communist threat as a useful tool in the suppression of dissent. In February, Minister of Defense and Security Edi Sudradjat maintained that the recent discovery of politicians in the Indonesian Democratic Party (PDI) with communist ties, (an unfounded allegation that had forced the head of the West Java chapter to step down in 1994), showed that government fears of a communist comeback were well-founded. In January, students in Central Java pushing for fewer speech restrictions on campus were accused of being the sons and daughters of communists by the deputy head of a parliamentary commission, Soerjo Handjono. In June, two officials in Bengkulu, Sumatra, reportedly intimidated thousands of people into paying for health cards that should have been free by threatening them with investigation for communist ties. In a justification for censorship, in April, a senior official in the ruling Golkar party, warned a seminar that frustrated communists could use literature for revenge. Suharto's government has banned some 2,000 books.

The report omits some other important issues and examples. As in last year's report, there is no reference to allegations of coercion in family planning, despite reports (including one by the Lawyers Committee) of declining but persistent human rights problems in the family planning program. Whereas earlier State Department instructions specifically directed that this issue be addressed, the most recent revisions appear to have dropped this requirement.

The discussion of academic freedom should be strengthened in future reports. In addition to the freedom of academic discussion, the report should include issues of pressure on faculty to join the ruling Golkar party, government interference in the selection of university rectors, the use of student militias (*Menwa*) and censorship of student newspapers as a means of stifling dissent. An important example has been omitted as well. Prominent government critic Dr. George Aditjondro, who in 1995 was charged with insulting a government body in a lecture the previous year, has opted to stay in Australia rather than return to face what he considers will be an unfair political trial.

As in past years, the report makes inadequate reference to U.N. instruments and findings. There is a passing reference to the visit by the U.N. High Commissioner for Human Rights to Jakarta and East Timor, but no reference to the content of discussions or to the recommendations made by previous thematic rapporteurs regarding torture and extrajudicial execution. The High Commissioner, José Ayala-Lasso, requested that the government implement the rapporteurs' recommendations and consider the repeal of the anti-subversion law; the reduction of troops in East

Timor; and clemency for all those civilians convicted for publicly expressing political dissent or revealing facts relating to the Dili Massacre and other more recent demonstrations. Also deserving of mention is the campaign by the National Commission on Human Rights and a coalition of Indonesian NGOs to secure ratification by the Indonesian government of the Convention on Torture, which it signed years ago.

The report mentions the matter of Sri Bintang Pamungkas, an outspoken parliamentarian suspended by his party and then brought up on charges relating to protests that greeted Suharto's visit to Germany in April 1995. It notes that Mr. Bintang was banned from traveling and was facing charges at the end of 1995 (he has since been sentenced to two years and 10 months in prison), but does not mention that two other prominent government critics — journalist Goenawan Mohamad and student activist Yeni Rosa Damayanti — were also publicly accused of instigating the protests in Germany. Following these demonstrations, the Indonesian government requested permission to collect evidence in Germany, a request that was rejected by Germany as "unreasonable." This attempt to reduce freedom of expression outside Indonesia is reminiscent of 1994 attempts to shut down seminars on East Timor in the Philippines, Thailand and Malaysia.

IRAQ

The human rights situation in Iraq showed no signs of improvement in 1995. The economic decline caused by sanctions and the government of Iraq's mismanagement of scarce resources brought continued suffering and deprivation to the majority of the population. At the same time, a wide range of civil and political rights continued to be denied. The re-election of Saddam Hussein in the presidential referendum in October 1995 was regarded by most observers as a mere formality. Internal protest as well as direct challenges to the government were suppressed. The predictions of an imminent collapse of the leadership which accompanied the defection to Jordan in August of Saddam Hussein's sons-in-law Hussein Kamil al-Majid and Saddam Kamil al-Majid and their families proved unfounded.

Crime and lawlessness reportedly remain at high levels despite draconian decrees passed in 1994, which included amputation and branding as punishments for some kinds of theft and army desertion. Described as cruel and unusual by the U.N. Special Rapporteur on Iraq, these punishments reportedly continued to be applied. Two general amnesties announced in July 1995 for those convicted of criminal and political offenses were viewed with skepticism by most human rights organizations.

Meanwhile, in the Kurdish-controlled areas of northern Iraq, fighting flared again during early 1995 between rival Kurdish parties, and concerns for the human rights situation in the region persisted.

The State Department's 1995 report covers most of the major human rights issues which arose during the year. There is less of an effort than in previous years to evade mention of abuses committed by parties other than the government of Iraq. However, the tone and emphasis of the report is at times questionable, and there is a tendency to gloss over issues which could be considered politically difficult. This problem relates particularly to reporting on the situation in northern Iraq, which appears to play down the significance of the internal conflict over the past two years, and the human rights abuses which have accompanied it.

The report does acknowledge more clearly than in 1994 that human rights abuses are being perpetrated by Iraqi Kurdish parties in the north.

It notes that civilians were killed in the course of the fighting in the first half of 1995, since which time a ceasefire has been in place. However, the report fails to provide a clear context for this information. Having described the establishment of the regional parliament and local administration in 1992, it merely states that: "This parliament last met in May 1995. Discussions among Kurdish and other northern Iraqi political groups continue on reconvening the parliament but tensions between the KDP and PUK continue to prevent parliamentary activity." The report does not say that since early 1995 the region has effectively been divided between areas in the northwest, including most of Dohuk governorate, controlled by the Kurdish Democratic Party (KDP), and those to the east and south of Arbil, including that city, which are controlled by the Patriotic Union of Kurdistan (PUK). It is the two major parties, rather than the administration or the parliament, that control most of the funds for "public" use.

No mention is made either of the U.S. government's interventions to achieve a resolution of this conflict. The United States initiated peace talks in August 1995, which brought together the PUK and KDP, representatives of the Turkish Government and the Iraqi National Congress (INC), and two meetings took place in Ireland. The first round of talks on August 10-11 reportedly led to the KDP and PUK agreeing in principle to the demilitarization of Arbil and to measures to ease the inter-party dispute over control of the region's finances. However, the second round of talks in Dublin on September 12-15 ended without an agreement on how to implement this plan. In early October, Iran hosted a rival round of talks between the PUK and KDP in Teheran, which, according to a joint communique, "achieved tangible progress" on issues similar to those discussed in Ireland. Further U.S. missions visited northern Iraq in mid-November and in early 1996.

The State Department report does not raise the more general issue of the conduct of the Kurdish protagonists to the conflict in the light of human rights principles. In a report issued in February 1995, Amnesty International expressed the view that the clashes between Kurdish parties in December 1993, and in particular those of May 1994, "signified . . . an abandonment of fundamental human rights principles to which the Kurdish leadership had publicly committed itself."

The Amnesty report highlighted two factors leading to abuses: the impunity enjoyed by the armed and special forces of the KDP and PUK; and the active undermining of the judiciary and lack of respect for its independence by these political parties. "From their respective positions of strength," Amnesty went on, "both parties have undermined many of the positive measures adopted in the name of the [Kurdish] administration." Thus, although the administration of justice is supposed to be carried out through the courts, the police service and recognized prisons, the Amnesty report states that the parties — especially the PUK, KDP and Islamic Movement of Iraqi Kurdistan (IMIK) — have usurped all these functions. The parties, especially the PUK and KDP, have prevented the arrest of suspects affiliated with them and for whom arrest warrants have been issued by investigating judges. Political interference has compromised the right to a fair trial. It does not seem that this situation has materially changed since the Amnesty report was written. The State Department does not include reference to the Amnesty report in its otherwise useful listing of the main organizations which issued human rights reports during 1995.

An additional criticism of the State Department's description of events in northern Iraq relates to the way in which the human rights abuses it records are in each instance juxtaposed and "balanced" with abuses committed by the Kurdistan Workers Party (PKK) in northern Iraq. The PKK is variously described as "a Turkish terrorist organisation" and a "Turkish Kurd terrorist group." The report notes that the fighting in early 1995 between the Iraqi Kurdish parties led to civilian deaths. The next sentence states that in the latter part of the year, the PKK "increased their activity in northern Iraq and reportedly killed local residents in an effort to control a territorial base." Similar juxtapositions of Iraqi Kurdish and PKK abuses are made in the summary in regard to kidnapping. The background here is crucial to an understanding of these events. The PKK has been using the areas of northern Iraq bordering on Turkey as a base for its operations inside southeastern Turkey. The KDP, which controls most of this border region, has from time to time, at the urging of the

Turkish government, launched attacks on the PKK, and there were frequent clashes between the two during the latter half of 1995. The report does not mentioned this.

In discussing the Turkish government's military incursions into northern Iraq, the report gives the Turkish authorities the benefit of the doubt. In March 1995 a large-scale Turkish military operation involving 35,000 troops backed by tanks, helicopters and F-16 fighter aircraft attacked PKK bases in northern Iraq. Turkish troops did not complete their withdrawal until May. According to Human Rights Watch, "Kurdish civilians from both Turkey and Iraq were casualties in the fighting." The State Department report, while including human rights organizations' "charges" that civilians were casualties, concludes by saying, "However, the Turkish government authorities stressed that the operation sought to avoid civilian casualties."

References to Turkish Kurdish refugees in northern Iraq suffer from some inconsistencies. For example, the report states that 14,000 Turkish Kurds fled civil strife in southeastern Turkey, adding that "The UNHCR is treating these displaced persons as refugees until it reaches an official determination of their status." It is unclear why they should be described as "displaced persons," since they have crossed an international border.

The report fails to mention a number of incidents in Iraqi Kurdistan which caused civilian casualties but whose perpetrators have not been identified. During 1995, Kurdish and Iraqi opposition sources reported several bomb explosions which caused death and injury. One, in a crowded market in Zakho, was said to have killed over 70 people. In Salah al-Din, a bomb explosion on October, 31 1995 at the security offices of the Iraqi National Congress was reported to have killed 28 people and wounded 70. Another explosion in Salah al-Din on November 14 was said to have injured the wife and child of a senior military officer working for the INC and another explosion, at a gas station on December 7, reportedly killed 13 people and injured 15. Human Rights Watch alleged that there had been "persistent reports" of Iraqi government agents using thallium sulfide poison against political opponents in Iraqi Kurdistan. In September 1995, the INC alleged that one man had died and six others were in a serious condition in a Tehran hospital after reportedly being poisoned with thallium. In his March 1996 report, the U.N. Special Rapporteur also speaks of receiving "credible allegations" of thallium poisoning "supported by certification of medical diagnosis." This refers to the case of Major Safa al-Battat, an Iraqi Special Forces officer who defected to northern Iraq. He allegedly developed symptoms after drinking a beverage said to be laced with thallium while in Shaqlawa, northern Iraq. He was taken to Cardiff, Wales, where he was treated for thallium poisoning.

The format of the State Department report gives rise to frequent repetition of material under different headings, sometimes resulting in inconsistencies. Surprisingly, one example is the report's inconsistent and even inaccurate descriptions of the "safe haven" and "no fly zones." In the initial summary, the international protection afforded to northern Iraq is described as "an internationally enforced safe haven." A more accurate formulation refers to Operation Provide Comfort as "continued enforcement of a 'no fly zone' to inhibit government aerial activity to repress citizens in northern Iraq." However, another reference on the same page says both the northern and southern no-fly zones were established in 1992. In fact, the northern no-fly zone was established in April 1991, and the southern in August 1992.

The report gives a rather misleading impression of both the role of U.N. guards in the protection of aid workers and the threats faced by U.N. personnel. Few international NGOs still work in government-controlled areas; most work in the Kurdish-controlled north. There have been attacks and threats ascribed to Iraqi government agents against aid workers in the north, but in 1994 and 1995, the major security concern hampering aid work in the north related to the internal fighting, particularly affecting Arbil and Sulaimaniya governorates. This is not mentioned in the report. In Dohuk governorate, security problems related more to Turkish military incursions and shelling across the border and PKK activities. The report says that: "Throughout 1995 the government harassed and assaulted employees of the U.N. and non-governmental organizations in Iraq." However, it cites only the single case of a U.N. guard who was denied entry to Iraq because he was carrying a foreign newspaper with unfavorable references to Saddam

Hussein. The report's other example of harassment of U.N. personnel refers to the kidnapping of eight U.N. aid workers by the PKK at the Atrush camp.

Social and economic conditions in Iraq continued to deteriorate during 1995, as highlighted in reports from the Food and Agriculture Organization and the Center for Economic and Social Rights. In May 1996, the Iraqi government finally agreed to accept the terms of U.N. Security Council Resolution 986 (adopted on April 14, 1995). This allows for the sale of $2 billion worth of Iraqi oil over a six-month period, with the possibility of renewing the arrangement thereafter. Thirty percent of this amount is earmarked for the U.N. Compensation Fund for victims of the 1991 Gulf War and further amounts are deducted for U.N. expenses. Under the resolution, $150 million is set aside every 90 days for humanitarian aid to the Kurdish-controlled areas. This aid is to be distributed through the U.N., while humanitarian aid within government-controlled areas is to be distributed through Iraqi government channels.

The resolution itself does not specify any form of monitoring of how the Iraqi government distributes this aid, referring only to "observation" by U.N. personnel of "whether Iraq has ensured the equitable distribution of medicine, health supplies, foodstuffs and supplies for essential civilian needs" (para 11). However, a detailed Memorandum of Understanding signed between the government of Iraq and the U.N. has outlined in more detail monitoring by U.N. personnel. It remains to be seen whether these provisions can address the criticisms raised by both the State Department and the Special Rapporteur about inequities in the distribution of rations and other goods between different groups in Iraq.

Despite the agreement on Resolution 986, there is still a sense in which the humanitarian needs of the Iraqi people remain a political football, with no party to the conflict willing to give them primacy. The resolution allows the leading protagonists of continued sanctions to say that they are addressing concerns over the impact of sanctions on the Iraqi population. The new flow of humanitarian goods may, if equitably distributed, alleviate extremes of hunger and lack of basic medical supplies. However, as the Center for Economic and Social Rights remarks, it will not solve the crisis of economic collapse, brought about by five years of sanctions and the economic policies of the Iraqi government. For the government, acceptance of Resolution 986 was probably a matter of necessity, not a result of concern over humanitarian needs, and it will be used to bolster the government if possible.

The report quotes Iraqi government officials as linking arbitrary arrest and detention to the impact of international sanctions. These are said to be "a temporary preventive measure." Human Rights Watch/Middle East, in its report on decrees relating to amputations, gives a more explicit example of this line of argument by Iraqi officials: "Ambassador Hamdoon said that 'the measures were not human rights abuses. . . . They are temporary measures that have to do with the current circumstances. . . . When the economic sanctions are lifted (by the United Nations), there will be no need for such measures.'" However, as Human Rights Watch concludes, "Difficult economic conditions that have caused a rise in crime and military desertion cannot justify Iraq's violation of its citizens' basic human rights."

The State Department report covers the major internal developments of the year, including the defection of Hussein Kamil al-Majid, Saddam Kamil al-Majid and their families to Jordan in August 1995, and their return to their deaths in February 1996. It also deals with the October 1995 presidential "referendum," in which Saddam Hussein received 99.9% of the vote. Like most other commentators, the report dismisses this vote as "not democratic."

The report rightly notes the difficulty in getting accurate information on events in Iraq. This may explain its rather brief references to opposition activity. It mentions "uprisings" by former General Wafiq Samara'i and General Turk Dulaimi but should also have explained the background to these events. Samara'i had already defected to the opposition in northern Iraq in early 1995. This unsuccessful army insurrection in March was apparently organized from outside government-controlled areas. The attack on Abu Ghraib prison in June, reportedly led by General Turk Dulaimi, stemmed from earlier events in Ramadi governorate which are not mentioned in the report. According to the U.N. Special Rapporteur, an uprising took place in the city of al-Ramadi in May 1995 after the body of Brigadier General Muhammad

Critique 1995

Madhloum Dulaimi was returned to his family in Ramadi, allegedly bearing the marks of torture. The riots which followed this event led to an "allegedly disproportionate and indiscriminate use of force" by the authorities, including arbitrary killings and numerous arrests, said to include women, children and elderly people. The attack on Abu Ghraib prison by General Turk Dulaimi was apparently aimed at freeing these detainees.

On developments in the southern marshes, the Special Rapporteur confirms the State Department report, adding that in October 1995, Iraqi military attacks on villages in Misan and Basra provinces were said to have resulted in the killing and wounding of many civilians. It should be reiterated in reference to Iraqi refugees in southwestern Iran that all the official refugee camps are run by the Iranian authorities, not by NGOs as the report suggests.

The report notes the continued use of punitive amputation during 1995. Additional evidence was gathered by the Special Rapporteur during his mission to Kuwait "that penal amputations continued to be enforced in the spring and early summer of 1995." A number of witnesses spoke of amputation of ears and branding on the foreheads of deserters. While anaesthetics were generally said to be given for the amputations, post-operative treatment was denied, sometimes leading to septicaemia. Reports suggested that doctors continued to be coerced into performing these amputations. The Special Rapporteur also received a report that in 1994 a large number of imams from mosques and prayer halls in Baghdad had been arrested, incarcerated or executed. One of the reasons cited was their opposition to the application of amputation decrees.

In his March 1996 report, the Special Rapporteur also confirmed the State Department's findings when he noted the application of the death penalty during 1995 "in a wholly disproportionate way" against persons convicted of minor offenses such as pickpocketing or illegally exchanging money. In his February 1995 report, the Special Rapporteur also raised the issue of decrees which gave judicial or quasi-judicial authority to non-judicial bodies. In the Special Rapporteur's view this "creates a private and personal 'judicial' prosecutorial mechanism in the person of the

Iraq

President's Principal Private Secretary who, of course is wholly dependent upon and partial to the President."

In July 1995, the RCC announced two general amnesties. The report appropriately shares the skepticism of human rights organizations about their validity. The Special Rapporteur remarked that these amnesties inspired "little confidence." The first, RCC decree No. 61 dated July 22, 1995, "remits the remainder of the sentences of Iraqi prisoners and detainees, commutes death sentences to life imprisonment and pardons persons liable to the penalty of amputation of the hand or the auricle of the ear." The second, decree No. 64, dated July 30, 1995 was said to grant "a general amnesty to Iraqis living in or outside Iraq in respect of the penalties imposed on them following their conviction for political reasons." However, a number of conditions are attached to each amnesty decree. For example, in Decree No. 61, a condition of remission of sentence is "if [the detainee's] relatives undertake to ensure their good conduct, provided that the said undertaking is endorsed by a member of the Arab Ba'ath Socialist Party." In both decrees a number of categories of offenders are not eligible for amnesty. One of these categories is espionage, which the Special Rapporteur noted is "a particularly important exclusion . . . because so many laws refer to 'espionage' and because the crime applies to a wide variety of behavior."

In referring to foreign nationals in detention in Iraq, the report alters the previous year's wording from "several" to "numerous foreigners." However it only gives details of two U.S. citizens arrested in March for crossing the border from Kuwait and released in July. In addition, press reports say that four Sudanese nationals were executed in Iraq in mid-1995, one allegedly for manslaughter, the other three for receiving stolen cars.

Israeli Occupied Territories/ Palestinian Authority

As in previous years, the State Department's 1995 report includes separate sections on Israel and the Occupied Territories. The body of the report briefly mentions Israeli violations related to Palestinians and the Occupied Territories, while an annex details human rights issues of both Israel and the Palestinian Authority (PA) in the territories. This division — always an obfuscation of Israel's responsibility for its human rights practices — is increasingly problematic, as two authorities are now discussed in a single section.

The division of the report into two separate sections suggests that Israel's occupation of the territories is far removed, and can be neatly divorced, from events inside Israel. This may be wishful thinking on the part of the Israeli and U.S. governments. The reality, however, is that such a division is artificial. Many human rights violations against Palestinians take place inside Israel. Virtually all instances of torture and ill-treatment occur in interrogations conducted inside Israel. Of the six Palestinians whom the report cites as having died in Israeli custody, at least four were held in detention facilities inside Israel, including 'Abd a-Samed Harizat, who was tortured to death by the Israeli General Security Service in West Jerusalem. Administrative detainees were also held inside Israel.

Furthermore, violence by Israeli civilians against Palestinians is only discussed in the annex, although one Palestinian was shot to death and another injured by an Israeli civilian inside Israel. In contrast, Palestinian extremist violence is mentioned in the sections dealing with both Israel and the Occupied Territories.

Regarding most rights, Israel has identical human rights obligations inside the state and in occupied territory. Article 2 of the ICCPR (to which Israel is a signatory) requires states parties to respect and ensure the human rights of "all individuals within its territory and subject to its jurisdiction. . . ."

To avoid inconsistencies, future reports should address all of Israel's obligations and practices in one chapter, with a separate section on the Palestinian Authority. At a minimum, those events which took place inside Israel, such as detentions and interrogations, should be detailed in the body of the chapter on Israel, rather than in the annex.

The State Department continues the trend, begun in the 1993 report, of equating political and diplomatic developments with human rights. Thus it asserts that: "[p]ositive human rights developments flowed naturally as peace agreements were implemented." Despite the report's conflation of the two, the relationship between peace agreements and human rights observance is often far from clear. On one hand, the withdrawal of Israeli military forces from the Gaza Strip and West Bank cities as a result of the Oslo and Cairo Accords has dramatically reduced the number of Palestinian deaths and injuries. Yet human rights problems remain, and in some cases they are the direct result of the implementation of the peace accords.

Support for the political process was a pre-condition to enjoy many of the positive developments in the territories. Signing a statement of support for the peace accords was a pre-condition for the release of every prisoner released in the framework of the agreements. Signing such a statement was also a pre-condition for Gaza students to obtain the necessary permits to attend West Bank universities.

The targeting of Palestinians who are opposed to the political process increased in 1995. In June Israeli sources said that 3,200 Palestinians had been arrested in the previous seven months, most of them said to be members of Hamas or Islamic Jihad. The enormous number of arrests suggests that they were motivated by a person's suspected political sympathies rather than evidence that the individual had engaged in illegal activity. In addition to its praise for the positive human rights developments, the report should have acknowledged that the peace process has also heightened suppression of non-violent political opposition.

Last year's edition of the *Critique* suggested that many distortions could be avoided by measuring human rights conditions against the consistent standard of applicable international human rights and humanitarian law. This year's report has decreased even further its reliance on international legal standards. For example, the report has deleted both references to the fact that transfer of prisoners from occupied territory into Israel is a violation of the Fourth Geneva Convention. The introduction to the annex no longer states that "Israel is not recognized to have sovereignty over any of the occupied territories."

The release of Palestinian prisoners — an element of the Oslo Accords — is discussed in detail in the report, although such releases are not necessarily mandated by human rights law. While the report continues to mention the applicability of the Hague and Geneva Conventions, the deletion of certain international legal standards together with the reporting on Israel's implementation of the peace accords implicitly suggests that diplomatic negotiations make human rights principles obsolete. The report should have made clear that, regardless of its agreements with the Palestinians, Israel is obligated to respect international human rights and humanitarian law.

The report demonstrates bias by reporting positive political developments even if they occurred after the end of the calendar year. At the same time, the report does not mention negative events which occurred in the same time period. For example, the report includes a detailed and favorable description of the Palestinian elections, held on January 20, 1996. Yet the arrest and 24-hour detention of B'Tselem field worker Bassem 'Eid by the Palestinian police on January 2, 1996 is not mentioned.

Furthermore, in its discussion of legal challenges against the use of force in interrogations, the report states that the Supreme Court issued an injunction against the use of physical force in interrogation. Yet this petition was canceled on January 11, 1996, enabling the General Security Service (GSS) to continue to use torture in its interrogation of the detainee. These events are not mentioned in the report, although they occurred well prior to the elections, which are discussed.

With regard to the release of Palestinian political prisoners, the report states that "another 1,200 detainees were scheduled to be released in January 1996." According to Israeli Defense Force (IDF) statistics, the prison population only decreased by approximately 900 prisoners in that month. To avoid such inaccuracies, the report should consistently report only those events which occurred in the year under discussion.

While it mentions certain developments from 1996, the report shirks its obligation to follow up on cases pending from 1995. Despite explicit instructions by the State Department that the *Country Reports* should provide an update into cases of extrajudicial killing from previous years, the report does not mention that there was no significant progress in the investigation into the killing of six Palestinians by Israeli undercover units in Jabalya. (In February 1996, the Chief Military Prosecutor ordered the file against the five soldiers closed for lack of evidence against them.) Nor does it update the two trials pending of members of the Palestinian security forces suspected of killing Palestinians.

The State Department does a good job of reporting on the use of excessive force constituting violations of humanitarian law. The report first provides IDF open-fire regulations, which allow soldiers only to fire at a suspect's legs and forbid firing in the direction of children and women unless a soldier's life is in danger. The report then states, "[i]n practice, soldiers, police and undercover units used live ammunition in situations other than when their lives were in danger . . . and sometimes shot suspects in the upper body and head." The contrasting of official policy with a succinct statement about what actually occurs in this instance is a welcome departure from the reliance on euphemisms and third party sources in other places throughout the text.

In many instances, the report continues to provide official government justifications for abuses. For example, in a discussion of violence by Israeli settlers against Palestinians, the report states that "[t]he IDF has imposed protective curfews on the Palestinian population when it expects violence from settlers." The report does not comment on the injustice of placing the victims rather than the perpetrators of violence under curfew. In fact, in response both to Israeli and Palestinian acts of violence, the IDF invariably places mobility restrictions solely on Palestinian communities.

The repeated mention of acts of violence by Palestinian extremists seems to be presented as an excuse for Israeli violations. The introduction to the annex discusses torture in the sentence immediately following reference to "lethal terrorist attacks." The report later states that the government approved the continued use of special interrogation measures "arguing that they were vital because their use had prevented numerous terrorist attacks." The inclusion of these rationales with no comment or criticism gives the impression that the United States agrees that torture and ill-treatment are acceptable under these circumstances. Yet according to the U.N. Convention Against Torture (to which both Israel and the United States are signatories), "[n]o exceptional circumstances whatsoever, whether a state of war or a threat of war, internal political instability or any other public emergency, may be invoked as a justification of torture." (Article 2(2)). Political violence should be mentioned in the introduction to the report and in the section on political and extrajudicial killing. It is irrelevant to the discussion of torture.

Last year's edition of the *Critique* cited a lack of candor in reporting on human rights violations by relying on "credible reports" of torture and extrajudicial killings. This report duplicates last year's language in both these cases. With regard to torture, the report states that "[i]nternational, Israeli and Palestinian human rights groups and diplomats continue to provide credible reports indicating that Israeli security forces are responsible for widespread abuse, and in some cases torture, of Palestinian detainees." The sheer bulk of evidence warrants a definitive opinion on the part of the State Department. Last year's edition of the *Critique* compared the language on Israel with the language on Syria, where the report states categorically that "[t]he police and security forces continue to use torture systematically." The report should simply state that Israeli security forces are responsible for widespread torture and ill-treatment of Palestinian detainees.

The report correctly attributes the death of one detainee to torture by the Israeli GSS. However, according to B'Tselem, a total of ten Palestinians died in Israeli custody, and not six as cited in the report. Two Palestinians died in the Ketziot military detention camp between August and October, apparently as a result of torture by other Palestinian detainees. Testimonies gathered by B'Tselem reveal that dozens of prisoners were severely tortured by other inmates during this three-month period. The large number of prisoners involved, and the fact that prison authorities took no action even after the deaths, raises the concern that

Israeli prison authorities were aware of these events yet did not intervene. The inaccuracy in reporting deaths in detention and the failure to report on the deaths in Ketziot represent a serious oversight.

An important omission in this year's report is any discussion of land confiscation and discriminatory land use policies. While the introduction to the annex states that "[d]iscriminatory policies on land and resource use . . . remained in place," there is no elaboration of this sentence anywhere in the report. In fact, not only did discriminatory policies continue, at least one pattern of discriminatory land use — confiscation of land for the construction of settler by-pass roads — intensified in 1995.

According to Land and Water Establishment, tens of thousands of dunams of land were confiscated from private Palestinian landowners in order to construct roads connecting Israeli settlements without traversing Palestinian cities. In addition to the loss to the landowners, this policy violates both international humanitarian law and an Israeli legal precedent against confiscation of the local population's property for permanent use. In addition, the report should have mentioned renewed land confiscations in East Jerusalem, particularly as B'Tselem released a report in May documenting systematic discrimination against Palestinians in all matters relating to land expropriation, planning and building in East Jerusalem.

While this year's report is significantly longer than in past years, several important items have been deleted. The introduction to the annex no longer mentions the problems of administrative detention and family reunification. The section of the report on freedom of movement contains a much abbreviated discussion of restrictions imposed on Palestinians, although the problems of curfew and family reunification remain. Among the passages deleted is the fact that curfews and closures of the territories do not apply to settlers, although this remains true. The deletions may be due to space limitations, as the chapter now addresses Palestinian as well as Israeli human rights practices. These same space considerations may have resulted in abbreviated attention to certain PA violations as well, although on the whole the report does a fairly good job of covering most issues related to the PA.

Israeli Occupied Territories/Palestinian Authority

As with Israel, much of the critique of the PA is attributed to human rights organizations rather than to the State Department itself. For example, the report states that "local and international human rights groups have criticized the PA State Security Court arguing that it is subordinate to the power of the executive, undermines the independence of the judiciary and violates defendants' rights to a fair and open trial." The report omits mention of the fact that the military judges who preside over these courts do not necessarily have legal training. However, the report's own description of the State Security Court demonstrates that it violates minimum requirements of fair trial.

The fact that the State Department relies on third parties to criticize the State Security Court may be related to the court's role in trying those suspected of violent opposition to the peace accords. The report notes that the State Security Court was created "in response to Israeli and international pressure." Israel's pressure on the PA to crack down on violent opposition should have been mentioned in the context of a variety of PA abuses, including mass detentions following bomb attacks. In addition, the United States played a central role in pressuring the PA to crack down on violent opponents, and specifically encouraged unfair trials. During and following his March visit to the Palestinian areas, U.S. Vice President Al Gore specifically praised the State Security Court and the sentences it had handed down.

As with the discussion of torture by Israeli officials, the report also refers to "credible sources" to report on ill-treatment and torture by the PA. While the report accurately describes the treatment of detainees in Palestinian custody — including hooding, beating and tying in painful positions — it abstains from labeling this treatment torture. Furthermore, the report mentions five cases of death in PA custody with no reference to allegations that these deaths were the result of torture and ill-treatment.

It is disingenuous of the report to mention disciplinary actions and investigations into these cases without mentioning that no result of any investigation has ever been made public and that in certain cases (such as the 1994 death of Farid Abu Jarbu') interrogators who were arrested were later released and reinstated to their posts.

Critique 1995

Despite the State Department's instructions that those preparing the *Country Reports* avoid comparisons with other countries, the report states that "[t]he PA Press Law . . . has been described by Palestinian journalists as the best in the Arab world." Two paragraphs later the report states that Reporters Without Frontiers has labeled the press law restrictive. The report should measure practices according to the universal standards of international human rights law, rather than the practices of specific countries or regions.

The report devotes a lot of space to restrictions on the press. Certain important incidents are absent, however, including the fire bombing of the leftist, opposition newspaper, *al-Umma*, allegedly by Palestinian security forces; and the arrest of five journalists from the pro-Islamist *Istiqlal* newspaper. Both in the context of press freedom and rights to fair trial, the report should have mentioned the midnight trial by the State Security Court of Sayed Abu Musameh, editor in chief of *al-Watan*, the pro-Hamas weekly. According to Amnesty International, Abu Musameh was convicted of writing "seditious" newspaper articles and incitement and libel against the PA. He was reportedly arrested after publishing an article comparing the Palestinian police to the IDF and accusing them of torturing suspects.

Israel enjoys a special relationship with the United States and is the recipient of tremendous financial and political support. The United States has played an active and highly visible role as mediator and supporter of the peace accords. Given the extent of U.S. involvement in the territories, the pressures to produce less than objective reporting of the human rights situation may be expected to be greater than when dealing with other parts of the world. Nonetheless, the report provides a great deal of accurate information. However, it is flawed by a persistent habit of appearing to justify both Israel and the Palestinian Authority's violations of human rights, and by a reluctance to criticize directly clear violations of international human rights norms.

KENYA

During 1995, internationally recognized human rights became increasingly imperiled in Kenya. Detainees were tortured; opposition politicians were arrested and sometimes held incommunicado; peaceful political rallies were dispersed by police with gunfire and tear gas; lawyers investigating human rights abuses were arrested and their documents were seized; violence against women increased; and journalists were harassed and threatened. True to form, the Kenyan government continued its increasingly harsh crackdown on dissent.

The State Department should be applauded for the overall tone of its 1995 report on human rights in Kenya and for its detailed approach to chronicling the many abuses perpetrated during the last year by the government and its security forces. In particular, the State Department deserves commendation for using the active voice and not mincing words, as in years past, when describing the deteriorating state of human rights in Kenya. In the introduction, the report unequivocally states that the government's "human rights record worsened in 1995" and that "[m]embers of the internal security forces committed numerous serious human rights abuses." Further, the report pronounces that the police "committed several extrajudicial killings and tortured and beat detainees" and that the Kenyan government "continued to harass and intimidate those opposed to the ruling party."

Like its immediate predecessor, the 1995 report is full of specific examples of human rights abuses committed during the year. Unfortunately, however, this year's report suffers from the same weakness as the 1994 report in that it takes a laundry-list approach to the recitation of abuses instead of providing an overarching framework within which to analyze and understand these disconnected facts. Succinctly stated, the Kenyan government is doggedly determined to silence its critics. By failing to present the chronicle of abuses within the context of intentional, institutionalized disregard for the rights of Kenyans who oppose the current government and for those who have no voice in the political realm (such as prisoners and refugees), the State Department trivializes the significance of the abuses it reports and minimizes the efficacy of the report as an analytic tool. This is particularly troubling as citizens throughout the country attempt to prepare for multi-party elections in 1997.

The list of abuses provided by the State Department in its 1995 report cannot be understood without reviewing the larger political context. President Daniel Arap Moi and other members of the ruling KANU Party have never been strong champions of multi-party democracy and the freedoms associated with it. It was not until millions of dollars of critical foreign assistance were withheld that Moi reluctantly agreed in 1991 — 13 years after coming to power — to allow opposition parties to form and participate in multi-party elections. Even so, as the report correctly notes, "the 1992 presidential and parliamentary elections were marked by violence, intimidation, fraud and other irregularities . . . . " Curiously, the report fails to mention that the next multi-party elections are scheduled for 1997. Now that its coffers have been replenished with foreign assistance and the 1997 elections are looming on the horizon, the Kenyan government is more openly and brazenly committed than ever before to silencing its critics. It is within this context that many of the abuses chronicled in the report can be seen as inextricably linked together as part of a coherent strategy of government repression. These abuses include: denial of registration to newly-formed opposition parties; denial of licenses to allow opposition MPs to meet with their constituents; detentions and arrests of opposition activists and human rights advocates who dare to question the Moi government; seizure of documents from human rights advocates investigating improprieties by public officials; intimidation of journalists; abuse of the judiciary; and incitement of ethnic clashes.

Unquestionably, President Moi and the ruling KANU Party are turning to increasingly harsh and oppressive tactics to silence their opponents. Critics of the government never know when they may be arrested, how long they may be held incommunicado, or how they will be treated. In February 1995, the government announced that insulting the president is now an arrestable offense. As the report accurately notes, several opposition activists have already been arrested and accused of such an offense. Given that most criticism of Moi or his government's policies can be perceived as an insult, it is becoming increasingly difficult for critics to voice their opinions without fear of significant reprisals.

In January 1995, police arrested three opposition members of parliament as they were about to attend a church service in memory of people recently killed in political violence. Each of the MPs was charged with promoting "warlike activities" and "uttering words with seditious intent." Two of the MPs were released in mid-February, when the charges were withdrawn. Before this happened, however, one of them had become so ill and had been denied medical treatment while in prison that over 300 inmates reportedly staged a hunger strike and refused to return to their cells until he received hospital care. The report makes no mention of the MP's ill-health or of the denial of medical care. The report acknowledges that the third MP was held for four months and admitted to the hospital three times, but fails to note that the government doctors in the Nakuru hospital refused to treat him and that while ill in the hospital he was chained to his bed at night. The chilling effect of such degrading treatment of opposition politicians is incalculable.

In August 1995, plainclothes police officers, prison guards dressed in full riot gear and members of the ruling KANU Party youth wing whipped, beat and stoned leaders of the opposition Safina Party and journalists who were with them as they approached the courthouse in Nakuru. While there were numerous eyewitnesses to the attacks and the involvement of the police, the prison guards and the KANU youth wing, the strongest statement that the report makes about this incident is that "police failed to protect members of the Safina Political Party from a mob attack." Given the amount of evidence, the report should have directly linked the government security apparatus and the ruling party to this horrifying event, and placed the abuse within the greater context of government suppression of dissent.

The report accurately notes that security forces "employ various means of surveillance, including a network of informants to monitor the activities of opposition politicians and human rights advocates." While it provides a few telling examples of such surveillance, it does not indicate the frequency and gravity of this abuse. Given the tremendous chilling effect of being followed and having one's correspondence and telephone calls potentially monitored, the report should have been placed greater emphasis on this abuse.

The State Department should be commended for unequivocally stating that "[a]lthough the Constitution provides for an independent judiciary, it is subject to executive branch influence in practice." However, it would have been even more commendable for the report to have stated that the judiciary is often treated as another tool in the government's arsenal of weapons to silence and discourage critics. Opposition activists are frequently charged with a host of imprecise crimes, with these charges usually dropped later without any investigation as to whether they were brought simply as a form of harassment. The judicial system is also used to subvert investigations of improprieties by government officials. As the report notes, the Kenyan Constitution permits the Attorney General to take over and discontinue proceedings in private prosecution cases. The Attorney General used this constitutional power in 1995 to terminate a public corruption case filed against Vice President George Saitoti and to stop an incitement case related to ethnic clashes brought against Local Government Minister William Ntimama.

The most publicized political trial in 1995 continued to be that of Koigi Wa Wamwere, a former MP from Nakuru, and three co-defendants, who were charged with attacking a police station in 1993. Influenced by the international outcry condemning the trial as a political witchhunt lacking any credibility, the Chief Magistrate decided against sentencing Wamwere and two of his co-defendants to death; instead, they were each sentenced to two concurrent four-year terms plus three strokes of the cane. In a peculiar and troublesome shift from the 1994 State Department report, in which the Wamwere trial was forcefully described as a "political trial" during which the prosecutor failed to "produc[e] credible evidence tying Wamwere to the alleged attack," the 1995 report makes no reference to the political character of the trial, and takes a much more passive stance on the credibility of the evidence presented by the state prosecutor. The report also fails to note that the four-year sentence imposed on Wamwere, a seasoned opposition activist popular among Rift

Kenya

Valley Kikuyus who are considered political rivals of President Moi, effectively removes Wamwere from any involvement in the 1997 elections.

In its efforts to suppress dissent in 1995, the government also resorted to its old practice of imposing outright bans. In February, the government banned all past, present and future issues of *Inooro*, a Kikuyu-language newspaper published by the Catholic Church, which contained certain articles critical of the government. The report makes no mention of this blatant suppression of dissent. The Kenyan government also banned CLARION, a non-governmental think tank, after it published a detailed report on corruption in Kenya. According to the government, the think tank was banned because it exposed "to ridicule and contempt the image and integrity of the Kenyan government."

As part of its overriding objective of silencing critics, state harassment of the independent press increased in 1995. As in 1994, this year's report grossly minimizes the pressure on the print media to conduct self-censorship, which continues to be flagrant. The 1995 report provides numerous examples of gross state harassment and intimidation of the press, including arrests, detentions, beatings and threats of deportation, but then blithely states only that "[n]ewspaper and magazine editors continued to feel varying degrees of government pressure to self-censor." Given the severity and regularity of harassment suffered by print journalists who wrote articles on topics deemed sensitive by the government, there is no question that the print media is under extreme pressure to self-censor.

The report's treatment of torture and other inhuman treatment is at best incomplete. While it describes several specific instances of torture by the police, the report undercuts the importance and impact of this section by stating in a passive voice only that there "continued to be credible reports that police resorted to torture and brutality." According to Amnesty International, which sent a team of medical delegates to Kenya in March 1995, "[t]orture and ill-treatment are widespread in Kenya." Amnesty concluded that the purpose of such treatment "appears to be to intimidate detainees and dissuade them from engaging in political activities, and to obtain (often false) admissions of guilt which can be used in court." According to Amnesty International, torture methods are frequently very brutal, including beatings on different parts of the body with knobbed sticks, fists, the handles of hoes and gun butts.

On the other hand, the State Department should be applauded for its discussion of a number of topics, including the treatment of refugees, discrimination against Rift Valley Kikuyus, prison conditions (although it provides two very different numbers for those who died while imprisoned), flagrant abuses of the right of peaceful assembly, and violations of International Labour Organisation (ILO) labor conventions. In particular, the report deserves praise for its discussion of the problem of mob justice. The State Department cites statistics from the Kenya Human Rights Commission quantifying the number of suspected criminals murdered by angry crowds, and then intelligently delves beneath government rhetoric, stating "[t]he Government condemned the practice but has taken no action to address the problem, nor arrested anyone who participated in the violence." The fact that the government has taken no action to address the problem destroys any pretense that it is committed to eradicating this serious problem.

In its discussion of female genital mutilation, the report notes the government's stated opposition to the procedure but fails to go the further step to indicate that the authorities have taken no action to address this "widespread" problem. Similarly, in its discussion of violence against women, the report acknowledges that this "is a serious and widespread problem," but then repeats the government position that it "condemns violence against women" without indicating the lack of leadership and action from the government to address the problem. As it did in its discussion of mob justice, the report should much more frequently go beyond government rhetoric and indicate where the government is doing little or nothing to address a particular human rights violation.

The report should be heartily commended for its analysis of the use of excessive force and other violations of humanitarian law related to internal conflicts. Unlike reports in previous years, the 1995 report admirably proclaims that "[s]ubstantial evidence indicates that high-level government officials were complicit in instigating and promoting the ethnic clashes of 1991-1994, which claimed over 1,000 lives and displaced 250,000 people." Moreover, the report explicitly states that

Kenya

"[g]overnment officials, particularly [Local Government] Minister [William] Ntimama, continued to make inciteful and threatening statements against non-Maasai living in the Rift Valley." This is particularly significant given that the Kenyan government frequently arrests its critics for allegedly making inciteful and threatening statements. The report also deserves praise for providing several telling examples of governmental disregard for the rights of displaced persons, and for drawing attention to the fact that the UNDP program to assist thousands of displaced victims of ethnic clashes drew to a standstill in 1995 as a direct result of the withdrawal of support from the Kenyan government.

The report should have mentioned that President Moi and his supporters repeatedly accuse critics and human rights lawyers of being in league with guerrilla groups committed to the overthrow of the government. In early April, the normally conservative Roman Catholic Church leaders in Kenya issued a stinging condemnation of the government. They spoke of a state of fear in the country in which there was no law, justice or protection except for the powerful. In what has become a typical response of the government to criticism, the government accused the church leaders of colluding with guerrilla groups.

Despite its claims to the contrary, the Kenyan government has neither embraced multi-party democracy nor recently improved its human rights record. Until President Moi and his government make genuine strides toward upholding the full panoply of civil and political freedoms, democracy will continue to falter in Kenya. The government's attitude to the opposition in the run-up to the 1997 elections will undoubtedly prove to be an invaluable gauge of the future for human rights in Kenya.

LIBERIA

The State Department's 1995 report on human rights in Liberia is a generally accurate and comprehensive picture of the complicated situation in that country. While this year's report improved in certain areas that were identified in the 1994 issue of the *Critique*, it nonetheless continues to be lacking in other respects. Particularly troubling are those problem areas that were identified in prior editions of the *Critique*. Specifically, the report continues to display bias in its characterization of the conduct of the Economic Community of West African States (ECOWAS) Ceasefire Monitoring Group (ECOMOG). The report should also have made much stronger summary statements about the situation of women in Liberia, given that so many of the individual incidents of killings, torture and gender-specific abuse reflect a clear pattern of targeted attacks against women.

There are several improvements in this year's report. Its introduction is clearer now that it identifies the various factions involved in the civil war. The report also includes a more accurate section on freedom of speech and the press. Last year's edition of the *Critique* noted the inconsistencies in this section between topic sentences and the paragraphs that followed. In contrast, this year's section is written in a much more consistent manner. A particular improvement is the listing of specific examples of problems facing journalists, which thereby inhibited a free press. These examples included the beating of a British Broadcasting Corporation (BBC) journalist by a police major associated with the Labor Ministry, and the beating of another journalist with *The News* by United Liberation Movement for Democracy in Liberia (ULIMO)-Krahn fighters.

Nonetheless, the section on freedom of speech and the press could be further improved. Specifically, the report should have noted that reporters outside Monrovia ran the risk of attack and harassment by ECOMOG soldiers who confiscated equipment and otherwise prevented journalists from reporting on events. Similarly, while the report states that journalist James Momo received death threats, it neglects to mention that Momo was beaten and had his camera confiscated by ECOMOG soldiers. The report also fails to mention an incident involving freedom of speech that would have cast doubt on its assertion that no member of the Monrovia-based consortium of human rights NGOs reported any governmental interference with its activities in 1995. In fact, according to the Catholic Justice and Peace Commission (CJPC), the management of the official Liberian Broadcasting System interfered with a CPJC radio program entitled "The Justice and Peace Forum." The program, which reported on human rights abuses by the various warring factions, was canceled without explanation in mid-September.

Several other parts of the report could also have been improved. Specifically, the report still demonstrates bias in favor of ECOMOG. This bias is particularly troubling since this weakness has been identified in previous editions of the *Critique*. For instance, while abuses perpetrated by certain factions are set forth as undisputed facts, ECOMOG's participation in human rights abuses is couched in more equivocal language.

Similarly, the report downplays human rights abuses committed by ECOMOG soldiers by sandwiching its descriptions of negative situations between positive statements, or by describing the negative act in a tone that belies the seriousness of the act. This is frequently apparent by the use of topic sentences that do not conform to the body of the paragraph. For example, the report states that ECOMOG is the military force supporting the transitional government, that it continued its humanitarian role and maintained a protective cordon around the cities of Monrovia and Buchanan. Yet the paragraph ends with the terse statement: "[t]here were reports that a few ECOMOG soldiers committed human rights abuses such as arbitrary detention." As written, this statement minimizes the seriousness of arbitrary detention carried out by ECOMOG.

The report also states that "there were reports that some ECOMOG soldiers beat individuals at checkpoints," but this comment is made after being couched in a paragraph which states that "to protect the 1.2 million people in Monrovia and Buchanan from rampant lawlessness and banditry ECOMOG established a protective cordon around those cities."

The report is also inaccurate in maintaining that "ECOMOG generally discouraged large scale parades or demonstrations for security reasons." In fact, demonstrations were not merely discouraged, but prohibited; as reported by the BBC, ECOMOG banned such "protests, demonstrations, and other potentially riotous forms of rallies as directed by the Liberian National Transitional Government" (LNTG). The report also fails to note that ECOMOG troops have developed a notorious reputation for extortion and looting, such that some Liberians contend that ECOMOG is an acronym for "every car or moveable object gone."

Finally, the discussion of ECOMOG would have been improved if it had accurately described the structure — or perhaps more precisely the *lack* of structure — within which ECOMOG operates. Currently, there is no official document that delineates the precise relationship between ECOMOG and the state of Liberia. In practice, ECOMOG has often carried out functions which should be the responsibility of the Liberian government, and when an organization challenges its authority, ECOMOG resists, as it did when the Liberian human rights community attempted to define ECOMOG's jurisdiction.

Similarly, the report should have also indicated that ECOMOG forces are in principle answerable to the ECOWAS defense commission. Yet ECOWAS has done little to ensure ECOMOG troops are properly trained, briefed on their roles as peacekeepers or made aware of international humanitarian law. In addition, there is no organized ECOMOG structure to discipline ECOMOG forces. The report could have also noted that Liberian courts have no jurisdiction over ECOMOG soldiers, and therefore those soldiers likely have no fear that their acts may be punished.

Besides the inadequate discussion of ECOMOG, the report should have also noted the lack of human rights provisions in the August 19 peace agreement and in the structure of the second transitional government (LNTG-II). As pointed out by both Amnesty International and Human Rights Watch/Africa, a failure to include provisions guaranteeing human rights and to provide a mechanism to address past human rights violations makes it more likely that the various factions will engage in further human rights violations to gain power.

The report also does not adequately address the ineffectiveness of the peacekeeping forces and the government in reporting or investigating human rights abuses. The April 9, 1995 massacre at Yosi, where

62 civilians were killed, is illustrative of this failure. After the Yosi massacre, the report of the United Nations Observer Mission in Liberia (UNOMIL) merely repeated observations made by UNICEF workers, while also stating that UNOMIL only had limited abilities to document such incidents. (The effort to create a human rights monitoring role within UNOMIL has apparently been abandoned.) LNTG-I similarly failed to pursue perpetrators of various human rights abuses. For instance, LNTG-I announced that it would set up a commission of inquiry to investigate the massacre of 50 civilians in Paynesville in December 1993. Subsequently, LNTG-I did nothing to pursue the alleged perpetrators.

The report should also have noted the danger of faction leaders assuming positions of power in LNTG-II. As Samuel K. Woods, a Liberian human rights activist, has stated: "To have criminals and warlords who have killed our people, to then emerge as the leaders of our people, is a contradiction." Illustrating this problem is a statement by Charles Taylor, leader of the National Patriotic Front of Liberia (NPFL) and a Council of State member, who maintained that only two people were killed in a massacre around Kakata on October 8, 1995, instead of the 60 that were widely reported to have died. Similarly, the Liberian Peace Council (LPC), another Council of State member, executed four of its own commanders for human rights abuses. Yet as Amnesty International stated: "If the long-standing disregard for human rights is to be reversed, justice not further human rights abuses is needed."

The report should also have expanded its explanation of the status of the Armed Forces of Liberia (AFL). It maintains that the AFL was "largely inactive," although this is contradicted by reports that the AFL warned against holding demonstrations and public meetings during scheduled peace talks.

Finally, contrary to the State Department's own instructions to those preparing the *Country Reports*, the report should have identified the various actions taken by the U.N. For instance, the report should have noted that the U.N. named a chairman, Gerardo Martínez Blanco, to implement a mandatory arms embargo against Liberia, and that UNOMIL had a new military observer, Mahmud Muhammad Talah appointed. And in June 1995, the U.N. Secretary General recommended that UNOMIL's presence be terminated if peace talks did not progress. The need for an expanded discussion of the U.N.'s actions in Liberia is important, since UNOMIL, as an independent international presence, is in a critical position to implement peace agreements and to report on human rights violations.

Mexico

The State Department's 1996 report on human rights practices in Mexico reproduces many of the same errors and weaknesses identified by previous editions of the *Critique*. The report relies excessively on the National Commission for Human Rights (*Comisión Nacional de Derechos Humanos*: CNDH) and other official sources for information, and excludes other independent and reliable sources. Furthermore, the report overemphasizes formal guarantees afforded under Mexican law, without assessing their vigor in practice. As in previous years, it also discusses certain abuses without providing much context. In spite of its breadth, the report omits important incidents as well as crucial facts in cases which are cited. Its assessments of government responsibility for abuse are often ambiguous, contradictory and at times misleading.

Tensions in U.S. policy toward Mexico between concern for human rights and other political and economic interests continue to be apparent in the report. It is generally cautious in ascribing responsibility for human rights violations to the Mexican government, the ruling Institutional Revolutionary Party (*Partido Revolucionario Institucional*: PRI) and the administration of President Ernesto Zedillo. U.S. trade and investment interests and geopolitical concerns are secured by the commitment of President Zedillo and his party to continue Mexico's course of economic and institutional reform. The PRI also offers some measure of political stability, in spite of its selective use of anti-democratic and authoritarian practices. Not surprisingly, the conflict between U.S. political and economic interests and the State Department's human rights mandate is evident in the report's lack of sharpness and clarity.

During more than 60 years in power, the PRI has developed a complex political structure that is still often synonymous with state power (hereinafter sometimes reflected by the expression "PRI/government"). The PRI political machine incorporates, either formally or through alliances, multiple social organizations, including opposition political parties. At present, Mexican civil society is pressing for reform and democratization of the country's political institutions. The PRI has been sensitive to some pressures, as evidenced, for example, by greater electoral transparency; however, government officials continue to use authoritarian means to control opposition forces. The PRI also uses its social organizations to divide civil society and stifle or co-opt opposition voices.

In spite of the report's deficient analysis, government responsibility for human rights abuses emerges from a close reading of the data it presents. For example, the report notes that at least 34 extrajudicial killings in 1995 are either attributable to government security forces or contain some indications of government complicity, and that another 100 politically motivated killings have gone unprosecuted. The report mentions over 50 cases of alleged torture by security forces and another 50 rape charges against government officials. Some 160 arbitrary arrests and detentions are mentioned, as well as a number of forced disappearances. Meanwhile, independent human rights NGOs report that the actual number of violations in these areas is even higher. The report describes a severely flawed judicial system, with problems of corruption, lack of judicial independence and lack of due process. Also mentioned are cases of involuntary sterilization of women, intimidation and persecution of members of the press, complaints of electoral fraud and unpunished violence against homosexuals. The report repeats the CNDH's disturbing conclusion that 280 different government agencies were "presumably responsible" for human rights abuses. But the report offers scant evaluation of the Mexican government's responsibility for such abuses. Instead, the introduction asserts: "[t]he Government generally respected the human rights of its citizens. . . ." Such vague conclusory statements prove to be disingenuous when independent sources of information are consulted and critical analysis is applied to the facts.

The impunity of military personnel for well-documented human rights violations committed in Chiapas, and of judicial officers for corruption and violation of due process, clearly implicate the government in these violations. The report brings critical analysis to bear on issues of discrimination, such as the combination of prejudice and state action regarding women and homosexuals, but slips noticeably when the focus turns to issues such as the impunity of state agents.

The report's only yardstick for measuring government efforts to reduce human rights abuse is the work of the CNDH and government compliance with its recommendations. Such practice is unfortunate given the CNDH's limited resources, autonomy and involvement in much of the actual human rights reporting in Mexico. As a creation of the government, the CNDH's power is limited to making recommendations; other officials and agencies must decide whether to heed them. Most importantly, the CNDH was divested of much of its responsibility by the creation of state level human rights commissions (*Comisiones Estatales de Derechos Humanos*: CEDH). For example, the CNDH has issued no recommendations concerning the military's conduct in the Chiapas conflict. Meanwhile, the CEDH have been largely ineffective. Though technically responsible for collecting and reporting on the vast majority of abuses in Mexico, they have often been negligent in investigating complaints, and are politically compromised by their relationships with state and local authorities.

The report's review of government compliance with the CNDH's recommendations offers no hint of the substance of those that were followed and those that were not, or the probable explanations for the governmental response. Some evidence suggests that in politically sensitive areas, the compliance rate is rather dismal. The National Network of Non-Governmental Human Rights Organizations (*La Red Nacional de Organismos Civiles de Derechos Humanos "Todos los derechos para todos"*) found that in Chiapas the government had complied with only 27% of the CNDH's recommendations.

The report's only references to non-governmental sources, other than newspaper accounts, are to Amnesty International, the International Labour Organisation (ILO), a women's organization in Chiapas, and a report on free speech published by a Mexican magazine. The Inter-American Commission on Human Rights (IACHR) of the Organization of American States currently has approximately 30 pending human rights cases regarding Mexico, yet no reference is made to this fact or to the IACHR as a potential source of information. Numerous complaints have been filed against Mexico with the U.N. Commission on Human Rights, to which the report makes no reference. The report mentions that ministerial consultations were held under the North American Agreement on Labor Cooperation (NAALC), the labor side agreement to the North American Free Trade Agreement (NAFTA). However, the decision by the National Administrative Office (NAO) which led to such consultations, and reflected poorly on Mexico, is not mentioned in the report's section on labor rights. Human Rights Watch/Americas and the Minnesota Advocates for Human Rights published significant reports on human rights violations in Mexico in 1995, but the State Department fails to mention these sources. NGOs working in the area of human rights in Mexico number over 150, yet only one Mexican NGO is cited by the report as a source of information. There is no indication that additional Mexico-based human rights groups were consulted.

The section on political and other extrajudicial killings contains a particular focus on violence in the state of Guerrero, but provides only a cursory review of other prominent cases which arose in 1995. For example, the report addresses too superficially the persecution and acts of violence against the Revolutionary Democratic Party (*Partido Revolucionario Democrático:* PRD). The "Miguel Agustín Pro" Human Rights Center (*Centro de Derechos Humanos Miguel Agustín Pro Juárez, A.C.:* PRODH) maintains that in the first year of President Zedillo's administration more than 100 members of the PRD were assassinated. According to the PRODH, the frequency of such killings has doubled since the administration of Zedillo's predecessor, Carlos Salinas de Gortari. CNDH figures cited by the report, referring to the number of cases investigated by CNDH since 1992, give the impression of a problem which is much smaller in scale.

By selectively reporting statistics, the report also downplays the problem of torture. CNDH figures cited by the State Department suggest a marked decrease in the number of torture complaints filed with that entity in 1995; however, since the creation of 33 state and Federal District (Mexico City) human rights commissions (all of whose statistics are not cited by the report), the CNDH no longer receives the majority of complaints. For example, the report does not mention that the Veracruz State Human Rights Commission has received almost 6,000 complaints, including many of torture, against members of the police and the judicial system. The report recognizes structural difficulties with bringing to justice those responsible for torture, such as the high burden of proof on the victim, but generally ignores the Mexican government's responsibility for such incidents.

The report does not adequately address the PRI/government's use of the legal system to weaken the political opposition. It states ambiguously that the detention of opposition political activists is "neither widespread nor systematic, but does occur frequently for short periods of time." For example, a court in the Federal District ordered the arrest of leaders of the traditionally oppositionist labor union of the Ruta-100 bus company in Mexico City (*Sindicato Único de Trabajadores de la Ruta-100*: SUTAUR) on charges of internal union corruption. The report did not mention that Judge Polo Uscanga (who was later murdered under circumstances suggesting that he was assassinated) resigned from the court due to pressure he received from the President of Federal District Superior Court. This pressure came after Judge Polo Uscanga refused three times to order the arrests of the union leaders because of insufficient evidence. The judge appointed in Polo Uscanga's place issued arrest orders only three days after entering office, which raised reasonable doubts as to whether the new judge actually reviewed the eleven volumes of transcripts concerning the case before making his decision.

Persecution by prosecution also occurs in many rural areas where local officials wield unbridled power. Government and PRI party officials often fabricate charges against rural, indigenous, labor and political party leaders to weaken their opposition. In Oaxaca, for example, prosecutors brought a series of questionable charges of crimes of moral turpitude against leaders of the Union of Indigenous Communities of the Northern Zone of the Isthmus (*Unión de Comunidades Indígenas de la Zona Norte del Istmo*: UCIZONI), which is based in the town of Matías Romero. UCIZONI leaders claim the charges have been brought to impede and distract attention from the investigation of the murders of UCIZONI leader Armando Augustín Bonifacio and other UCIZONI officials by local bosses (*caciques*).

The report ignores the widespread persecution of debtors after the peso devaluation in 1994. Banks in Mexico have collaborated with the police, courts and prosecutors to extort and intimidate individuals to pay loan interest rates that are among the highest in the world. The *Unión Nacional de Productores Agropecuarios, Industriales, Comerciantes y Prestadores de Servicios "El Barzón,"* a large association of indebted merchants, farmers and business entities, was organized to challenge bank practices of charging exorbitant interest rates, repossessing property and instigating legal actions against the debtors. *El Barzón* also claims that vandalism to offices, threats and attacks against its members have occurred on the orders of creditors and with the complicity of government authorities. Some *El Barzón* leaders were reportedly jailed illegally by the government in the last year. Another debtor organization, the National Association of Credit Card Users, requested the intervention of the Federal District Human Rights Commission (with jurisdiction in Mexico City) against the legal departments of certain banks, which had threatened to utilize the judicial system to imprison thousands of credit card users and embargo goods and services. According to the PRODH, half of the six million credit card users in Mexico have no possibility of repaying their debts.

The recent economic reforms and devaluation have had noticeably negative effects on public safety and civil liberties, and exacerbated the general feeling of lawlessness in Mexico. The report understates these trends. The Mexican government has responded with new public safety legislation, including the recently approved Law of the System of National Public Security, and the proposed Law against Organized Crime. Human rights observers in Mexico consider the legislation to be authoritarian and threatening to civil liberties. Some of the developments not mentioned by the report are the result of U.S. pressure for Mexico to combat drug traffickers. Articles 16, 20, 21 and 22 of the Mexican Constitution, which guarantee individual rights and liberties, have been reformed in anticipation of the proposed Law against Organized Crime, modeled after the far-reaching Racketeering Influence and Corrupt Organizations (RICO) statute in the United States. Given the pattern of human rights abuse in Mexico, human rights observers fear the new law, if passed, will be used as an additional pretext for the persecution of political and social opposition to the PRI/government.

The militarization of civil police forces in several areas also bears mention. Because of widespread corruption, military officers have been given authority over police forces in Chihuahua, Morelos and Mexico City. Military personnel also have been used as agents of the Public Ministry (*Ministerio Público*). This measure is highly threatening to civil liberties, because the Mexican military has been the source of many human rights violations and alleged corruption, and enjoys considerable impunity and independence from the civilian court system.

The report concludes that the Mexican government generally respects freedom of speech and the press. It does not mention that journalists are routinely harassed by police and government officials and private citizens who enjoy official protection. For example, in Nuevo Laredo, Tamaulipas, the newspaper *El Mañana* has faced censorship and harassment as a result of its opposition to the PRI. *El Mañana*'s publisher has also claimed that she and reporters have received death threats in response to the paper's consistent and open criticism of the PRI/government.

The report asserts that the Mexican government has not forced a radio or television station off the air; however, Radio Huayacocotla, a short-wave radio station which broadcasts to indigenous communities in the northern sierra of Veracruz, and Radio Polanco, in Guadalajara, were forced off the air last year for alleged "technical violations." Radio Huayacocotla's manager is convinced, based upon past incidents of harassment, that the alleged violations were fabricated. In the last two years, the director of the station has been accused of broadcasting "coded messages" and promoting violence among indigenous communities, without substantiation.

Government pressure on the media via its regulatory authority is a serious issue in Mexico, which the State Department downplays. Without an examination of actual incidents, the report's brief discussion is not particularly illuminating. It repeats suggestions by critics that the government's power to grant or revoke licenses, which can pose a problem in almost all countries, has a chilling effect on free expression; however, the evidence suggests that the Mexican government is using this power excessively, and the report should have discussed this. Radio Huayacocotla, for instance, maintains that it has repeatedly been denied a license to broadcast over the AM-band because of the viewpoints aired by the station. Manipulation of the licensing power may well chill the competition needed to diminish the influence of the pro-government media company, Televisa, which controls 80% of Mexico's television market.

The report does not mention the government's large purchases of advertising space and provision of subsidized newsprint to papers, which undermine the independence of the press in Mexico. Such practices have had the effect of making newspapers financially accountable to the government. Threats to deny such government privileges have often proven useful for the government to maintain control over the press. Only four national print outlets have dared to be openly defiant and independent of the government: the dailies *El Financiero*, *El Norte* and *Reforma* and the weekly news magazine *Proceso*.

Rural Mexico saw numerous violent acts and human rights violations in 1995, especially in the southern states with large indigenous populations. The government has used these outbreaks of violence to justify an increased militarization of the countryside; military posts and checkpoints have become increasingly common. The report dedicates a lengthy section to the well publicized massacre of 17 peasants in the state of Guerrero, but does not capture the dimension of the problem in the countryside. Human rights groups, peasant organizations and indigenous rights groups describe a persistent conflict over land and other issues between peasants and ranchers. Local authorities, under the control of the ranchers, are generally recalcitrant in adjudicating and enforcing peasants' claims. The political manipulation of local bosses, the resort to violence by rural strongmen, and the denial of judicial remedies generate conflict, confrontation, violence and multiple human rights violations.

The report suggests that "local political rivalries," "family feuds" and peasant "invasions" of private property are at the root of rural violence; however, it fails to recognize the links between local *caciques*, the PRI and government officials. Private militias, such as the *guardias blancas* ("white guards") in Chiapas, operate with impunity, often with the acquiescence of state security forces, as in the case of the municipality of Chicomuselo. On January 10, 1995, *guardias blancas* armed with semi-automatic weapons confronted indigenous protesters who had occupied Chicomuselo's city hall. Violence erupted and at least six individuals were killed. State and local police officers observing the event failed to intervene in a timely manner to prevent the violence, and, according to some reports, joined with the private militia in their attack on the protesters. The case remains open, but lack of cooperation from state authorities has slowed the work of a special federal prosecutor.

Peasant invasions usually occur after long and frustrated attempts by the peasants to obtain government adjudication of land disputes. Even after a favorable adjudication, government officials often fail to implement the decrees, which leads to further violence. Three cases of human rights abuse against members of UCIZONI in 1995 illustrate various levels of government responsibility and complicity. In early 1995, a 30-year-old land dispute with local ranchers was finally adjudicated in favor of the indigenous peasants, but the ranchers blocked execution of the decree. In November 1995, Blas Santos Vásquez of UCIZONI was assassinated, allegedly by some of the ranchers. UCIZONI sees the assassination as part of the ranchers' ongoing intimidation of the peasants and resistance to the execution of the decree. Formal accusations have been filed against members of a particular ranching family, but no arrests have been made. As of April 1996, the peasants had still had not received possession of the land at issue.

The same month, Armando Agustín Bonifacio, a member of UCIZONI's board and a prominent leader in Mexico's indigenous rights movement, was assassinated under similar circumstances. He had been defending a group of peasants who fled from their village of origin, Santiago Tutla, because of harassment by local political bosses aligned with the PRI. Agustín was murdered on November 30 by a group of five armed men. The police thus far have failed to apprehend the gunmen, despite their being identified by witnesses. At the same time, local officials continue to intimidate members of the peasant community, alleging that UCIZONI leaders are members of the Chiapas-based rebel

Critique 1995

Zapatista Army of National Liberation *(Ejército Zapatista de Liberación Nacional*: EZLN).

Finally, in December 1995, Juan Carlos Beas Torres, an officer of UCIZONI, and 12 other members of that group received numerous death threats. Beas's case has been marred with confusion because of official government reports that he was under investigation for fraud and corruption against his own organization. Allegedly such charges were filed by UCIZONI's president, but this was untrue. The Public Ministry later admitted that no charges against Beas were pending. The case demonstrates the same pattern of harassment found in other cases, consisting of attempts to divide an independent organization and damage the prestige of its leaders.

Patterns of government neglect with respect to the claims of indigenous peasants, and false accusations against their organizations and leaders, were similarly at the root of the Guerrero massacre. The report mentions the work of CNDH, but fails to mention the allegations against Governor Rubén Figueroa for planning the repression and participating in his administration's subsequent state-level cover-up. The report also fails to assess critically the delays and other deficiencies and irregularities in the state-level investigation, such as the failure to take statements from many witnesses, threats against witnesses and the state's failure to comply with CNDH recommendations. In 1996, Figueroa was forced to resign, and was found by a two-judge commission of the Mexican Supreme Court to share, at a minimum, responsibility for the cover-up. Independent human rights organizations had alleged his involvement since the beginning of the investigation, supported by testimony from a local mayor. Progress in the Guerrero case was obtained primarily as result of public pressure. The Supreme Court and federal authorities refused to become involved with the case until recently, even though their intervention was solicited from the start by human rights advocates and the victims' families, who argued that the matter fell within the court's authority over cases affecting the well-being of the nation.

Notwithstanding official resignations, dismissals and the criminal proceedings currently underway, the case is still indicative of problems within the judicial system of investigating and prosecuting human rights

154

violators. In spite of recommendations by the CNDH, no measures have been implemented to restructure the police force or prevent the recurrence of similar acts of abuse and cover-up. In the 12-month period following the June 28 massacre, over 100 extrajudicial killings occurred in the same region of Guerrero. All have remained unsolved. In light of these facts, the report's general reference to "family feuds" as the source of more killings is grossly misleading.

Another example of the report's failure to assess meaningfully governmental non-compliance with CNDH recommendations concerns the killing of two peasant leaders in the community of Plan de Encinal, Veracruz. The report mentions only that state officials blocked attempts by Amnesty International to conduct autopsies on the victims, and states that authorities have made no progress on the case. The report fails to mention that the Veracruz State Human Rights Commission identified the probable guilty parties and asked that arrest warrants be issued, but authorities have failed to act. The case was presented to the IACHR by PRODH and the Center for Justice and International Law. In April 1996, the offices of PRODH were burglarized, and the file of this case was the only item taken.

The report correctly identifies the conflict in Chiapas as an internal conflict in which international humanitarian law is applicable; however, it fails to mention that the Mexican government refuses to take such a view. The government styled their military offensive a "judicial operation," with "support" by the army to carry out arrest warrants against the Zapatista leadership. During the offensive, the Mexican Army invaded and ransacked the homes of peasants who had fled out of fear of the army's advance.

The report's account of the expulsion of U.S. clergyman Loren Riebe, along with other priests working in Chiapas, is misleading. The case should have been easy to report since Riebe provided thorough information regarding the situation to the State Department. The Mexican government alleges he was inciting peasants in Chiapas to participate in land invasions, based on testimony by a woman who claims she overheard Riebe planning peasant land invasions with Bishop Samuel Ruíz at a local religious celebration. The content of the claim lacks credibility on its face. Riebe has documentation, submitted to the State Department, that proves he was in the United States at the time the conversation is alleged to have occurred. The report fails to assess the Mexican government's claims. The report also is misleading when it states out of context that Church leaders were "pleased" with their meeting with government officials on the matter.

The passage dealing with the Chiapas conflict recites the official military version of events concerning three heavily documented cases of extrajudicial killings committed by the Mexican Army during the January 1994 hostilities. At the beginning of its discussion of the cases, the report states: "The law does not require civil trial of soldiers involved in civil crimes, and the military continues to handle such cases." This is erroneous. Article 13 of the Constitution states that military personnel should be judged by civil tribunals for crimes against civilians. The practice of submitting military personnel only to military tribunals for crimes against civilians is contrary to Article 13. The three cases included in the report concern: five men shot at close range at the Ocosingo market with their hands bound behind their backs; the murder of 11 individuals at an Ocosingo medical clinic; and the disappearance of three men from the community of Morelia in the municipality of Altamirano. The report begins the account of each case with a similar phrase: "the military alleges. . . , the army claims. . . , the army continues to stand by its assertion. . . ." It makes no attempt to critically assess the military's claims, and fails to shed light on the incidents, despite information readily available from independent sources.

The report repeats the army's claim that Second Lieutenant Arturo Jiménez Morales, the officer allegedly responsible for killing eight civilians at the Ocosingo clinic, committed suicide after being questioned by military authorities. It ignores the fact that eleven individuals were killed, not just the eight attributed to Jiménez, and fails to critique the military's version of the events and the suspicious "suicide" of Jiménez. Human Rights Watch/Americas issued a report in 1995 which found serious irregularities and contradictions in the army investigations and reports on these matters. The army prosecutor's report on the clinic deaths does not take into account any of the testimony provided by civilians. Jiménez is

156

not listed among those interviewed by the prosecutor. He was only later questioned in April 1994 by high-ranking officers at the Ministry of National Defense in Mexico City, after which he allegedly committed suicide.

The army prosecutor also did not report the contents of Jiménez's confession. The report from a separate internal investigation of the alleged suicide does not explain why Jiménez was not immediately disarmed and placed into custody after confessing the crime. Other questions casting doubt upon the alleged suicide are not adequately answered by the army's report. In fact, the alleged responsibility and suicide of Jiménez only became public after it was revealed by military authorities to the director of Human Rights Watch/Americas in April 1995.

In the case of the three men disappeared from Morelia, forensic experts from Physicians for Human Rights have positively identified their remains in a clandestine grave. The report admits their remains were discovered, but fails to note that the CNDH has refused to recognize the experts' work and continues to officially list the cases from Morelia as unresolved "disappearances." The government, meanwhile, has closed its investigation of the "disappearances" without seeking to bring anyone to justice.

With respect to human rights violations, the report includes no analysis of the failings of the internal army investigations, the lack of public accountability and the failure of the army to prosecute any of its members for crimes against civilians. The repetition of skeletal, official military versions is again misleading. The report offers no critical assessment of the work of the CNDH in response to human rights violations committed during the Chiapas conflict, and the CNDH's failure to make recommendations concerning the Mexican military.

In the area of labor rights, most problems in Mexico stem from the PRI/government's efforts to control the labor movement through "corporative" unions affiliated with the PRI or otherwise aligned with it. The report recognizes the link between the major unions and the PRI, but fails to analyze complaints concerning the right to free association and the right to organize and bargain collectively in this context. A pattern of violations of the rights of independent unions and their organizers is discernible from the complaints brought before domestic human rights groups and international fora such as the ILO and the NAO. This pattern includes: the government's failure to protect workers from intimidation and unjust dismissal which result from their attempts to form independent unions; inadequate access to judicial remedies or, in some cases, deficiencies in the remedies themselves; and the imposition of technical obstacles to the registration of independent unions. The report does not adequately recognize this systematic infringement of the rights of the independent labor movement.

The report credits Mexico for the formal guarantees of labor rights contained in the Constitution and the Federal Labor Law (LFT), without critiquing sufficiently their application. Pro-union provisions of the law work favorably for pro-government unions aligned with the dominant Confederation of Mexican Workers (*Confederación de Trabajadores Mexicanos*: CTM), which is affiliated with the PRI. As the NAO's findings suggest, the protections of the law are enforced unequally. The LFT is supposed to protect unions from government interference in their internal affairs; however, from a practical standpoint, this enables pro-government union leaders to consolidate power, stifle internal opposition and act undemocratically. The complaint submitted to the NAO by workers at the SONY subsidiary, Magnáticos de México (a *maquiladora* in Nuevo Laredo, Tamaulipas), included allegations against the official, CTM-backed union for the use of strong-arm tactics in collaboration with the employer. The local labor tribunal also placed technical obstacles to the registration of an independent union. The report recognizes the problem of internal union democracy and transparency, but fails to link it to PRI corporativism and government complicity in the infringement of labor rights.

Independent social organizations regularly complain of intervention by the government and the PRI to "divide and conquer," or effectively co-opt their organizations. Usually members are recruited inside the organizations and provided with money and resources to create parallel leadership or organizations. Such tactics facilitate the legal recognition of pro-government factions and the denunciation of independent leaders as corrupt, or in some cases the filing of criminal charges against the independent leaders of these organizations. The Fray Bartolomé de las Casas Human Rights Center of the Diocese of San Cristóbal, Chiapas, has received numerous complaints of such tactics from local chapters of the Regional Association of Collective Interest *(Asociación Regional de Interés Colectivo)*, an association of indigenous *ejido* cooperatives. Charges of corruption against PRI-backed union leaders are rarely, if ever, prosecuted, while charges of corruption against independent leaders allow selective persecution by prosecution of the opposition.

The debate over social security reforms in 1995 provided another example of how rights to freedom of association and expression are restricted. Reforms to Mexico's social security law provoked serious divisions, including within the PRI-aligned labor movement. Labor activists and union leaders who vigorously opposed the reforms and the official position taken by the CTM hierarchy were intimidated and accused by government officials of having links with the Zapatista guerrillas. In general, the government program to privatize public entities has met with significant opposition and protest from independent labor groups and leaders. Complaints of selective measures being used to intimidate such opponents of privatization have increased.

Some of the problems in the area of labor rights may have technical legal solutions, as suggested by the ILO and NAO recommendations, but past practice suggests that technical perfection of the law will not suffice to end the pattern of abuse of labor rights in Mexico. The report fails to take this context into account in its assessment of the Mexican government's respect for the right of association and the right to organize and bargain collectively.

In its assessment of Mexico's respect for political rights, the report states that the government no longer restricts the activities of political opponents. Such a statement is not completely true; continued violence against PRD activists suggests that the government's old habits die hard. Moreover, the PRI continues to manipulate elections in a variety of ways. For example, the PRI overspends its opponents by large margins in campaigns, which the opposition alleges illegally include government funds. In the 1995 Tabasco election, for example, the PRI candidate for governor allegedly spent US$70 million, which was 60 times over the legal limit on campaign spending. Opposition candidates commonly claim that the PRI uses its vast resources to buy elections and even opposition candidates. Ledgers leaked to the press from the PRI's 1995 Tabasco gubernatorial campaign indicate that PRD leaders were among those paid off.

Furthermore, the government intimidates opposition candidates by auditing or conducting criminal investigations against candidates or family members before an election. Opposition candidates often find it difficult to acquire advertising space in the media and must cope with negative media reports from pro-government television prior to an election, as occurred in Tamaulipas during November, 1995. The PRI also mobilizes its affiliated labor unions and social organizations to garner support for party candidates and pressure members to support party candidates by linking job security to voting for the PRI.

The report does not thoroughly assess the accuracy and fairness of the election process during recent federal and state elections. Though the Mexican government attempted to demonstrate the legitimacy of the elections by having election monitors from participating parties and civic organizations, there have been credible reports of irregularities in the monitoring process. In Tamaulipas, for example, a non-governmental report cited that one half of the monitors from the PRD were denied observer status by electoral officials on election day due to technical errors in documents improperly completed by the Federal Electoral Institute, which runs and monitors the elections.

The report also omits important criticism of the selection process for voting place officers. The District Boards of the Federal Electoral Institute randomly select 15% of registered voters from a voting district to be included in a pool of potential voting-place monitors. The District Board then selects those who will be invited to take a special training course; however, District Boards have been accused of manipulating the process to fill the pool with their personal selections. The report also fails to mention problems posed by Mexico's process of invalidating votes from polling places where fraud is alleged to have occurred. By voiding all results from such polls, the Federal Electoral Institute effectively disenfranchises a whole bloc of voters. This process could be used to neutralize entire blocks of support for opposition parties simply by alleging (or committing) fraud in particular districts.

The State Department's 1995 report on Mexico lacks in depth what it has in breadth. Its continued excessive reliance on governmental sources appears to reinforce a tendency to eschew critical analysis. As suggested in previous editions of the *Critique*, future reports would benefit from greater attention to non-governmental sources, especially Mexican human rights groups. Their reporting may compel the State Department to take a fresh look at its analysis of a situation that now requires more probing attention than it has so far received.

NIGERIA

When the State Department reported the state of human rights in Nigeria in 1994 as "dismal," it apparently did not foresee the need for a description of "worse than dismal." Thus, in its 1995 report, it merely says that the human rights situation in Nigeria "worsened" in 1995. This is unfortunately correct. Human rights in Nigeria reached a new low in 1995, and the report has generally taken pains to detail the more significant abuses and to provide sufficient examples of other human rights violations. What is more disconcerting than any shortcomings in the report, however, is that the State Department's criticisms of human rights violations in Nigeria in 1995 was both too little and too late. In particular, U.S. condemnation came too late in the case of Ken Saro-Wiwa and his eight co-defendants who were executed in November. The public outcry and diplomatic initiatives that followed the execution of the nine Ogoni would have been better spent in an attempt to save their lives rather than to criticize their deaths. A principal purpose for the gathering by the U.S. government of this type of information concerning human rights abuses abroad must be not just to monitor human rights violations as they occur, but to predict and take steps to prevent events such as the senseless killing of Ken Saro-Wiwa and others like him.

The execution of Ken Saro-Wiwa and his eight Ogoni co-defendants received a great deal of international publicity and condemnation. The biased nature of the tribunal that convicted Saro-Wiwa and the others emphasizes one significant reason for concern over the escalation in executions in Nigeria in 1995. A majority, if not all, of those executed in 1995 were also convicted by special tribunals set up by the military government. The Committee for the Defence of Human Rights (CDHR), a local NGO, estimated that there are more than 800 convicted armed robbers on death row. Persons accused of armed robbery, for example, are tried before special Robbery and Firearms Tribunals that lack fundamental notions of due process, and there is no right of appeal from the decisions of these tribunals.

By October 1995, more than 86 persons had been executed for armed robbery. Between July and September, CDHR reported 75 executions: 43

in Lagos, 18 in Delta State, and 14 in Akwa-Ibom State. Amnesty International noted that in addition to the 43 persons executed in Lagos on July 22, six more were executed on July 26 and five in Adamawa State on the same day. The report, which notes that "in practice tribunal proceedings often deny defendants due process," fails to mention the increasingly deadly results of proceedings in these tribunals. This does not mean the State Department has to take a stand in opposition to the death penalty, which lies outside the mandate of the *Country Reports*. Rather, the alarming rate of executions in Nigeria must be placed within the context of the report's discussion of the denial of fair public trial stemming from specially formed tribunals.

The 1995 report provides an excellent discussion of extrajudicial killings in Nigeria. Occasionally in past years, the *Critique* has noted a lack of attention to the extremely serious problem of frequent killings of Nigerian citizens by police and other security service personnel. This year's report not only states forthrightly that the police and security forces "commonly engaged in" extrajudicial killings, but also emphasizes the Nigerian government's failure to hold its security personnel accountable for their excessive uses of force. In addition, the report provides a detailed list of examples of extrajudicial killings that occurred in 1995. Clearly, the Abacha government has done nothing to improve upon the atrocious record of its predecessor in this area. In fact, it appears that Abacha's own willingness to resort to violations of fundamental human rights to repress his critics is paralleled by the lower ranks of the police and the security forces, who also abuse their authority with impunity. One statistic reported by CDHR that the report does not include is that between April and June, 1995, 34 persons were killed by police in Lagos and Oyo states alone. The police apparently claimed that all of those killed were armed robbery suspects. One of the deceased was aged 16.

For those of its critics that the Abacha government chose not to kill — judicially or otherwise — extended incarceration increasingly became the norm. One major flaw in the reporting of arbitrary detentions and arrests is the report's frequent failure to state whether those persons incarcerated during the course of 1995 had been released at year end.

Nigeria

Although the report does recount the names of persons who were arrested in 1993 and remained in detention at the end of 1995, it often does not provide the same information for those arrested in 1995. It was often the case with the persecution of political figures that they were imprisoned briefly and then released. Therefore, it was often difficult to know whether someone sentenced to five years in prison is still actually imprisoned in any given year. The Abacha government, on the other hand, has demonstrated an increasing willingness to leave its critics in prison indefinitely.

The report notes that Sylvester Odion-Akhaine, secretary general of the Campaign for Democracy, was arrested on January 17, 1995. No further explanation is given as to whether, by the end of the year, Mr. Odion remained in prison and whether he had been charged with any crime. This type of reporting is essential and should in any event be part of the State Department's efforts throughout the year to track the status of political prisoners.

A number of examples of arbitrary arrests escaped the State Department's attention in 1995. For instance, Dr. Charles Ugboma, a doctor who treated M.K.O. Abiola, legitimate winner of the 1993 elections, in prison, was arrested and held incommunicado. CDHR reported the arrest on February 20 of Samson Ranti, chairman of the Kwara State Public Service Joint Negotiating Council, and on March 27 of Bisi Fakayode, chairman of the Nigerian Labour Congress in Kwara State. On June 13, government forces arrested Alao Aka-Bashorun, chairman of the Democratic Alternative (DA), and Dr. Onje Gye-Wado, a member of DA's National Coordinating Committee. Aka-Bashorun was arraigned 12 days later and charged with conduct likely to breach public peace. Ayo Opadokun, general secretary of the National Democratic Coalition (NADECO), was also arrested by government forces in 1995. The Lawyers Committee is not currently aware whether any of these men have been released from jail.

Some of the details recounted in the report are confusing, misleading or simply inaccurate, and a number of proper names are misspelled. For instance, the description of the arrest of CLO employees Steve Aluko and Tunde Akanni (misspelled "Akannu") is confusing in that it is unclear when, if at all, both men were released from detention. According to at least one source, Akanni remained in detention for 17 days before being granted bail. Dr. Beko Ransome-Kuti was arrested and sentenced to life imprisonment for being an "accessory after the fact of treason." His offense was to distribute the statement of a suspect in an alleged coup plot, Ralph Bello Fadile, to international human rights organizations and diplomatic missions. Furthermore, the report's discussion of the Ogoni arrested in 1995 lends the improper impression that only a handful of Ogoni were detained. Although the exact number is unavailable, credible reports say that at least 100 Ogoni were detained by the government and that even after the execution of Saro-Wiwa and his co-defendants in November, the number of Ogoni who remained in detention far exceeded the dozen or so noted in the report.

Those imprisoned by the Abacha government were often at risk of bodily harm from torture in addition to the hardships normally associated with the abysmal prison conditions found in Nigeria. The constant stream of credible allegations of torture in Nigerian prisons is of particular concern to the Lawyers Committee. This is an issue that has received little attention from the State Department, although it has consistently acknowledged over the years that there are credible reports of torture in Nigeria. In 1995, international organizations recounted that both Ken Saro-Wiwa and his co-defendant Baribor Bera were beaten in detention. Bera allegedly showed the special tribunal scars from the beatings inflicted upon him and stated that he had been stripped naked, tied to a pillar, flogged with a horsewhip, and forced to swallow teeth knocked out by the beatings. CDHR related meanwhile that Clement Tusima, who died in detention, had also been tortured by his detainers. Finally, both Lt. Col. M.A. Igwe and Col. G.A. Ajayi alleged that they were subjected to torture and vicious interrogation after their arrests for involvement in an alleged coup plot.

The Abacha government has done little or nothing to ameliorate the problem of prisoners awaiting trial for years. The State Department report, while consistently recognizing the problem of lengthy pre-trial detention, just as consistently fails to emphasize the seriousness of this problem given the length of the detentions and the poor conditions in

Nigeria

Nigerian prisons. In the past, the *Critique* has pointed out that lengthy pre-trial detention affects a number of important rights such as the presumption of innocence, the right to a fair trial and even the right to life. The efforts of local NGOs have been successful in a limited number of cases, but these cases remain sad examples of the magnitude of this problem. Thus, for example, on January 5, the Constitutional Rights Project secured the release from detention of four persons who had each been detained without trial for between seven and nine years. Nevertheless, it will require a commitment by the government to make a significant impact on the number of persons awaiting trial for extended periods of time.

The report once again notes that accusations that the Nigerian government is engaged in a "genocidal campaign against the Ogoni are unfounded." The 1994 edition of the *Critique* pointed out that although the campaign against the Ogoni has not reached the level of genocide, it should not take a genocidal campaign to evoke a stronger condemnation from the United States government. In July 1995, Human Rights Watch/Africa released an extensive report documenting flagrant human rights abuses by the Nigerian government against the Ogoni people and, to a lesser extent, other ethnic groups in Nigeria's oil-producing region. The Human Rights Watch report details such abuses as extrajudicial killings, indiscriminate shootings, rape, torture, and looting by Nigerian security forces, particularly by the Rivers State Internal Security Task Force commanded by Lt.-Col. Paul Okuntimo. Furthermore, the Unrepresented Nations and Peoples Organization (UNPO) stated in March that: "There appears to be a government policy aimed at strangling the Ogoni community's social, political and economic life. Daily, gross human rights violations are being perpetrated against the Ogoni people by the security forces." UNPO noted that during the Saro-Wiwa trial, gatherings of Ogoni women who were fasting and holding prayer meetings were broken up by security forces using excessive force, including teargas. Clearly, the State Department should be more concerned with the very serious abuses inflicted upon the Ogoni people than with the repeated reminder that those abuses have not yet reached the level of "genocide."

The Abacha government did not spare members of the press who dared to criticize the military government's actions in 1995. The State Department report lists a number of journalists who were arrested for writing, publishing or airing stories critical of the government. But naming other cases would have given a more complete picture of the scope of abuse of press freedom. For example, CDHR reported the arrest of Ocheriome Nnanna, deputy political editor of Vanguard Newspapers on February 20 at his Apapa office. Also in March, police attempted to arrest Dapo Olorunyomi, editor in chief of *THENEWS*. Not finding Olorunyomi at home, the police detained his wife and three-month-old infant. Olorunyomi apparently went into hiding. In the same month, Olufisayo Alabi, publisher of *Osun Voice*, was arrested by security agents in Osun State after publication of a story on a regional official entitled "Udofia's Administration: The Reign of Agony." Bala Dan Abu, editor in chief of *Majestic Weekly*, was imprisoned in April by security forces in Lagos. He was released two days later. Dan Abu's arrest was reportedly in connection with an article called "Problem Pure Abiola." In July, the government detained Lekam Otufodunrin, a reporter for *A.M. News*.

In less drastic actions, Fidel Egwuche, editor of the Kogi State government-owned newspaper, *The Graphic*, was suspended indefinitely by the state's military administrator, Colonel Paul Omeruo, who complained of negative attacks on the state and federal governments. In addition, the government announced on July 3 that all newspapers and magazines would have to register with a Newspaper Registration Board and deposit 250,000 *naira* (approximately U.S.$11,423) and pay 100,000 *naira* (approximately U.S.$4,569) fee.

The report also notes that a 1991 decree provides that only sitting or retired civilian judges may preside over tribunals hearing "nonmilitary cases." Assuming that this means proceedings in which the accused are civilians, this decree would conflict with the State Department's report that the special military tribunal convened to examine the alleged coup plot convicted and sentenced seven civilians as well as a number of soldiers. The report should have condemned such a contradiction in the Nigerian government's implementation of its own decrees.

Nigeria

Over the years, this *Critique* has paid particular attention to the State Department's description of whether a Constitution is actually in effect in Nigeria, in part because of the confusing nature of the interplay between constitutional provisions and military decrees, which supersede the Constitution. Unfortunately, the language in this year's report is once again confusing and perhaps deceptive. The report notes that "some provisions of the 1979 and 1989 constitutions were observed, although the decree suspending the 1979 constitution was not repealed, and the 1989 constitution was never implemented." It would seem pointless at this writing, in 1996, to continue to reference the proposed 1989 Constitution which has never been implemented or promulgated into law by a civilian government. Furthermore, the decree suspending the 1979 Constitution specifically suspended the chapter providing for fundamental human rights. The report does not explain what constitutional provisions were actually "observed" and by whom, thereby leaving the incorrect inference that there is some recourse in Nigerian courts to a federal constitution. Finally, the report omits appropriate language in the introduction that was included in last year's report indicating that the government expressly made reference to the continued suspension of constitutional rights, lest there be any doubt on the part of the public. Rather, as the report only notes much later in its section on the denial of a fair public trial, the military government reiterated in 1995 that Decree No. 12 of 1994 divests the judiciary of any authority to question the actions of the federal government.

PERU

The 1995 report provides a largely accurate overview of Peru's principal human rights problems and supports its presentation, for the most part, with specific facts. Its central weakness is one of tone and emphasis. The report correctly indicates that there has been a "marked decrease in the number of extrajudicial killings and disappearances attributable to the security forces," although it does not emphasize that arbitrary executions and forced disappearances continued to occur in certain emergency zones. The report generally stresses "improvements," in Peru's human rights situation, while downplaying gross human rights violations perpetrated by the government, principally the routine torture of suspects by the military and police. Significantly, the report discusses, but fails to condemn directly, two crucial retrenchments by the government on human rights issues: its decision to protect human rights violators by passing Latin America's broadest general amnesty law for state agents in June 1995, and its refusal to eliminate "faceless" military and civilian courts in October despite prior commitments to do so. Although the report is factually accurate in most respects, it does not squarely identify or sufficiently analyze the question that lies at the heart of Peru's human rights problems — whether the government is truly committed to restoring civil and political rights in the wake of President Fujimori's "self-coup" (*autogolpe*) in 1992.

The report correctly notes that government security forces still routinely torture persons during interrogation, but inappropriately refers to the victims as "suspected subversives." The use of torture by Peru's security forces is more widespread, reaching to persons held on suspicion of a variety of criminal activities. Moreover, the victim's suspected affiliation is appropriate only if it sheds light on the motive for torture; as used here, it may be interpreted as implicitly condoning the practice. The systematic use of torture during interrogation has led many detainees to confess to crimes they did not commit, and has perpetuated false arrests of other persons who themselves become the victims of torture. The report does capture the horrors of torture by describing not only the forms of torture employed by the government (including beatings, electric shock, near-drownings, prolonged suspension by the arms bound behind the back, mock executions and death threats), but also the facts of specific cases. Consistent with State Department guidelines, the report focuses appropriately on the use of rape as a form of torture of female detainees. The report should have mentioned that rape with rifles is committed against male and female detainees in many instances. While citing claims by the Justice Minister that officers and non-commissioned officers have been punished for committing human rights abuses, including torture, the report fails to mention that the secrecy of military proceedings precludes corroboration of such claims. Human Rights Watch/Americas reported in July that it was not aware of a single case in which an agent of the state had been brought before a civilian court and punished for having carried out torture.

The report indicates that constitutional protections were suspended in state of emergency zones affecting 44% of Peru's population. It should have attempted to analyze the close connection between ongoing human rights abuses and the continuation of states of emergency. For example, according to the World Organization Against Torture, 41 residents of a village in an emergency zone were detained, interrogated and tortured by the military in August. Such abuses occur more readily where civilian control of government has been ceded to the military in these emergency zones. Nor does the report address whether states of emergency continued to be necessary in such zones, particularly in light of the government's repeated claim that guerrilla violence had been brought under control. While *Sendero Luminoso* (Shining Path) and other guerrilla groups continued to commit gross violations, and, according to most respected human rights organizations, killed more civilians than government security forces, these activities sharply declined in 1995, as compared to prior years. The government's broad adherence to states of emergency in the face of these changes has been questioned by most respected human rights advocates. The report should have directly confronted the government's policy, which forms part of the institutionalized core of Peru's human rights problem.

The report contains an extensive discussion of the Amnesty Law proposed by President Fujimori in June — two months after he was re-elected to a second term — and passage of that law the very next day by a Congress dominated by the president's party. It notes that the "summary manner" in which this and other laws were passed "revived concerns about an authoritarian approach to governance." However, the report stops short of directly condemning the Amnesty Law. That reticence is particularly troubling because, in June, the State Department forthrightly denounced the law, stating that it demonstrated a "lack of serious commitment to the protection of human rights." Among other things, the Amnesty Law resulted in the release of low-level military officers convicted of the 1992 La Cantuta massacre, whom the United States had insisted be prosecuted as a condition for renewed foreign assistance. The report's failure to criticize the Amnesty Law more directly is, in effect, a subtle retreat by the United States from its prior denunciation.

A subsequent law passed by Peru's Congress has equally disturbing implications for the rule of law. After a judge ruled that the amnesty was unconstitutional and could not be applied to the 1991 Barrios Altos massacre case before her, the legislature rushed passage of a law which prohibits judicial review of the amnesty law and mandates a mechanical application of its benefits. The report offers no evaluation of this action, which truncates the role of an independent judiciary. Few actions are as threatening to the protection of rights than a prohibition on the ability of courts to review governmental action against constitutional imperatives. This disturbing measure leaves little doubt about the government's attitude towards judicial independence.

Similarly, the report mentions, but fails to condemn, the government's one-year extension of its use of "faceless" courts, despite prior indications that it would eliminate such courts by October. Instead, the report spends considerable time discussing judicial reforms which, while important, do not counteract the fundamental due process violations committed under Peru's military and civilian faceless court system. The basic elements of that system are: military jurisdiction over civilians accused of treason; incommunicado and punitive detention; routine torture; denial of bail pending trial; severe restrictions on access to counsel; presentation of persons dressed in prison garb to the press before they have been convicted; secret trials by prosecutors and judges who remain behind one-way glass mirrors and whose identities are never revealed; denial of the opportunity to cross-examine security force witnesses; and sentencing that violates basic proportionality requirements. (Terrorism cases are tried by civilian tribunals and not, as the report suggests, military courts. The civilian tribunals follow procedures which are very similar to those described in the report and herein regarding treason cases.) As a July 1995 Human Rights Watch/Americas report aptly concluded:

> Since 1992, faceless courts have amassed a breathtaking record of human rights violations. To enumerate the particulars is to descend into a citizen's nightmare, where no rule is inviolable, no right guaranteed, no precedent honored. In Peru, the arbitrary permeates every stage of the judicial process: from arrest to charge, investigation, trial, sentencing, and appeal.

The State Department report describes the failings of that system but does not directly condemn it. Indeed, at one point it appears to attribute the decline in disappearances and extrajudicial killings approvingly to the "high conviction rate" obtained in military courts. The report does not mention the arrest on terrorism charges in December of Lori Berenson, a U.S. citizen, and her descent into Peru's faceless court system.

The report correctly indicates that most Peruvian NGOs are "independent and generally objective," and appropriately criticizes the government's "verbal attacks" against these organizations, as well as its attacks against journalists who criticize government policies. The State Department itself has been the subject of "verbal attacks" when it has publicly criticized Peru's human rights record. In the absence of sustained public pressure, however, it seems unlikely that the Peruvian government will take those steps that are minimally necessary to account for the disappeared, eliminate torture, and bring the administration of justice out into the open.

The actions of the Fujimori government — its continued use of the faceless court system; pushing through an amnesty law and then barring judicial review; and continued hostility to human rights advocacy — lead

174

to an inescapable conclusion: the Peruvian government has no demonstrable commitment to institutionalized improvement or to the rule of law. While the State Department's catalogue of facts is admirable, this obvious conclusion nonetheless remains muted.

Russia

The State Department's 1995 report on the Russian Federation presents the picture of a country that remains deeply troubled and divided, while still much freer than it was a decade ago. A practical consensus has yet to emerge in Russia over the priority that should be accorded to human rights, the rule of law and the nature and purposes of democracy. Democratic rule remained precarious at the end of 1995, even after the procedural step forward of the second free Duma elections on December 17. A symptom of that precariousness, which does not emerge clearly enough from the State Department report, was the increasing influence of the Communist Party and the continued fragmentation of the supporters of democracy and reform. The election results confirm the finding in last year's edition of the *Critique* of "the fragmentation of democratic reform parties in Parliament and around Yeltsin, and the increasing influence of nationalist, agrarian and neo-communist parties." The results confirm also the volatility of the electoral support.

The report is once again wide-ranging and detailed. It contains thorough accounts of serious violations in law enforcement and the administration of justice. These range from widespread police brutality to appalling conditions in pre-trial detention centers, persistent violations of defendants' rights to due process, the holdup in expanding the jury system, and sweeping new investigative powers for the security agencies, which once again have become a force unto themselves. The report expands its coverage of the mistreatment of army conscripts, which reportedly caused the deaths of some 4,000 to 5,000 in 1995.

Under the rubric of "discrimination based on race, sex, religion, etc.," the report notes the increasing violations of the rights of women, including inadequate protection against domestic violence and job discrimination; of children (notably the orphaned and homeless); of indigenous people — especially from the Caucasus; and of religious minorities, including Jews and "foreign" groups such as Jehovah's Witnesses. The coverage of worker rights brings out shortcomings in the protection of labor rights and occupational safety.

Critique 1995

Though detailed and balanced in its presentation of facts, the report contains significant omissions in analysis and coverage. It fails to assess the responsibility and impact of the president and his "power ministers" in matters of war and in the failure to provide adequate human rights protections. Analysis is also lacking on the Constitutional Court's guardianship of the rule of law.

The report's expansive coverage of civil liberties omitted three areas of governmental policy which bear on democratic freedoms and governance. These are: access to information; infringements on religious freedom and equality emanating from within the Russian Orthodox Church; and the growth of organized extremism. The report also passes lightly over other threats to democratic rights, such as organized crime and the deterioration in respect for economic and social rights.

The report provides substantial coverage of the extensive violations of humanitarian law by both sides in the Chechnya War, which has produced as many as "tens of thousands of civilians killed and some 500,000 people displaced." The report correctly concludes that: "Violations committed by Russian military forces occurred on a much greater scale than those of the Chechen separatists."

The report alludes to a "major debate over accountability in government for decisionmaking and the Government's commitment to the rights of its citizens and international norms." Yet it remains almost silent on the responsibility of the president and his ascendant conservative advisers and "power ministers" for waging war as a solution to Chechnya's separatism since November 1991. The report cites "Russia," "Russian military forces" or "Russian forces" — and, just once, "government forces" — as violators in the attack on Chechnya, while leaving unmentioned the responsibility of the president and the conservative cabal of security, police and military officials around him in Moscow. As the 1994 edition of the *Critique* found, "The effect of this is clearly to downplay criticism of President Yeltsin's actions and of his justification for the actions."

President Yeltsin's Human Rights Commission has declared that, "in the magnitude and severity of the human rights violations, in the sufferings of hundreds of thousands of Russian citizens, and in the brutalities perpetrated against the civilian population, the Chechen events are unparalleled since the era of mass political repressions in the USSR." The report's probing treatment of violations committed during the war on Chechnya bears out this view. However, it remains silent on the lukewarm criticisms of that war that have been offered by the U.N. Secretary-General, the European Union, and foreign governments including that of the United States.

The report does not evaluate the Constitutional Court's fulfillment of its mandate "to protect the foundations of the constitutional system and the basic rights and freedoms of the individual and the citizen, and . . . to ensure the supremacy and direct action of the Russian Federation Constitution on the entire territory of the Russian Federation." When the court finally reconvened in February 1995, after its suspension and reorganization by President Yeltsin in 1993-1994, the president had packed the court by raising its membership to 19 and by steering through the Federation Council the approval of six new justices.

Citizens may now complain directly to the court about legal norms, but only about laws, not about the more numerous decrees and resolutions with normative force issued by the president and the government. As last year's *Critique* noted: "This is a potentially crippling limitation since many major state actions are taken solely by decree or decision, including the Chechnya intervention and the Anti-Crime decree." Although citizens may now bring cases directly to the Constitutional Court, their complaints — or complaints by different state organs — may not concern *law application*, which is now beyond the competence of the court. For this reason, the Constitutional Court could not rule on the constitutionality of the government's violations of human rights and humanitarian law in Chechnya. It could only advise that civilians had the right to bring suit in ordinary courts for restitution of damage caused by the action of government forces. That recourse, the report fails to note, is hardly promising, given the dubious remedies provided by ordinary courts.

The 1994 statute reduced the court's legitimate powers of judicial review to the detriment of the rule of law and the separation of powers. The reduction in the length of a judicial term from life to 12 years for judges elected under the 1994 law makes the court more rather than less subject to political pressures and changes. The lack of explicit guarantees of the right of non-citizens to petition the court themselves threatens the constitutional recognition of equal rights. It leaves foreigners particularly at risk because of increasing discrimination against non-Russian minorities, especially favorite targets such as people from the Caucasus and Central Asia.

The report, as noted last year, "does not adequately set out the legal foundations for principled opposition to the Chechen events." It fails to give an independent assessment of the Constitutional Court's July 31 decision denying the suit of plaintiff parliamentary deputies and upholding President Yeltsin's decrees ordering the sending of troops to Chechnya to liquidate "illegal armed bands." The court did, as the report notes, ban the revoking of journalists' accreditation in the war zone without a court order as unconstitutional. But the flaunting of that ruling through the "detentions, beatings and sniper attacks" mentioned in the report, as well as the authorities' disregard of the court's and law's bans on residence permit requirements as a violation of the freedom of movement, only exemplify the limited enforcement of the court's decisions.

The requirement of residence permits contributes also to the violation of the human rights of forced migrants to freedom of movement. Forced migrants are Russian citizens returning from other parts of the former Soviet Union, and all permanent residents of Russia who are forced to resettle within Russia, to escape violence or persecution. Lack of a *propiska* is also one of the reasons given by the Federal Migration Service for the denial of asylum to refugees. Thousands of refugees have been granted asylum, but the report does not say that fewer than a hundred of these have come from countries outside the former Soviet Union. Contrary to the report's assertion that "most refugees do not want to remain in Russia," the majority of refugee asylum seekers polled in UNHCR accommodation centers in Moscow by the NGO *Equilibre* in early 1996 said that they would like to seek asylum in Russia. The denial of asylum, even often of asylum status hearings, has resulted in violations of Russia's obligations — under both international and (formally

180

generous) Russian law — to grant asylum seekers non-discriminatory due process in establishing refugee status and protection against *refoulement* to countries where they face persecution.

The Presidential Human Rights Commission has covered a gap in the report with data concerning limited access to government information, which the commission finds to be "among the critical problems in Russia today." By the end of 1995, 42 ministers and agency directors had been granted the right to restrict citizens' access to information. One disturbing example of secrecy is the Ministry of Atomic Industry's classification of information about the amount of nuclear wastes stored underground, as well as annual inspection reports on the country's nuclear and radiation safety. The Presidential Human Rights Commission also gives ample evidence of the unlawful denial of information to the media.

Access to many government archives is closed or disappearing — a trend the commission sees as "a step toward a new alienation of society from its history." Blows to independent human rights monitoring noted in the State Department report have been the interference by government forces with domestic and foreign human rights reporting from Chechnya, the Duma's dismissal of Sergei Kovalev as Ombudsman in March, and his resignation from the depleted and undermined Human Rights Commission of President Yeltsin in January 1996. Yelena Bonner, the widow of Andrei Sakharov and herself a prominent human rights activist, had resigned from the commission in protest against the Chechnya War in February 1995. The network of Russian human rights NGOs continued to expand in 1995 but remained heavily dependent on foreign funding.

The report mentions local violations of religious freedom, which were also alluded to in the 1994 report, such as the refusal to return non-Orthodox religious property. It also notes the proposed legal restrictions on proselytizing by foreign groups, which would have been endorsed by a draft law in parliament but were opposed by President Yeltsin. The report also fails to follow up on its predecessor's mention of the growing influence of the Russian Orthodox Church's influence in society and government and the reluctance of Patriarch Aleksy to condemn the anti-Semitic writings of Metropolitan Ioann of St. Petersburg.

Metropolitan Ioann's death on November 2, 1995 has not ended the threat of anti-Semitism or significantly advanced the interests of a liberal minority in the church which favors greater openness, parish outreach and dialogue with other religions and non-Russians, including Jews. The government has done little or nothing to implement constitutional and legal protections against hate speech and activities amidst the steppe-fire spread of extreme nationalist-racist organizations across Russia. Alexander Barshakov's Russian National Unity, for example, has its own publications, security forces and commercial enterprises, with branches in 350 cities.

Such extremism feeds on the growing poverty and economic insecurity that afflict Russia today. The report mentions that 13% of the labor force is unemployed and that 30% of the population lives below the poverty line. However, it stops short of detailing the calamitous deterioration in the sphere of economic and social rights to adequate living standards, for all but a flagrantly rich stratum of beneficiaries of reform. Specialists at the Ministry of Social Security estimate that by the end of 1995, real income had dropped to 46% of its 1991 level. The Presidential Commission on Human Rights concludes from citizen complaints and appeals that "violations of social and economic rights and citizens' legitimate interests constitute the most widespread form of human rights abuse and are the main source of social tension." Organized crime is a major contributor to that tension, yet the report gives even less space to this issue than it did a year ago.

Complicity with organized crime reaches into the government, parliament and police, to the point that criminal gangs have had little to fear from the police who are routinely paid off. Duma deputies have had shadowy and at times fatal connections to organized crime. During 1994-1995, mysterious assassins killed four Duma deputies, contract-style. One of the deputies, Sergei Skorochkin, was murdered by gangsters in early 1995 apparently in revenge for his killing of an organized crime leader in 1994.

Russia

Government inaction and complicity further undermines its shaky legitimacy. Attempts to challenge official complicity in the legislature were set back by the death in an unexplained traffic accident of Deputy Vitaly Savitsky, a leader of the Christian Democratic Union, just eight days before the 1995 elections, when he was expected to be re-elected. A prominent and respected member of the Duma, Savitsky served as vice-chair of the Committee on Social and Religious organizations. Among his controversial actions had been his support for repeal of norms that guaranteed legal immunity for Duma members.

Savitsky's death was reminiscent of the mysterious deaths in traffic accidents that occurred during the Stalin era. He suffered massive injuries after his driver suddenly and inexplicably swerved into a collision with oncoming traffic. While the driver was rushed to a military hospital with relatively minor injuries, Savitsky lay unattended on the street. He was then kept in isolation and later reported to have died from "medical complications."

Savitsky's suspicious death also resembles the hit-and-run death in January of the son of Sergei Grigoriants, head of the Glasnost Foundation, as well as an attack on Grigoriants himself in March. It adds to a growing record of suspicious behavior by police, prosecutorial and security agencies, including their inability to solve any of the scores of murders of bankers and business people. As the report indicates, the wave of contract killings, still unsolved, has struck the press as well, inhibiting crime reporting. Former KGB General Oleg Kalugin has commented that "[t]he government is filled with mafia people. Unfortunately this is the reality of our country." Grigory Yavlinsky, leader of the liberal Yabloko party, has said bitterly that the killing of Dmitry Kholodov, a journalist investigating army corruption, "shows what the future holds for people who speak the truth here." Responses to organized crime themselves pose a threat to human rights — whether in the form of procedural shortcomings in the arrest and processing of suspects or the proliferation of private armed groups in what the Presidential Commission has dubbed a "militarization of society."

Reports such as the Lawyers Committee's *Critique* draw heavily on information from a growing network of Russian human rights NGOs such as the Glasnost Foundation, Memorial, the Moscow Center for Prison Reform and the Soldiers' Mothers' Committees. Collaboration with these NGOs will remain possible to the extent that the Russian government in power continues to allow them and their affiliates across Russia to operate. They remain vulnerable, as the State Department report reveals, to harassment and worse from national and local security agencies. They will also remain vulnerable to the extent that they continue to rely heavily on funding by foreign foundations.

In summary, the 1995 State Department report covers the human rights situation in Russia even more thoroughly than its immediate predecessor. But as in 1994, this year's report falls short when it comes to analysis of responsibility and context. The report's format continues to be strong on the classification of violations by specific types of rights. But this format contributes to an overall sense of fragmentation and the loss of analytical thrust. Nevertheless, in casting such a wide net for its data, the State Department report is more than ever an indispensable source of information on human rights as Russia continues its uneasy transition toward democratic governance.

SAUDI ARABIA

The 1995 report on Saudi Arabia is marred by a very serious overall shortcoming, one that was raised in last year's edition of the *Critique*. This is the State Department's tendency to cheer for the unrepentantly fundamentalist Saudi government while subtly representing its opponents as extremists. The specious distinction which the report attempts to draw between the benign fundamentalism of an important U.S. ally — the Saudi government — and the malevolent fundamentalism of the religious opposition spoils an otherwise good discussion of human rights in the Kingdom. This is unfortunate because, in terms of detail, breadth and factual accuracy, this year's report otherwise continues a welcome trend of steady improvement in reporting on human rights in Saudi Arabia. Facts are presented clearly and most of the salient issues discussed frankly.

However, the report's insidious attempt to discredit the opposition to the Saudi regime by subtle shadings of meaning and tone has no place in a serious human rights report. This problem has ramifications for the report's discussions of Islam and Islamic law, two areas which are critical for evaluating the human rights situation in the Kingdom. It also leads the report's drafters to overstate in an irresponsible manner the existence of popular support for the current Saudi government. Finally, and most distressingly for a document that styles itself an objective report on human rights, the partisanship displayed on behalf of the Saudi government subtly imparts the suggestion that governments which support U.S. foreign policy initiatives are held to a lower standard than those that do not.

As in 1994, the introduction to this year's report omits the main item of interest in the Kingdom, namely the appearance of an organized opposition movement. This opposition, until recently represented principally but not exclusively by the Committee for the Defense of Legitimate Rights (CDLR) has a pronounced conservative religious character and apparently comprises a large number of clerics and intellectuals. Clearly it does not include all persons opposed to the government or all persons who urge reform, but it does constitute the one group which continues to speak out consistently against the Saudi government and whose supporters have become special targets of that government's oppressive practices.

Given the unprecedented fact of an opposition group operating within (and now also outside) Saudi Arabia, despite enormous obstacles in the form of Saudi laws prohibiting all forms of free speech and association (which the report describes in detail), it is simply incredible that the report's introduction should fail to mention the CDLR, or at least the phenomenon for which it stands. The introduction should have stated in no uncertain terms that a more or less organized opposition movement has formed, and that the Saudi government has responded to it with a disappointing and brutal pattern of human rights violations. That is a simple and indisputable fact of primary relevance, and precisely the sort of "key human rights development" that drafters of the *Country Reports* are instructed to include in their introductions.

If the State Department does not believe that the Saudi government considers the CDLR a serious threat, then its drafters should consider Saudi Arabia's widely reported attempts to have the CDLR's head, Dr. Abdullah al-Mas'ari, expelled from Britain for expressing and publicizing criticism of the Saudi government. Dr. al-Mas'ari was forced to secretly flee Saudi Arabia in 1994 after being detained and tortured for his public criticism of the Saudi government. In March the British Home Office rejected Dr. al-Mas'ari's asylum application, after British government spokesmen had alluded publicly to the potentially negative effect of Dr. al-Mas'ari's presence in Britain on British exports to Saudi Arabia. In January 1996, the Home Office ordered Dr. al-Mas'ari deported, which order was, however, rejected by Chief Immigration Appeals Adjudicator, Judge David Pearl, in March. Judge Pearl criticized the Home Office for attempting to circumvent the U.N. Convention on Refugees for "diplomatic and trade reasons." In April, after reconsidering its precarious legal position, the Home Office granted Dr. al-Mas'ari exceptional leave to stay in Britain for four years in a move that has been characterized as a grant of asylum in all but name. Furious over Dr. al-Mas'ari's presence in Britain, the Saudi government has publicly threatened to boycott British firms, most recently through its ambassador in London, Ghazi al-Ghosaibi, and its Interior Minister, Prince Nayef.

Saudi Arabia

According to one British engineering firm, Saudi Arabia began a de facto boycott of British contractors in November 1995 which was still in effect as of April 1996. Britain's Department of Trade and Industry has denied that British business has been adversely effected.

It is possible that the State Department shares the Saudi government's concern about the CDLR. Although the CDLR is not mentioned in the introduction, many unflattering references to it appear in the body of the report, which gives the following characterizations of the CDLR and other persons:

> "[The CDLR and Mohamed al-Mas'ari] were *associates* of Abdullah Bin Abd Al-Rahman Al-Hidaif, who was executed for *assaulting a security official with acid* . . ."

> "The *vociferously antigovernment* CDLR . . ."

> "[Al-Mas'ari's] publicized views have expressed *opposition to peace with Israel and to Saudi support for the peace process.*"

> "The CDLR *does not advocate internationally recognized human rights but takes a rigidly Islamic fundamentalist approach.* Statements by CDLR supporters have advocated policies and actions that are *antiwomen and anti-Shi'a.* [The group has expressed] *'understanding' of the National Guard headquarters bombing.*"

> "[One CDLR founder has] made strong *anti-Shi'a* statements."
> (all emphases added)

To label CDLR members "associates" of Mr. Hidaif is nothing less than an attempt to suggest guilt by association. To label CDLR "vociferous" is gratuitous and redundant. The CDLR's views on peace with Israel are so egregiously irrelevant to the human rights situation in the Kingdom that it is astonishing that this claim should appear in the report for the second year running. This claim serves solely to underline the (admittedly likely) fact that the CDLR may not agree with U.S. foreign policy objectives in the Middle East, which, it hardly needs saying, has no bearing whatsoever on the state of human rights in the Kingdom. The report might just as well have mentioned that *The Economist*, too, routinely criticizes the current incarnation of the Israeli-Arab peace process. Or, to be fair, it might speculate about how deep support for the Arab-Israeli peace process runs among the members of the Council of Senior Ulema.

In addition, the report could have presented a more balanced description of the trial and execution in mid-August of Mr. al-Hidaif. The report takes two swipes at the late Mr. al-Hidaif. In the first, it notes that he, "a supporter of [CDLR,] was sentenced to death by a Saudi court and executed for the 1994 attempted murder by acid of an Interior Ministry official." The second is quoted above. As noted already, both passages aim to discredit the CDLR by mentioning it and the word "acid" in the same sentence. (It bears emphasizing in this context that the CDLR's manifesto expressly eschews violence, though Dr. al-Mas'ari has made public statements which seem to contradict the principle of non-violence.) Neither passage states that the charges against Mr. al-Hidaif included his support for the CDLR, thus ignoring direct evidence of the Saudi government's prohibition of freedom of association and speech in his case. That fact is stated in more neutral territory where the charges against his co-defendants are mentioned, but where neither the word "acid" nor the name of Mr. al-Hidaif appear.

Now, it is important to condemn violence whatever its source, and if Mr. al-Hidaif attacked a Saudi security official with acid, that act ought rightly to be punished in accord with applicable criminal law, whatever the circumstances. But the circumstances, even if they do not excuse, are not therefore irrelevant, and in this particular case they should have been mentioned in the report. Human Rights Watch/Middle East reported that the victim of the attack had interrogated and tortured Mr. al-Hidaif during a previous detention and, further, that the Saudi government refused to return Mr. al-Hidaif's body to his family, suggesting that he had been tortured prior to his execution. The fact that Mr. al-Hidaif's alleged accomplices included several of his family members suggests a revenge motive and lends credence to the report by Human Rights Watch.

188

Saudi Arabia

Wholly irrelevant is the claim that the CDLR rejects international human rights norms. Paragraph 8.G of the State Department's instructions to those drafting the *Country Reports* requires them to discuss human rights violations by "guerrilla forces, terrorists or occupying forces of a foreign power" and by "rebel/insurgent forces." The CDLR is none of these. Neither is Saudi Arabia "affected by serious international or internal conflict," as spelled out in paragraph 12 of the State Department instructions. Thus, the CDLR, being neither a government nor an armed insurrection in progress, is not in a position to violate anyone's human rights. It is true that the distaste for international human rights norms which the CDLR seems to share with the Saudi government represents an interesting facet of political discourse in the Kingdom (although this is ignored in the report, as discussed below). Of primary relevance, however, is that the CDLR's supporters have been victims of human rights violations committed by the Saudi government (as noted in this year's and the previous two reports), which denies the validity of such norms (as noted by this year's report). Mention of the "anti-women" and "anti-Shi'a" tendencies of the CDLR is vulnerable to the same criticism of irrelevance.

Finally, the allegation that the CDLR exhibits a rigid Islamic fundamentalism presents a particularly pernicious drafting tactic in the report. Assuming that such a characterization is accurate, it would be relevant only if the report's drafters wished to make the point that the Saudi government holds itself out as a rigidly fundamentalist Islamic regime in the belief that this constitutes an effective claim to political legitimacy (the report could even go further and note that the Saudi government seems to understand its asserted fundamentalism as license to commit certain kinds of human rights abuses in the name of Islam). Then, it would make perfect sense to say that the CDLR challenges the asserted religious legitimacy of the Saudi regime, claiming for itself a more authentic or different form of Islamic fundamentalism (even assuming that "fundamentalism" is a meaningful term in this context). However, the report does not proceed in that manner, but rather labels the CDLR as "fundamentalist" while applying much less loaded descriptions (such as "rigorously conservative") to the Saudi government.

Critique 1995

As is apparent from the Saudi government's many human rights abuses in the name of Islam (including torture, maiming, discrimination against women, abuses by the religious police *(Mutawwi`in)*, discrimination against the *Shi`a*, executions for practicing "witchcraft" and for apostasy, use of government-sponsored religious organs to have opponents declared heretics, etc., most of which are described in this and past reports), the only meaningful difference between the respective "fundamentalisms" of the CDLR and the Saudi government is the latter's support of U.S. foreign policy initiatives in the Middle East. The strategy adopted in this year's report to discredit the CDLR violates the spirit of evenhandedness and fairness called for in the State Department's drafting instructions.

The report's kinder and gentler approach to dealing with the Saudi regime's "fundamentalism" infects its attempts to explain the application of Islamic law and precepts in Saudi Arabia. In its introduction, for example, the report notes that the Saudi government's "adherence to the precepts of a rigorously conservative form of Islam . . . enjoys near-consensus support among Saudi citizens." In addition, it states (echoing the unfortunate formulation of last year's report) that: "Most Saudis respect the legal system, which they believe is divinely inspired." It is quite obvious that neither of these statements is verifiable, especially in a country which has, as the report very competently notes, neither elections nor a free press, and where anti-government expression is strictly prohibited by law and routinely punished by arbitrary detention and torture. As the 1994 edition of the *Critique* pointed out, given the immunity in practice of the royal family before Saudi courts (noted again in this year's report), it is inconceivable that Saudis consider their legal system to be "divinely inspired," though it is very likely that they consider the *shari`a* to be so and therefore believe it should be applied. (It hardly needs stating that Islamic law and actual Saudi legal practice cannot be assumed to be identical. The asserted adherence of the Saudi legal system to Islamic precepts is precisely what the conservative religious opposition challenges; that challenge *is* a fact, but the report ignores it.) Such irresponsible generalizations constitute nothing less than cheerleading on behalf of the Saudi government and should be excised from the report.

Saudi Arabia

This year's report contains further problems along these lines. One is the attempt to explain away the inherent discrimination of the Islamic law of inheritance, in which female heirs receive only half the share of male heirs. The statement that such discrimination reflects the fact that "men have financial obligations to their mothers and sisters" is entirely inappropriate and misleading. The report apparently means to suggest that such inherent discrimination constitutes a benevolent paternalism, ensuring that women in fact receive their full inheritance via their male relatives, a patently absurd implication. In fact, Islamic law consistently views women as only half as valuable as men, since it is also the case — as the report notes — that "the testimony of one man equals that of two women." Such inherent gender-based discrimination in the Saudi interpretation of Islamic law should be stated as a brute fact without attempts to rationalize it away. The attempted rationalization of legally sanctioned polygamy is similarly fraught with difficulties. The literal sense of the Qu'ranic passage which serves as the basis for this rule is simply that polygamy is allowed, not necessarily that four is an upper limit. The point is that this rule is equivocal, or rather that it, too, is a brute fact requiring no exegesis from the report's drafters. Finally, the characterization of the Sunna as "authenticated actions and deeds of the Prophet Muhammad" correctly states a theological proposition, not a relevant fact. It would be more accurate to say that Muslims consider the Sunna to be authentic and leave it at that.

Also, the discussion of the application of "*ta'zeer*" in the case of the execution of Mr. al-Hidaif could have been clearer. *Ta'zeer* is a punishment left to the discretion of the judge and is ordinarily less severe than the corresponding capital or corporal punishment (*hadd*). *Ta'zeer* can be as mild as a verbal reprimand; in Mr. al-Hidaif's case it was, very unusually, death. It is also the prerogative of the sovereign to apply *ta'zeer* (hence the intervention of the Ministry of the Interior, which demanded that Mr. al-Hidaif receive a stiffer sentence than the prison term originally imposed). Thus, *ta'zeer* can serve as an instrument of political coercion. The claim that *ta'zeer* is also applied as a deterrent is correct, as is the accompanying analysis, namely that it was designed in Mr. al-Hidaif's case to "deter others who might . . . sympathize with acts of political resistance that bring disunity to the community." The report could have gone one step further in its analysis and noted this as an instance in which the Saudi government cynically invoked an idiosyncratic interpretation of Islamic law as a pretext for violating binding international human rights norms to serve its domestic political interests. Moreover, inasmuch as it notes problems relating to procedural safeguards in cases of arrest, defendants' lack of legal representation in court, rules of evidence which encourage forced confessions, interference by governors, royal family members and their associates with legal proceedings, and the perception that the royal family is above the law, one wonders how the report can again sanguinely state that "The independence of the judiciary is . . . usually respected in practice."

It is not the task of the report to explain Islamic law to its audience. The fact that it does so is pernicious; it represents a subtle exercise in slanting information in such a way as to suggest that reasonable principles underlie the Saudi government's brutal practices. It is both ironic and unfortunate that such rationalizations (even assuming for the sake of argument that they are well-intentioned) appear in a report on a country which seems to view maiming, beheading, and gender-based discrimination as the very essence of Islamic law. Such a drafting tactic insults Islam and, more important, directly undermines the report's own credibility as a serious human rights document.

The above points are important; the shortcomings they outline color the entire report. It is, however, also important to give credit where credit is due, and, the foregoing criticisms aside, this year's report is generally very good when describing concrete cases and general tendencies, excluding the difficulties it has in dealing with the related problems of Islam and the religious opposition. However, the following issues represent areas in which still further improvement is possible and, indeed, desirable.

One case which the report might have mentioned, whether under the rubric of foreign labor, the arbitrary and repressive character of the Saudi legal system, or cruel and inhuman punishment, is that of Egyptian national Muhammad Kamil Khalifa, which was raised in last year's edition of the *Critique*. In late 1994, Mr. Khalifa accused the headmaster

192

Saudi Arabia

of his son's school of sexually assaulting the boy, a charge later reportedly confirmed by medical examination. For making this medically supported allegation, Mr. Khalifa was imprisoned and sentenced to be flogged in front of the school's students. This sentence was later commuted to 80 lashes, which Mr. Khalifa received, before the student body, in May 1995. No doubt the students learned their lesson. While the State Department's instructions discourage the report's drafters from presenting a mere laundry list of incidents, the horrific experience of Mr. Khalifa underlines both the complete vulnerability of foreign workers under Saudi law, as well as the flawed and brutal functioning of the Saudi justice system. Since this case cuts across many of the report's different topics, it would have been appropriate to include it.

Continuing the unfortunate practice of ignoring U.N. human rights investigations concerning Saudi Arabia, this year's report also failed to mention the United Nations' interest in Mr. Khalifa's case. A Special Rapporteur to the U.N. Commission on Human Rights transmitted an official expression of concern to the Saudi government concerning this case, noting in particular that corporal punishment of the type inflicted on Mr. Khalifa was inconsistent with binding international human rights norms prohibiting torture and other cruel, inhuman or degrading treatment or punishment.

The report also ignores important findings of the U.N. Special Rapporteur Nigel S. Rodley regarding the mistreatment and abuse of Iraqi refugees. For the last two years the drafters of the report have offered a spirited defense of Saudi treatment of Iraqi refugees displaced by the Gulf War. In 1994 this was done in response to a devastating Amnesty International report which provided details of numerous disturbing abuses committed against Iraqi refugees in the Rafha and Artawiya camps between 1991 and 1993. The 1994 report went so far as to directly refute Amnesty's findings. This year's report ignores the Special Rapporteur's conclusions regarding the mistreatment of such refugees during the same period. The Special Rapporteur outlined the specifics of a number of different cases of mistreatment, torture, collective punishment, death and other abuses violative of international norms of human rights and humanitarian law. The Special Rapporteur concluded, contrary to the assertions made in the last two State Department reports, "that the allegations of torture and cruel and inhuman treatment and punishment of Iraqi refugees [appeared] well founded."

Another report concerning the same camps by UNHCR is cited by the report without editorial comment in order to refute a 1993 report by Human Rights Watch that such refugees had been forcibly repatriated to Iraq. The State Department instructions to drafters of the *Country Reports* requires them to "pay special attention to reports by the various UN human rights mechanisms." The self-serving and selective use of such sources made by this year's report is deplorable and violates the spirit of this instruction.

The fact that the Saudi government refused to cooperate with the Special Rapporteur regarding his inquiry into abuses against Iraqi refugees also deserved mention since it continues a pattern of disregard in practice of international human rights mechanisms. This fact would make a fitting addition to the report's otherwise adequate discussion of the Saudi government's rejection of international human rights norms as a matter of allegedly Islamic principle.

Another issue which the report continues to ignore, despite repeated urging in previous editions of the *Critique*, is the Saudi government's relentless efforts to stifle domestic and external criticism by acquiring or thwarting foreign broadcast and other media. The latest casualty in this campaign is a joint Saudi-BBC television venture which the Saudis forced to shut down in early 1996 after it broadcast a documentary featuring Dr. al-Mas'ari. In addition, the Egyptian Organization for Human Rights (EOHR) reported that the Saudi government had successfully pressured the Egyptian government to ban any and all books critical of the Saudi government. Also, in an article in the London *Sunday Telegraph*, noted author Said K. Aburish revealed that in 1993 a Saudi government advisor had offered him $600,000 to cancel publication of a book critical of the Saudi government. Aburish also recounted an incident in which the Saudi government successfully pressured the BBC to cancel an appearance by Aburish on a news program to discuss the November car-bombing in Riyadh of a National Guard training facility. The Saudi government's censorship extends abroad in order to prevent negative information about

194

itself reaching its citizens at home. Such practices are therefore appropriate for inclusion in the report.

It is difficult to divorce the State Department's reluctance to criticize the Kingdom's censorship of media located outside Saudi Arabia from the fact that the U.S. government, through the Voice of America (VOA), now assists the Saudis in broadcasting pro-Saudi propaganda in the Middle East and North America. VOA and Middle East Broadcasting Corp. (MBC), owned by King Fahd's brother-in-law, jointly produce a program called "Dialogue with the West." MBC reportedly has editorial control over the program's content. The program runs in the United States over the Arab Network of America, a Saudi-owned radio network noted in last year's edition of the *Critique* for its censorship of reports critical of the Saudi government. Aside from the U.S. government's dubious decision to aid dissemination of propaganda by a country routinely identified by the U.S. government itself as one that "commits or tolerates serious [human rights] abuses," this partnership bodes extremely ill for the many persons in the Middle East who rely on VOA for objective news reports.

Absent from this year's report is the fact that different elements among the Saudi security forces, some of which were responsible for human rights violations (as noted in the report's introduction), seem to represent competing constituencies within the Saudi government. Paragraph 13 of the State Department's instructions to drafters encourages them to note where security forces are not under the complete control of the government. This seems to be the case with the *Mutawwi'in*, who often overstep their authority and yet are only very rarely, if ever, reprimanded for doing so. In past years, the National Guard, under the command of the Crown Prince, have presented something of a counterbalance to the *Mutawwi'in*, as suggested by occasional incidents of conflict between the two groups. In any event, the fact that the *Mutawwi'in* are not entirely under the Saudi government's control should be stated more clearly. On a related note, this year's report is to be commended for correcting last year's questionable assertion that incidents involving the *Mutawwi'in* were on the decline, and instead noting this year a long-term increase in such incidents of abuse.

Critique 1995

The report could improve its section on arbitrary detention by providing an estimate of prisoners of conscience in one place; this is admittedly difficult in a country like Saudi Arabia where information is tightly controlled. However, the report's current approach is confusing. It appears to suggest that it could only confirm the detention of 38 persons for their anti-government activity (27 from an incident in 1994, nine in connection with the execution of Mr. al-Hidaif, and two clerics.) While the report is appropriately cautious in accepting the figures given by the CDLR, it might have mentioned the figure of 200 proposed by Amnesty International.

Parts of this year's report were very well done. For example, it offers a fine discussion of capital punishment in the Kingdom, noting the alarming increase in executions, the fact that most persons executed are non-Saudis, and the expansion of capital offenses. It would have been appropriate to note that a number of women were publicly beheaded in 1995 (12 as of mid-October). The beheading of women represents a new development in Saudi penal practice; according to last year's report women were formerly executed out of public view by firing squad.

Aside from the criticisms above, the discussion of women's rights in the Kingdom is detailed and accurate. Issues appropriately raised included: domestic violence; the use of religion as a pretext for legalized discrimination; discriminatory dress codes; harassment by the *Mutawwi'in*; restrictions on travel and freedom of movement; polygamy; and discrimination in the work place. Similarly complete, again subject to criticisms raised above, is the discussion of discrimination against the *Shi'a*. However, the report's wording ("Sunni clerics . . . and one CDLR founder have made strong anti-Shi'a statements") could suggest that only the religious opposition encourages such discrimination on the basis of religion. It would be helpful to note that state-sponsored clerics have in the past engaged in virulent public tirades against the *Shi'a*. That would clarify that the government encourages religiously motivated public expressions of anti-*Shi'a* sentiment. Also, the report's discussion of worker rights is thorough, noting among other things that Saudi Arabia has been suspended from the U.S. Overseas Private Investment Corporation for its failure to adhere to internationally recognized worker rights standards. A good summary of the abuses suffered by female foreign domestic servants, a problem of epidemic proportions in Saudi Arabia, appears in the section dealing with women's rights.

SERBIA AND MONTENEGRO

On November 22, 1995, media all over the world broadcast the image of U.S. Secretary of State Warren Christopher sitting at a long conference table with the presidents of Serbia, Bosnia-Herzegovina and Croatia as they initialed the Dayton Agreement. Notably, Christopher sat as far away from Slobodan Milosevic as was possible. Although the distance-measuring skills associated with Kremlinology get little use in the Balkans, they are unusually helpful in analyzing this State Department human rights report. The uncomfortable tableau at Dayton is reflected in the State Department's attempts to come up with language for its 1995 human rights report that reconciles policy and practice and can allow for the Secretary of State's year-end negotiations with Milosevic, who is described as "serving his second five-year term as President of Serbia," but is not president of "Serbia-Montenegro," an entity which is nonetheless "dominated by" him but not recognized by the United States and the international community as "the successor state to the former Yugoslavia."

The result of this linguistic exercise is often distractingly awkward — and telling. The carefully crafted language is so colored by political considerations that it dilutes — and, in some instances, negates — the effect of the State Department's revised instructions for drafting the country reports. In general, while describing extensive, brutal and systematic human rights abuses, the 1995 report subtly — and at times not so subtly — distances Milosevic, the government of Serbia, and the ruling Socialist Party of Serbia (SPS) from named responsibility for abuses conducted in Serbia-Montenegro and on the territory of former Yugoslavia. More often than not, the report cites "police" action to violate human rights, but it does not examine the political and legal infrastructure which supports police violence.

Nowhere is this distancing better illustrated than in comparing the 1994 and 1995 excerpts from the report's sections on the *Use of Excessive Force* and *Violations of Humanitarian Law in Internal Conflicts*, which deal with an issue crucial to the success of Dayton: the relationship between Belgrade and the Bosnian Serb headquarters at Pale. In 1994, the State Department noted that: "The Government's decision to close the border with Bosnia in August, exempting only food, clothing, and medicine, was an implicit acknowledgment of the support it has provided to the Bosnian Serbs and their policy of ethnic cleansing since the beginning of the Bosnian war." By 1995, however, the report observed simply that: "The Government officially closed the border with Bosnia in August 1994, exempting only food, clothing and medicine."

Not only did the "implicit acknowledgment" of support to Pale disappear in 1995, but so did references to actions by the government of Serbia that could be construed as involvement in any form of "ethnic cleansing." (The phrase "ethnic cleansing" has itself disappeared from the 1995 report.) For example, in 1994, the State Department charged that: "In Serbia itself [including Vojvodina and Kosovo] authorities frequently subjected members of ethnic minorities to intimidation, with the goal of provoking their emigration." By 1995, however, the actors cited in the report have altered: "Ethnic tensions were high . . . in Serbia, and ultranationalist Serbian elements encouraged hostile acts by private citizens against members of minority ethnic groups." These differences in emphasis and tone are particularly noteworthy in light of the State Department's guidelines to report drafters to "identify abusers, and to indicate whether they have been punished, or to indicate whether they have committed abuses with impunity."

The report consistently identifies one egregious abuser: the Serbian police, "a heavily armed force of perhaps 100,000." As it has done consistently in previous years, the report describes well the pervasive and systematic brutality of the police force, particularly in the Kosovo and Sandzak regions, and credits the work of several local NGOs in documenting individual cases. The report does not, however, make clear the relationship between the police and the ruling SPS party. It notes that Milosevic "controls the country through his [SPS]," and that he "wields strong control" over the police force, which is "a key element of [Milosevic's] hold on power." By neglecting to describe the relationship between police and the SPS, the report creates the impression that no such relationship exists. The report emphasizes the "arbitrary" behavior of the state security apparatus and the control of Milosevic over that apparatus to maintain his hold on power. The implication is that Serbia-

Serbia and Montenegro

Montenegro is a police state which is controlled by the one man who also controls the ruling party. (No other government officials, except for Montenegrin President Miomir Bulatovic, are mentioned by name, and even he is treated only in passing. The special issues raised by the "Montenegrin question" are discussed separately below.) A more realistic assessment is that the Federal Republic of Yugoslavia (FRY) is controlled by a single political party, which is controlled by one man, and that the state security apparatus is an instrument of that ruling party. The distinction is not just semantic. To suggest that rump Yugoslavia is a "party" state, as opposed to a police state, imparts a connection to history. It acknowledges that the police apparatus, not the army, serves the same purpose for the SPS that the Yugoslav National Army served for the League of Communists of Yugoslavia. It acknowledges a longstanding infrastructure of repression. It acknowledges that Milosevic is a product of the system, not a brilliantly manipulative historical aberration.

To acknowledge an infrastructure of repression or to draw the connection between effective one-party rule and the state security apparatus would significantly undermine the image and optimism presented at Dayton. An end to extraterritorial warfare among the Dayton participants is the immediate priority. However, as the report on Serbia-Montenegro shows and as other chapters in this volume describe, internal war against civilians continued to be waged throughout 1995. In the FRY, there is little evidence to suggest that the Dayton Agreement, which so colors this human rights report, affected the means by which institutionalized repression continues.

The report's emphasis on ethnicity as the grounds for repressive action by the state needs to be examined more closely. There is absolutely no question that Serbian police, party, and government officials take brutal and repressive measures as a matter of routine against persons on the basis of ethnicity alone. As widely reported by both intergovernmental and non-governmental organizations, in Kosovo these include police brutality against ethnic Albanians, killings, arbitrary searches, seizures and arrests, torture and ill-treatment of detainees and discrimination, arbitrary dismissals of ethnic Albanian civil servants, mass dismissals of ethnic Albanians and intimidation and imprisonment of ethnic Albanian journalists.

Given space limitations, the State Department report provides many individual examples of violence and discrimination against ethnic Albanians. Reports of independent human rights monitoring and advocacy organizations throughout the FRY contain many others. However, especially in the context of the mass trials of Albanians, which are described briefly in the State Department report, two additional examples deserve mention here. In spring, charges were brought in Prizren against 44 persons — including 43 ethnic Albanian, former Ministry of Internal Affairs security officers — accused of conspiring to form a parallel ministry of internal affairs for the "self-proclaimed Kosovo Republic," whose purpose was the "surveillance and liquidation of prominent Serbs." The 44th man so charged, whom the State Department report does not mention, was Sezair Shaipi, leader of the Turkish national minority party in Kosovo, who had no ties to his fellow defendants. Shaipi was arrested and subjected to heavy, as opposed to customary, torture; before Shaipi's arrest, the only leader of a political party within the FRY who had been tortured so severely was Vuk Draskovic, leader of the Serbian Renewal Movement (SPO). Defense attorneys speculate that Shaipi's arrest and torture was an attempt to decapitate the Turkish political party.

In another instance noteworthy for its display of extraterritorial cooperation, ethnic Albanian Djeljalj Canziba was kidnapped from his workplace in Skopje by Macedonian and Serbian police. After interrogation in Skopje by the Macedonian police, Canziba was transported by representatives of both police across the territorial border to Serbia, where he was further interrogated and tortured by Serbian police. The Canziba case sets a troubling and potentially ominous precedent which the report should not ignore.

These two cases, as well as the findings of the U.N. Special Rapporteur, point out the political nature of violence against Albanians in a manner that differs from the presentation of such violence in the State Department report. By simply listing brutalities committed against ethnic Albanians, the report makes no distinction between traditionally criminal violence conducted in a politicized atmosphere and coherent political violence conducted by state and party officials. The distinction is by no means obvious on the territories of the former Yugoslavia; no less a judicial body than the international war crimes tribunal is grappling with its complexities. However, even if it cannot resolve the matter for all individual cases, the report should at least acknowledge the existence of the distinction and attempt to address its significance. To that end, the State Department should pay closer attention to the methodology and form of reports by the U.N. Special Rapporteur.

The report's presentation of ethnic violence and discrimination also fails to make seminal distinctions of degree and duration. For example, the report notes that: "Police repression continued at a high level against the ethnic Albanians of Kosovo and the Muslims of Sandzak and reflected a general campaign to keep the one-third of the population who are not ethnic Serbs intimidated and unable to exercise basic human and civil rights."

Various human rights advocates, both inside and outside the former Yugoslavia, have taken issue with the use of ethnic categorizations to define an individual's legal status. (They include some of those described in the report as the "[e]thnic Serb lawyers who were part of the defense team for the trials in Prizren." Setting aside that issue as debatable, and setting aside the fact that the report does not appear to acknowledge the special problems faced by persons of mixed ethnicity, the State Department's description of ethnic conflict in the FRY still misses several important subtleties. Albanians and Muslims make up the majority of the total population of national minorities in the FRY. The level of repression experienced by these two groups is, in general terms, much greater and more pervasive than that experienced by other national minorities, such as Hungarians, Croats, Slovaks, Romanians and others. The report's summary sentence quoted above creates the impression that national minorities within the FRY experience repression equally. In fact, throughout the FRY, there are significant differences in the level of repression experienced by Albanians and Muslims: Albanians have been the victims of organized repression for decades, while the repression of non-Albanian Muslims is of relatively recent vintage, dating back approximately to the start of hostilities in Bosnia. Albanian Muslims in the FRY today generally experience more repression than non-Albanian Muslims in the FRY except, of course, in those areas on the Bosnian border. Moreover, the situations of Albanians and Muslim Slavs differ in Serbia and in Montenegro. And, when discussing the situation in Sandzak, an even finer distinction can be made, since that region falls into both Serbia and northern Montenegro. The State Department's instructions for drafters of the *Country Reports* stress the need for specificity and "what happens in actual practice." In view of the sensitivity and vast importance of the issues involved, the report's failure to address subtle and not-so-subtle differences in ethnic violence and discrimination is disappointing.

It is not surprising, then, that the State Department report cannot decide what to do about Montenegro. It notes that "Milosevic greatly circumscribes the Montenegrin government's sphere for independent action and does not tolerate significant divergence from the ruling Socialist Party of Serbia line." However, the first we hear of the president of Montenegro, he is "at year's end," i.e., post-Dayton, freeing his republic's political prisoners. And last summer, while police in Serbia were rounding up refugees and sending them to serve against their will in Serbian forces in the Krajina and Bosnia (across the closed border described above), the "[g]overnment of Montenegro refused to allow refugees within its borders to be forcibly mobilized." References to actions by the government of Montenegro are generally positive, while negative actions are attributed to its police force and to unnamed actors threatening Croats in and around Kotor. It is clear that, while the State Department appears to welcome independent initiative on the part of Montenegrin government and party officials, it has not determined the extent of the sphere circumscribed by Milosevic. Judging by the passing attention devoted to Montenegro, we can conclude that the State Department does not deem events there to be of much significance. The report should devote more careful attention to why and how the Montenegrin government has been able to introduce economic reforms and maintain comparatively stable relationships among ethnic groups, including the amnesty granted Muslims originally tried for weapons possession in Bijelo Polje and the reasons for successful resettlement of Muslim refugees from Bosnia in Montenegro. It should assess the currency of the relationship between Serbia and Montenegro and the mechanisms of state power within Montenegro itself.

When the report does attempt to describe practical means by which the FRY state and party apparatus exerts internal control, it makes grave errors of fact in several places, exposing fundamental flaws in the State Department's understanding of the FRY's legal code and criminal justice system. Given the report's general emphasis on actions taken by police, these serious errors suggest that the drafters are interested in anecdotal information on arbitrary violence but not in the infrastructure that supports such violence.

The report is simply wrong in describing prison conditions in the FRY as "adequate." In addition to interrogation cells in local police stations, criminal detention facilities established by law fall into two categories: investigative detention jails (*istrazni zatvori*) and prisons for long-term incarceration *(zatvori za izdrzavanje kazne)*. Both are filthy, insufferably hot in summer and unheated in winter. But these are the least of detainees' problems. Each detention facility has an official physician who is required by law to attend to the health and physical conditions of detainees and to certify whether a prisoner who is to be transferred from jail to prison is fit for long-term incarceration. According to eyewitness reports of defense attorneys, both jail and prison physicians do not describe injuries received by detainees during interrogation, even when those injuries are patently obvious, and do not provide adequate medical treatment. The usual medical treatment for victims of police torture is cold water and aspirin. Jail and prison physicians are often themselves witnesses to torture and mistreatment of prisoners and nonetheless protect the actions of police by certifying that tortured prisoners are fit for incarceration. By law, prisoners have the right to complain of such treatment, but do not do so for fear of provoking even more violence and torture.

The physical conditions endured by detainees are also far from adequate. Vehicles used to transport prisoners have no windows or ventilation. In addition to the rank filth and temperature extremes noted above, jails and interrogation cells in police stations are often subterranean. They are routinely bloodstained. Physical conditions in longer-term facilities are only slightly better.

The report is also wrong about the length of time police hold suspects incommunicado without charging them or granting them access to attorneys. It is correct that, by law, police can hold suspects under those conditions for three days. However, by law the police can hold suspects for an *additional* day "to determine identity." Police do so even when an individual is arrested at home and is carrying an identity card. In the Kosovo mass trials, Serbian police held their ethnic Albanian former colleagues, even those who had worked with them in the same local police station, for that extra day "to determine identity." As a rule, suspects — particularly those charged with ethnic-based or political crimes — are held incommunicado and interrogated for four days, not three, as the report states.

The report does not mention that, in Kosovo and Sandzak, a large number of defense attorneys are themselves former police officials. It is difficult for others to be certified for defense practice in those areas and, as a result, those defense attorneys who were police officials bring to the job their experience and identification with the tactics of repression.

The report presents an incomplete explanation of the Ministry of the Interior's routine examination of mail, arbitrary searches of vehicles and homes, and monitoring of contacts from abroad. In the 1970s, Minister of the Interior Stane Dolanc pronounced all of Yugoslavia a single customs zone; in view of this, neither a warrant nor suspicion of criminal activity was required to justify a search. In 1971, after crushing the liberal movement in Serbia and the national movement in Croatia, Tito and Dolanc wished to expand police activity without making it appear that police power was unlimited. When the entire country was proclaimed a customs zone, police surveillance and harassment could masquerade as assistance to customs officials. The law is still in effect in most parts of the former Yugoslavia, which is procedurally why police who wish to search a vehicle nowhere near any international border still ask those they have stopped where their journey originated.

Serbia and Montenegro

When discussing the means used to repress civil liberties, the report correctly describes the economic pressure used by the authorities to threaten or shut down independent media. However, it does not even hint at the effect on independent media of the sanctions imposed against the FRY, nor does it mention that the drastic deterioration of living standards and skyrocketing costs of basic necessities have made the purchase of a more expensive independent publication a luxury few can afford. The FRY's ruling party was able to exploit the country's isolation under sanctions to strengthen its control not only over media and educational institutions, but over all aspects of cultural life. Future reports should consider the effect of repression not just on political and social institutions, but on cultural institutions, including popular (as opposed to "high") culture, and especially the cultural forms accessible to children and young people.

The rigid format prescribed by the drafting instructions fragments the presentation of issues relating to freedom of assembly and association, particularly if persons wish to associate in order to advocate political change or to investigate violations of human rights. As a result, the report's section on freedom of assembly focuses exclusively on members of ethnic minorities, creating the impression that those who are not members of ethnic minorities face no restrictions in their attempts at political association. (Even more curious is the fact that the only public assemblies described in this section are soccer matches.) Other sections of the report describe the consequences of attempts at association or assembly by persons who express opposition to the SPS. In describing the harassment in May of members of the Belgrade Circle, however, the report minimizes police reaction to the activity of NGOs. It notes that, after a larger campaign of threatening phone calls, "one young woman was called to the police station for questioning." In fact, hundreds of persons involved in NGOs were called in by the police for "informative conversations" — an "invitation" which can by law be issued only in the event of criminal conduct or to gather information on criminal activity. According to one of the invitees, the large-scale questioning appears to have been intended to disrupt NGO and opposition activity in Belgrade and to create suspicions among those questioned that others had begun to cooperate with the police.

In 1995, the FRY faced a massive challenge to its mechanisms of internal control when, as the State Department estimates, 170,000 persons expelled from the Krajina arrived in the FRY, adding to the hundreds of thousands of refugees already in Serbia-Montenegro. Although the report does intermittently describe the problems faced by refugees within the FRY, it does not coherently address their exploitation by the authorities, their forced resettlement, their mass abduction and forced conscription into military service, their arbitrary treatment by government authorities, their widespread difficulties in obtaining official refugee status, and the lack of clarity in their citizenship status. As the refugees continue to stretch already overburdened social services within the FRY, they challenge the government to maintain internal control and, as the forced conscriptions indicate, foreshadow human rights violations on a massive scale.

In conclusion, the State Department report on Serbia-Montenegro is so colored by considerations of policy in the wake of the Dayton Agreement that it is far more useful as a political document than as a description of the state of human rights in the FRY. Although it provides extensive detail on individual violations of human rights, it does so without sufficiently linking those incidents to a longstanding infrastructure of repression based on what is effectively one-party rule. As long as Slobodan Milosevic holds out the promise of cooperation in ending extraterritorial hostilities in Bosnia-Herzegovina, future reports are unlikely to change this politicized approach.

SOUTH AFRICA

Like its immediate predecessors, the State Department's 1995 report provides a fairly comprehensive overview of human rights practices in post-apartheid South Africa. With the election of the Government of National Unity led by the African National Congress (ANC) in April 1994, South Africa is experiencing a social, political and economic renaissance. No longer accorded pariah status in the international community, post-apartheid South Africa is well on its way to transforming itself into a significant global actor.

In the international media, post-apartheid South Africa is often portrayed as the catalyst that will speed up democratization and development efforts throughout the Continent. In particular, through the Southern African Development Committee (SADC), South African cooperation will be key to the success of regional economic development projects. Unfortunately, discussion of such economic development efforts is noticeably absent from the report, and this constitutes its major flaw — the failure to locate its discussion of human rights within the context of South Africa's economic, social and political development.

In post-apartheid South Africa, the practical realization of first-generation civil and political rights will largely turn on whether the new nation has the capacity to provide an economic environment in which the basic human needs of its citizens can be met. Further, future compliance with first-generation civil and political rights standards will largely depend on whether the Government of National Unity is able to eradicate the vestiges of apartheid, which are starkly apparent in the separate and widely divergent lives that blacks and whites in South Africa still lead. While the report does acknowledge some of the disparities between black and white living standards in the new South Africa, it does not challenge these economic inequalities as human rights issues that may compromise South Africa's future development.

Despite these flaws, the report correctly includes discussion of the interim Constitution and the plans to finalize the Constitution in 1996. But it does not examine South Africans' conception of human rights as revealed through the extraordinary ongoing public discourse concerning the principles and ideals that should be included in the Constitution.

Because South Africa is still at the initial stages of building a post-apartheid society, discussing the constitutional law making process within the context of the current political environment is crucial to an assessment of South Africa's commitment to human rights in the future.

A prime example of such political discourse involves separation of church and state concerns. It has been argued that South Africa should be a secular state — meaning that there would be no official religion but that the state would value the principles of religious tolerance, freedom and diversity. Although this appears to be a fundamental democratic and human rights principle, it was met with some resistance from some South African Christians. According to an article in *Constitutional Talk*, the official newsletter of the Constitutional Assembly, there was a campaign to give the Constitution an overtly Christian character, led by the African Christian Democratic Party (ACDP) and a group called the Christian Voice. Among other things, these groups were concerned that the interim Constitution does not acknowledge the authority of a Christian God in its preamble, permits abortion and upholds freedom of sexual orientation as a basic right.

There is also widespread discussion as to whether the Constitution's equality provisions will undermine traditional African customary law. As the new South Africa becomes a signatory to international human rights instruments, immediate questions arise as to whether adherence to customary law means that South Africa, the putative leader of the African world, will embrace cultural relativism in its conception of human rights or join the global trend toward a more universal understanding of human rights. Unfortunately, the report does not address these important questions.

Additionally, apart from limited children's and labor rights, the interim Constitution does not protect social and economic rights. Nevertheless, at the Constitutional Assembly, both the Congress of South African Trade Unions (COSATU) and the National Congress of Trade Unions (NACTU) advocated the inclusion of second-generation social and economic rights in the final Constitution. COSATU, however, tempered its position by stating that the inclusion of social and economic rights should not impose a legal obligation on the state, but should be provided for in light of available resources. With this in mind, it is evident that many South Africans are concerned with religion, traditional African ways of life, and social and economic rights. Accordingly, as some of this popular thinking could be enshrined as principles in the new Constitution, the report is remiss in not examining the constitutional lawmaking process within the context of the debates that surround it.

The report also fails to examine human rights within the broader context of economic development. Future reports should monitor the South African government's efforts to foster sustainable development and alleviate poverty, particularly in predominantly African communities. The Government of National Unity has introduced a number of policies designed to reduce government expenditures, relax exchange controls, remove barriers to competition and foster infrastructural development. South Africa's public corporations are of particular importance to the government's infrastructural development program. Transnet, the state-owned transport group, and ESKOM, the public utility agency that supplies electricity, are ranked as South Africa's 10th and 11th largest businesses respectively, in terms of assets. The expansion of government infrastructural development programs and comparable initiatives in the private sector will create new jobs which will have direct bearing on South Africa's chronic unemployment problem. At present, the unemployment rate in South Africa is a staggering 40% in the formal economy.

The most difficult challenges facing the new South Africa as it strives for economic development involve the enduring vestiges of apartheid, particularly the disparity between black and white living standards. According to a 1995 "Country Profile and a Fact Sheet" distributed by The Africa Fund, a research group established by the American Committee on Africa in 1966, South Africa's per capita GDP of $3,885 compares favorably with those of many nations within the industrialized world. The gross disparity of income, however, between black and white is significant, with the white GDP per capita being $14,920 compared to a paltry $1,710 for blacks. Further, whites continue to control approximately 54% of post-apartheid South Africa's national income, even though they comprise only about 13% of the population. Africans, on the other hand, have only a 36% share of the national income. In short, whites have personal incomes per capita about 9.5 times those of Africans, 4.5 times those formerly designated as "Coloureds" and three times those of Asians. Ultimately, to be black in South Africa still largely coincides with economic disadvantage. It is a significant omission for the report to ignore these economic inequalities.

The   report correctly notes that South Africa experienced less politically motivated violence in 1995 than in 1994, according to the Human Rights Committee of South Africa, with less than half the number of violent deaths. The committee, which is an independent monitoring group, has found that an average of 97 politically motivated killings occurred every month in 1995, compared to 223 a month in the previous year.

Although the report focuses attention on KwaZulu Natal, where over two-thirds of the country's political killings occurred in 1995, it fails to mention the Human Rights Committee's explanation for the falling rate of political violence. Specifically, the monthly death toll in KwaZulu Natal has dropped by one-half. The Human Rights Committee stated that "the continued presence of the police and the army in trouble spots is an important factor which, taken together with the political will of the Inkatha Freedom Party to demonstrate the province is governable, helps to provide an explanation." Nevertheless, the Human Rights Committee also pointed out that while deaths in KwaZulu Natal had dropped, political intolerance remained high. In short, the report fails to consider the committee's plausible explanation for the drop in the number of political killings in KwaZulu Natal, which is that "large-scale indiscriminate attacks have given way to more well-organized targeted attacks against specific individuals."

Additionally, the report fails to state that the political violence in KwaZulu Natal continues to have a devastating impact on daily life in that region. The political violence has had a particularly severe impact on the Mandisi/Isithebe industrial complex region on the north coast of KwaZulu Natal, which has seen production slide by as much as 50% at some of its textile, clothing and metal factories. The violence has caused workers to fear for their lives. Consequently, workers are routinely absent from work and either report to work late or leave early to avoid traveling to or from work when it is dark.

The report provides a scant overview of the Truth and Reconciliation Commission created through the legislative action of Parliament and signed into law by President Nelson Mandela. Archbishop Desmond Tutu, the Anglican Archbishop of Cape Town and 1984 Nobel Peace Laureate, was appointed to head the commission by President Mandela's Cabinet on November 29, 1995. Sixteen others were also named to the commission, which began its hearings in April 1996. Charged with probing human rights abuses committed during the apartheid era, dating back to 1960, the commission's examination of the past will have serious political ramifications for South Africa's future.

At present the commission is organized into three sub-committees. The body will investigate all politically motivated crimes committed by members and allies of the former apartheid regime, as well as violations perpetrated by members of the liberation movements. In exchange for full disclosure of their crimes, one committee has the discretionary power to offer former human rights violators amnesty and indemnity from prosecution. Finally, another committee is charged with the administration of a reparations program for victims, the families of deceased or living victims and those who lost property during the struggle for freedom.

The report correctly states that on December 15, 1995, South Africa ratified the 1979 Convention on the Elimination of All Forms of Discrimination Against Women (CEDAW), which came into force on September 3, 1981. There is no mention, however, of the practical effect of this ratification. Section 8(1), commonly referred to as the equality clause, guarantees to every person the right to "equality before the law" and to "equal protection of the law." Adoption of the CEDAW will have an impact on the ongoing tension between many South African women who seek to fully participate in South African society on an equal footing with men and more traditional leaders who argue that application of the interim Constitution's equality clause and universal human rights standards to customary law will undermine African culture.

In particular, at least one commentator, Fulbright Scholar Kim L. Robinson, formerly a Visiting Researcher at the Gender Research Project of the Centre for Applied Legal Studies at the University of Witwatersrand, has called for the new Government of National Unity to pay particular attention to the constitutionality of section 11(3)(b) of the Black Administration Act 38 of 1927 (section11(3)(b) of the Black Administration Act) and section 27(3) of the KwaZulu Act of the Code of Zulu Law and the Natal Code of Zulu Law (section 27(3) of the KwaZulu Act). Section 11(3)(b) of the Black Administration Act provides that African women married under customary law have the legal status of minors. Under section 27(3) of the KwaZulu Act, women are subject to the marital authority of their husbands. Robinson argues that it is highly questionable whether these provisions are truly customary law. Nevertheless, notwithstanding the putative cultural basis for such laws, Robinson correctly argues that such laws should be repealed because they are incompatible with the development of a post-apartheid democracy, have severe social and economic consequences for African women, impede African women's participation in the Reconstruction and Development Programme and contravene the basic constitutional promise of equality. In short, the report does not discuss these important legal and social questions that have direct bearing on whether women, particularly African women, will be able to fully participate in South African society.

One of the first announcements made by President Nelson Mandela after the April 1994 election was related to the domestic application of principles enshrined in the Convention on the Rights of the Child (1989). The report fails to state that South Africa, through its Ambassador to the United Nations, Josiah Jele, ratified the convention on June 16, 1995. The report correctly notes that several of President Mandela's "Presidential Initiatives" under the Reconstruction and Development Programme (RDP) are directed toward child welfare. In particular, the report correctly states that there are now programs in place to provide free health care to pregnant mothers and children under the age of six, as well as school nutrition programs to provide meals to primary school children. However, the report does not state whether these programs are comprehensive. According to Minister Jay Naidoo, who until recently was in charge of the Reconstruction and Development Programme, some 4.5 million children from 8,000 schools were benefitting from the school nutrition scheme. However, according to an article published by the Washington Office on Africa, 5.5 million children are receiving the "Mandela sandwich" of peanut butter and a cup of soup, which provides 25% of the minimum daily nutritional requirements in some of South Africa's poorest areas and results in increased classroom attendance. In light of these differing estimates, next year's report should focus on whether such programs are comprehensive and made available to all South African children, particularly those in remote rural areas.

The report should have also included discussion of the White Paper on the RDP tabled on November 15, 1994, in which the new government discussed its intention to ratify the Convention on the Rights of the Child within the context of its reconstruction of the welfare and educational systems. The White Paper appeared in draft form on September 23, 1994, and was published in final version in March 1995. Representing the Government of National Unity's most comprehensive statement on education and child welfare, the White Paper states that South African children will be entitled to ten years of free and compulsory education. This proposal, however, was not fully implemented in 1995 due to financial constraints. The White Paper also proposes equal access to all educational institutions and the equalization of per capita expenditures per student, irrespective of race. Additionally, the report does not provide any background information whatsoever on the larger social conditions that constrained black access to education and destabilized schools and educational programs throughout South Africa, particularly in African communities. According to the Institute of Multi-Party Democracy, in the two decades prior to the April 1994 elections, educational inequities gave rise to massive resistance by black students and teachers that resulted in a deep crisis in the education system, which was most severely felt in African schools.

In short, the years of activism against apartheid education and other educational disparities through school boycotts, strikes and other protest tactics has made it difficult for educators to establish a new culture of learning in some South African schools. Future reports should focus attention on black access to educational opportunity and inequitable funding of schools in predominantly African areas as compared to schools in predominantly white areas. It should further include updates on the efforts of Minister of Education Professor Bengu to create a responsive national Ministry of Education with nine semi-independent provincial ministries.

Although the report states that the Constitution explicitly prohibits discrimination on the grounds of sexual orientation, it does not elaborate on the importance of the inclusion of this provision. While pervasive social discrimination against lesbians and gay men in South Africa exists, it appears that the Government of National Unity, as well as those involved in the constitutional lawmaking process, are committed to ensuring that such discrimination is not sanctioned by law and is legally prohibited. According to the International Gay and Lesbian Human Rights Commission, South Africa's interim Constitution is the only national constitution which prohibits discrimination based on sexual orientation. Moreover, the African National Congress has proposed allowing lesbians and gay men to serve openly in the military. The atmosphere of relative tolerance for diversity in South Africa has allowed a vocal gay rights community to develop, galvanized in part by the virulently anti-gay statements made in August 1995 by Zimbabwean President Robert Mugabe, who was subsequently the target of highly visible protests when he arrived at Johannesburg airport for a SADC summit.

The report makes only fleeting references to South Africa's notoriously high rate of violent crime, which escalated in 1995 and threatens to inhibit future international investment and consequently economic development. According to the South African Police Service's National Crime Information Management Centre, in the first seven months of 1995, 1,126,101 serious crimes were reported across the country, excluding the old homelands. This included more than 10,000 murders — or one every 29 minutes.

The report fails to mention that the Human Rights Committee of South Africa (HRC) stated that at least 507 people died in police custody in South Africa during 1995 — a figure confirmed by police authorities.

216

South Africa

HRC National Director Patrick Kelly commented: "I would call it a national crisis that such a high number of people are dying in police custody whatever the reason may be." The police did not challenge the figure other than to add that it included deaths at the hands of other prisoners, detainees dying of natural causes and people shot by the police during escape attempts.

The report should also have paid greater attention to land issues, which are charged with intense socio-historical resonance in South Africa. Under apartheid, blacks were denied ownership access to 87% of the land in the country because it was reserved for whites. Further, an estimated 3.5 million blacks were forcibly removed from land that was allocated to whites. In 1995, South African Land Affairs Minster Derek Hanekom proposed legislation intended to offer security to millions of blacks denied land ownership rights under apartheid. Hanekom also proposed related legislation to set up a number of land reform mechanisms including the establishment of a Land Claims Court and Commission. Briefly, these mechanisms were intended to give tenants the right to apply to buy land over which they historically had constructive possession, which will have the effect of increasing the number of black farmers and landowners. But, according to South Africa's premier public interest law organization, the Legal Resources Centre (LRC), "removal of legal impediments represents nothing but the unlocking of a door." Recognizing the inevitability that poor South Africans will have difficulty gaining access to such land reform mechanisms, the LRC has established a special Land and Development Unit, and in every LRC office across South Africa at least one lawyer is involved in preparing submissions to the Land Claims Commission. Future reports should monitor developments in the area of land reform with an emphasis on whether poor South Africans, particularly those living in rural areas, have meaningful access to mechanisms intended to counteract the vestiges of apartheid land policies.

In sum, the State Department's 1995 report is comprehensive in listing the various human rights concerns facing post-apartheid South Africa. However, the listing of these concerns appears disjointed, as if the rights discussed have no relationship to one another. Given the nascent stage of development of post-apartheid South Africa, it is apparent that all of the human rights interests discussed in the report should be understood and examined within an integrated context. Where the interests of a new nation are involved, human rights observers must be especially cognizant of the intersection between human rights and development. Ultimately, in post-apartheid South Africa, the protection of first generation civil and political rights largely depends on continued reconstruction and economic development.

SUDAN

The Sudanese government's apparent involvement in a failed attempt to assassinate the president of Egypt on Ethiopian soil in June 1995, together with allegations that Sudanese officials were involved in assisting those who bombed the World Trade Center in 1993, have raised considerable international interest in Sudan's involvement in terrorist activities outside its borders. Much less attention has been paid, however, to the Sudanese government's responsibility for myriad and systematic human rights abuses within Sudan. By 1995, the government headed by Lt.-Gen. Omar Hassan al-Bashir had established sufficient hold over the country to be able to reduce the extent of outright torture, especially in northern Sudan, where abuses are more visible than in the war zones of the south. However, its frequent resort to violence and its general hostility to civil liberties were evident throughout the year, and were exemplified by a rise in reports of slavery and by the killing of at least 15 demonstrators in the capital, Khartoum, in September.

The 1995 State Department report is more sharply focused than in previous years. Its forthrightness, accuracy and attention to detail are welcome and timely in shifting attention to the Sudanese government's domestic human rights practices. Nevertheless, the report takes a piecemeal approach which fails to provide an integrated picture or convey the enormity of the problem of human rights violations in Sudan. In adhering to point-by-point legal categories, the report still shies away from addressing the intrinsic incompatibility of the government's ideological drive — heavily influenced by the ostensibly illegal National Islamic Front (NIF) — with respect for basic human rights, including those theoretically afforded by Islam to Muslims and non-Muslims under the jurisdiction of Islamic rulers. (Khartoum continues to claim that it is being victimized by Western antagonism to "Sudan's Islamic orientation," but this assertion is becoming less convincing to non-Sudanese Muslims and is already ridiculed by many ordinary Sudanese.) The report refers to the "Arabization and Islamization drive" on non-Muslims, but does not tackle the government's double-talk about Islam. The NIF asserts that, since the Qu'ran says there can be no compulsion in Islam, then forced Islamization is a contradiction in terms and therefore cannot exist. In practice, of course, it does exist, and many abuses are carried out in the name of the religion. The background to this and many similar issues is tackled in depth by Human Rights Watch/Africa in its 260-page report, *Behind the Red Line: Political Repression in Sudan*, released in May 1996. Human Rights Watch and the Lawyers Committee for Human Rights were the only international human rights NGOs to gain official access to Sudan in 1995.

The U.N. Special Rapporteur on Human Rights in Sudan, Dr. Gaspar Biro, has felt able to criticize the 1991 Penal Code in terms of its incompatibility with international law while rebutting the regime's claim that he is anti-Islamic. Cruel and inhuman penalties have been enshrined in the 1991 law. The State Department, however, appears to accept the conventional wisdom (and the Sudanese government's claim) that the 1991 Penal Code, which includes some traditional *huddud* punishments, is based on the Islamic *shari'a*. This implies acceptance of the assertion by absolutists that the religion demands the penalties. Many Sudanese Muslims would argue that the Bashir government has used such concepts solely for its own political advantage, and has degraded Islam in the process. Meanwhile, elements within the NIF and the government dismiss human rights as a "Western" invention of no validity to Muslims, and is building what Amnesty International calls "a culture of impunity." This is, of course, sensitive territory for any non-Muslim observer, but its implications cannot continue to be avoided as fastidiously as they are in this report.

Where the State Department report does succeed is in combining brevity with information content. Presumably because of the restrictions on the report's format and size, pertinent questions are left unasked concerning the ability of a religious state to serve the needs of a multi-ethnic, multi-cultural and multi-religious society. From a scattering of references to the "uneven" application of the law, one can infer that some of the Sudanese government's many-layered security organizations operate beyond its control with impunity. However, it lacks a statement as clear as the one put forward by the Islamist intellectual and former London embassy cultural attaché Abd al-Wahab al-Effendi, that one

220

function of the civil state machinery is to put a public relations gloss on the excesses of the security apparatus that effectively runs the country.

No mention is made of the NIF's patronage system, which permeates Sudan's "reforms aimed at privatizing state-run firms and stimulating private investment" and turns them into cut-price opportunities for friends of the government to enrich themselves. It is not made clear that opponents of the regime and members of minority groups are deliberately targeted by the selective use of the law, ranging from arrests for alcohol consumption to conscription into militia service. (The proportion of alcohol drinkers to abstainers is not necessarily any different from that in the United States during the Prohibition era, and the opportunities for abuse of the law are similar. Any NIF insider wishing to drink alcohol can do so without fear of punishment.)

However, the report does establish from the outset that "NIF members and supporters hold most key positions in the Government, security forces, judiciary, academia and the media." It also points out that the government-appointed Transitional National Assembly, which "theoretically" had legislative authority, did nothing in 1995 to lift restrictions on civil liberties — including the state of emergency — imposed by the military Revolutionary Command Council which first seized power in 1989.

Describing a "dismal human rights situation" in which "little improvement" is apparent (apart from a limited ceasefire in the civil war, brokered by former U.S. President Jimmy Carter in mid-1995), the report catalogues serious abuses by the Khartoum government and also by the insurgent Sudan People's Liberation Army (SPLA) and smaller rebel factions. All sides share responsibility for massacres, other extrajudicial killings, forced labor and almost total restriction of civil liberties, although, as the report notes, these have been carried out "on a broader scale" by the government. Hundreds of political detainees were held incommunicado without charge or trial, and detainees continued to be tortured and ill-treated. Civilians in the war zones have been deliberately attacked; thousands have been driven from their homes and hundreds — including many women and children — have been killed or kidnapped.

Almost seven years since the Revolutionary Command Council seized power, these events have a recurrent nature which threatens to exhaust the descriptive vocabulary, and it is perhaps not surprising that the phrase "dismal human rights situation" is repeated from the 1994 report. Other repetitions are less understandable, however, and suggest that this is a revision of last year's report rather than a complete overhaul. Although the revised State Department instructions to drafters of the *Country Reports* encourage the repetition of stock language where conditions remain unchanged, the danger here is that such language is no substitute for fresh consideration. Thus, the State Department report must be the only publication outside Sudan to continue referring to the governmental human rights body as the Sudan Human Rights Organization (SHRO), when that title properly belongs to the original banned SHRO which now operates in exile in Cairo and London.

Other repetitions from the previous report include the assertion that "among some southern ethnic groups rape is common. No blame is attached to the process." This contentious, inaccurate and implicitly racist remark is at best a gross over-simplification of both social relations and customary law. It employs the word "rape" with no indication as to the degree of force employed, and overlooks the cultural context in which adultery may be called rape in order to preserve the illusion of marital dignity. In no way is this comparable with the use of mass rape as a weapon of war elsewhere in Sudan, or with the rapes that occur in police stations.

The report's section on freedom of movement needs some clarification. The climate of intimidation and harassment faced by educated and professional Sudanese has prompted many of them to flee the country, creating a disempowered diaspora and isolating the few intellectual activists who remain. There is every sign of a deliberate policy at work here, in which opponents of the government are classified into two groups. Those with the highest profile and sufficient international contacts to be useful outside the country are not allowed to leave. Former Prime Minister Sadiq al-Mahdi has been denied an exit visa despite repeated requests, as has human rights activist Dr. Ushari

Mahmoud, co-author of the 1987 report on slavery and the massacre at Ad-Daein under civilian rule.

Travel inside the country is not only restricted for non-Sudanese, as the report suggests. Known opponents of the regime cannot make in-country journeys without permission. Individuals who are regarded as troublesome inside the country but who are less influential abroad are continuously harassed until they leave, and no obstacle is then put in their way. Once driven abroad, their energies are often absorbed by the everyday difficulties presented by immigration controls, asylum appeals and making a living in a foreign country. In this way they are both demoralized and disconnected from developments inside Sudan. In the longer term, as the period of exile extends and educated Sudanese settle into life in the diaspora, the likelihood of their returning to assist in the reconstruction of their country diminishes with every year that the present Sudanese government remains in power.

The "pervasive surveillance" described in the section dealing with arbitrary interference with privacy, home or correspondence, also has an international dimension. Expert witness submissions to British asylum tribunals have confirmed that the Sudanese government has a network of informers among the exiled and expatriate Sudanese population, NIF members who liaise with security officers operating out of Sudanese embassies. According to SHRO, lists of people wanted for interrogation are circulated to officers at principal points of entry to Sudan. NIF supporters are also being sent for training in information technology, according to SHRO sources, and the security forces are relatively well supplied with computer systems, including the best database in the country. Meanwhile, the University of Khartoum has been obliged to launch an appeal for equipment of its own.

The report gives insufficient attention to the government's deployment of NIF "mass organizations" — for which the government can disclaim responsibility — in putting down the unrest that spread through Khartoum and other main northern towns in September 1995, involving thousands of people. Responding to accusations by the German Ambassador that detained demonstrators had been killed, Khartoum said three people were killed in the demonstrations, but maintained that counter-demonstrators, not security forces, were responsible for their deaths. In fact, armed plain-clothes security men fired into the crowds, and the government incited the "mass organizations" through its use of the media.

The report's illustration of the draconian treatment meted out to anti-government demonstrators in late 1995 might have been more complete if it had made reference to Majdoline Haj al-Tahir and Shihab Yousif Ali. Ms. Haj-al-Tahir, a student of agriculture at the University of Khartoum and a part-time translator at the British Embassy, was a member of the small group whose arrest sparked the huge public demonstrations in September. She was maltreated in detention for two days until a relative, none other than Army Chief of Staff Lt.-Gen. Ibrahim Suliman, located her. After her personal beating was halted, she was reportedly forced to watch while those arrested with her were tortured. The British Embassy made no official mention of her treatment — and her case is overlooked by the State Department report, too.

Shihab Yousif, a student at Omdurman's private Ahliya University, was accused of tearing a copy of the Qu'ran in public. The NIF has targeted Ahliya University because of its resistance to government purges of opponents in education and the official Arabization program. While in detention Shihab Yousif was subjected to severe torture, to the extent that he was repeatedly hospitalized in between beatings. After his release four months later he detailed his treatment in a handwritten statement. This treatment was in part an attempt to extract a confession from him, since the government had no other material or witnesses to support its case. Indeed, the Sudanese Ambassador in London wrote to the Chairman of the British Parliamentary Committee on Human Rights, Lord Avebury, inadvertently contradicting Khartoum by saying there was no evidence against Shihab and that the student was being held in custody for his own protection. Shihab was also subjected to media vilification for his allegedly "anti-Islamic" act, and was warned on his release not to appear in public, since he might be eliminated by an extremist group — an act for which the government would disclaim responsibility. Shihab Yousif is effectively a marked man.

Sudan

The detention of three students and nine others which prompted the protests of September 9-15 immediately followed the government's much-publicized "amnesty" of political and criminal detainees and prisoners, timed to coincide with the visit of a European Parliament delegation and under which former Prime Minister Sadiq al-Mahdi was also released. (Dozens of detainees are known to have remained in jail or in the detention places known as "ghost houses" after the amnesty. One not released and whose fate was already causing particular concern was Brigadier Muhammad Ahmad al-Rayah, who had taken the unprecedented step of suing the government, alleging torture and rape.)

The insurgent forces in southern Sudan — above all the SPLA and the splinter groups led by defecting SPLA commanders, principally the Southern Sudan Independence Movement (SSIM) — have been responsible for many deaths and abuses of southern Sudanese civilians, which have often alienated the very people they claim to be liberating. Despite an announcement in 1994 that it would establish civilian control over its military and humanitarian wings, the SPLA has taken no action to lend credence to its promises. Regional military commanders continue to hold what the report calls "secret and basically political" trials, and are not accountable to the civilian population. Western Equatoria is the only region under rebel control which appears to be attempting to implement civilian rule.

The momentum of inter-factional fighting continues. On July 30, SPLA soldiers took part in a massacre of over 200 Nuer villagers in the Ganyliel area of south Sudan. Pressure from the international community and NGOs prompted the SPLA leadership to announce in August that it would investigate the massacre, but by the end of the year no such investigation had begun. In addition to the killing of civilians and the abduction and rape of women, acts of torture by the SPLA and SSIM are frequently reported.

The State Department report blames the absence of monitors in the south for the difficulty in verifying such allegations. Although the international relief agencies often have staff in the area, they are frequently withdrawn when clashes start, not least because of the risk of hostage-taking by the antagonists. The hostages are then exchanged for relief supplies.

The report regards the treatment of refugees as "relatively good," without further elaboration. It does not specify which refugee groups it has in mind, so the assumption must be that it refers to Ethiopians and Eritreans, who constitute the majority. The report does not clearly state whether the comparison is with the government's treatment of its own citizens, with the treatment of refugees by prior governments, or with the treatment of refugees in neighboring countries. Certainly, most refugees in Sudan enjoy greater protection and provision of more generous assistance than internally displaced Sudanese, and the government sees political advantage in their well-being.

The 600,000 Eritreans and Ethiopians who have not returned to their countries since the fall of the Mengistu regime in Addis Ababa are often those who do not trust their new governments, and as such are potentially useful to Khartoum, which has fallen out with both Eritrea and Ethiopia. Muslim recruits to the Eritrean Islamic Jihad, which attempted an incursion into Eritrea in 1994, have been encouraged by the NIF.

The question of discrimination against disabled people should not merely be seen in terms of "disability awareness" and access to buildings and transport, which, as the report notes, are non-existent. Organizations set up to assist the victims of amputation — mostly from former President Numeiri's experiment with *huddud* punishments in 1983-1985 — have been harassed, obstructed, deprived of funds or closed down. The amputees were mostly southerners and impoverished before they were mutilated, in what constituted a grotesque parody of Islamic practice notable for its display of social prejudice. Now they are being denied practical help on the apparent grounds that any alleviation of their suffering will undermine the punishment.

In its discussion of female genital mutilation (FGM), the report says that the practice is illegal. This is disingenuous, given that 90% of females in the north undergo the operation. (The report correctly notes that "women displaced from the south to the north reportedly are increasingly imposing [FGM] on their daughters, even if they themselves have not been subjected to it.") The severest form of FGM, infibulation, is certainly illegal, but no one has been arrested for performing it in recent years. The commonest form, known as *Sunna* ("Tradition"), is not, in practice, treated as unlawful. Enforcement of the law is non-existent, in contrast with the enforcement of laws concerning dress, female behavior in public or the consumption of alcohol.

The routine use of harassment, detention and torture to retain the government's monopoly of power is devastating Sudanese society, just as the relentless pursuit of an impossible victory in the civil war is destroying the economy. In the same way, the damage to the fragile social fabric of Sudan will persist long after the oft-predicted downfall of the regime that has caused it.

It may be argued that the Bashir government has sown the seeds of its own destruction by arousing unprecedented levels of international hostility, with neighbors such as Eritrea and Ethiopia calling openly for its overthrow. If and when it falls, dominant international concerns such as the detention of prominent politicians and Sudan's destabilization of its neighbors through support for dissident Islamist groups — or terrorism — might be ended. At the domestic level, however, the corrosion of attitudes toward human rights — and not only among the security and police forces — will not be healed overnight.

The NIF-dominated Sudanese government has certainly pushed human rights violations to extreme levels, but its behavior often has more historical precedent than the party politicians now in opposition care to admit. It should not be forgotten that ex-Prime Minister Sadiq al-Mahdi's civilian government in the mid-1980s began arming tribal militias with automatic weapons, and detained Ushari Mahmud and Suliman Baldo, the authors of a revealing, almost premonitory report on child slavery and the massacre of southern Sudanese in the town of Ad-Daein in 1987. The National Democratic Alliance (NDA), an umbrella group for those now waiting to resume their places in government, has not closely examined its own policy toward Sudan's diverse peoples. In its discussions with Sudanese opposition elements — chiefly the SPLA and the NDA — the State Department should make clear that its insistence on human rights does not apply only to the present government, and that those now seeking power must also accept responsibility for their share of past abuses and set out their plans for guaranteeing full respect for human rights in the future.

TURKEY

The State Department's report on Turkey is one of the longest and most detailed of the 1995 *Country Reports*. Only the report on China occupies as many pages. The report succeeds in identifying the major human rights problems in Turkey. However, the language describing the human rights violations is relatively mild, given the context. The report is thorough in describing what changes took place in Turkey in 1995 in the area of human rights and what remained the same. However, it downplays the seriousness of the issues it discusses. Some areas of gross human rights violations are mentioned without any indication of how widespread they are; other areas are discussed without any commentary. In an effort to address all the topics covered in previous *Country Reports*, some serious human rights violations are mentioned only superficially. The facts reported, which are thorough and accurate, add up to a picture much more serious than the conclusions of the report imply. These discrepancies appear to reflect the variety of authorial hands and institutional interests that have gone into drafting and editing the report on Turkey, a key U.S. ally and aid recipient.

As a consequence of this discrepancy between its facts and its conclusions, the report contradicts itself in many places. For example, in one of its introductory sentences, the report states: "Civilian authorities remain publicly committed to the establishment of a state of law and respect for human rights but torture, excessive use of force, and other serious human rights abuses by the security forces persisted through 1995." The statement gives the impression that the security forces are the only violators of human rights; no law, no government and no court has any involvement in the numerous violations listed in the pages that follow. But one does not have to read very far into the report to find out that this is not the case. However, the report repeats this contradictory formulation in later sections — for example, in its discussion of torture.

The report's introduction discusses the armed conflict between the government and the Kurdistan Workers Party (PKK) which has been going on for over a decade. As in previous years, the report refers to the PKK as a "terrorist" organization and refers to its goal of creating a separate state of Kurdistan in southeastern Turkey — even though this is no longer the PKK's stated aim. The State Department never acknowledges that this "armed conflict" is a significant source of the human rights violations that are discussed at great length in the rest of the report. The disproportionate effect of the government's human rights violations on the Turkish Kurds is not acknowledged by the State Department.

The strongest sections of the 1995 report are those that deal with torture and infringements on freedom of speech. The Turkish Constitution specifically bans torture, as do the European and U.N. Conventions to which Turkey is a party. Given the high number of cases, the report takes allegations of torture seriously and discusses certain cases of torture in great detail. Despite this, the report repeats the Turkish government's claim that torture is not "systematic," without comment or qualification. This is strange coming from a government which also states that torture is "closely tied to the State's fight against terrorism." The report does not question how, if this is the case, torture can be anything but systematic on the state's part. The rest of the section provides ample evidence that even if torture itself is not systematic, the state's intentional blind eye to torture certainly is. It is impossible to be convinced of the Turkish government's determination to fight torture if, of the 547 complaints of torture and mistreatment filed in the first seven months of 1995, only 337 reached the administrative investigation stage and only 15 resulted in convictions.

The report lists positive improvements throughout the year in Turkish law without commenting on their lack of implementation. This problem is apparent in the section on freedom of expression, an area the report focuses on in some detail. However, here again the report introduces the topic positively, continues to discuss some clear-cut violations of human rights, but does not directly qualify the positive opening to this section. The year's most positive development in this regard was the reform of Article 8 of the Turkish Anti-Terror Law. Instead of making "separatist propaganda" a crime "irrespective of the methods, aims and ideas," the law now requires the courts to prove intent. While, as the report mentions, certain imprisoned writers were freed as a result of the change in Article 8, at the end of 1995 about 100 people remained in prison as a result of their writings or spoken words, with thousands more still on trial. The report fails to mention that some of those released after the amendment to Article 8 were in fact prosecuted again for the same offenses, using the amended version of the law. For example, Lawyer Erin Keskin, former Secretary General of the Istanbul Branch of the Human Rights Association, was released in November 1995 only to be indicted for the same offenses relating to articles she published on the Kurdish issue in 1993. The revised version of Article 8 still permits the prosecution of people for their non-violent opinions. At the time the reform was introduced, Amnesty International made the following statement in a press release:

> It is difficult to believe in the sincerity of a democracy package which permits Turkish citizens to be imprisoned for the expression of their non-violent opinions, exposed to secret detention and brutality in police stations, or abducted by plainclothes policemen, never to be seen again. It is difficult not to believe that the package was designed principally in order to deflect international and domestic criticism of a worsening human rights record.

(It should be noted that Amnesty issued this statement before the reforms were enacted, and that some 90 prisoners were in fact released when the reforms became law in October 1995 — even though many of them were subsequently rearrested.)

Moreover, prosecutors now use lesser known provisions of the Anti-Terror Law to restrict freedom of expression. For example, in 1995, more cases were brought under Articles 6 and 7 of the Anti-Terror Law, which ban publishing of propaganda by "terrorist" organizations. The Turkish Penal Code's Article 312, which makes it a crime to "provoke enmity," has also been the source of a higher number of court cases recently. The report fails to mention that Turkey has the dubious honor of imprisoning more journalists than any other country for the second consecutive year.

In December 1995, a Turkish State Security Court confiscated all copies of the December issue of the magazine *Savasa Karsi Baris* (Peace

Against War). The issue contained an excerpt of a November 1995 report by the Arms Project of Human Rights Watch, entitled *Weapons Transfers and Violations of the Laws of War in Turkey*. This was an internationally visible example of the many confiscations of newspapers, magazines and other publications throughout 1995 for violating one of many Turkish code provisions restricting freedom of speech. While the confiscations of pro-Kurdish publications have decreased markedly since the repeal of Article 8 of the Anti-Terror Law, confiscation of publications still goes on regularly as a consequence of the laws restricting freedom of expression described in the report.

In almost all areas, the report makes comparisons between the situation in Turkey in 1995 and the situation in the preceding year. While this is helpful to the reader, in some areas it detracts from the significance of the problem. Since each area is analyzed in terms of whether the total number of incidents has increased or decreased since 1994, those areas in which incidents have decreased tend to lose their importance in the overall scheme of the report. With no commentary to follow these observations, the report loses sight of how certain human rights violations in Turkey remain serious, even if the overall numbers are lower. For example, in the introduction to the section on Political and Other Extrajudicial Killings, the report states that: "The number of deaths in detention and mystery killings was down significantly in 1995"; however, it goes on to state that six deaths in detention were reported in the first nine months of 1995, as well as 98 political killings of civilians by "unknown perpetrators."

In the same way, the section on disappearances opens with the statement: "The [Human Rights Foundation of Turkey] reports three disappearances, which ended in death." The third paragraph of the section finally discusses the hundreds of other disappearances in 1995. While it is correct that the number of disappearances in 1995 is down compared to 1994, the report does not say that the number of disappearances in 1994 was the highest recorded by Amnesty International for any country in the world that year. While the numbers decreased in the beginning of 1995, October and November saw a significant increase. On October 30, six people, including three children, reportedly "disappeared" after being detained near Dargecit, in the Mardin province. Two people "disappeared" in Istanbul in circumstances that suggested they were abducted by police.

The report states that "two million persons have been displaced." It also mentions that there have been no adequate government programs to take care of these people. However, the report falls short of elaborating on the problems that arise when two million people are displaced by the security forces of their government. The Human Rights Watch *World Report* for 1995 points out that 2,200 villages have been either partially or totally depopulated, most of them burned down by Turkish security forces.

The report admits that United States weapons have "been used in operations against the PKK during which human rights abuses have occurred," and adds: "It is highly likely that such equipment was used in support of the evacuation and/or destruction of villages." However, it does not discuss (at any greater length than what is implied by the above statement) what a February 1996 article in the *San Francisco Chronicle* called "the mountain of evidence that most of the aircraft, helicopters, tanks, artillery pieces, mortars, machine guns and assault rifles used to bomb and burn those Kurdish villages and kill and scatter the people came out of American factories and were paid by U.S. government loans and grants." Human Rights Watch has stated that "the Clinton administration, which is fully aware of Turkey's misuse of U.S. weaponry, has consistently refused to link arms transfers to improvements in Turkey's human rights record, and has downplayed Turkish violations for strategic reasons." According to Human Rights Watch, the U.S. government has adopted a significantly less critical attitude toward Turkey than have other governments.

The State Department report also fails to discuss the broader relationship between the United States and Turkey. It ignores the fact that Turkey, having received $5.3 billion in military aid from the United States over the past decade, is now the third largest recipient of U.S. aid (after Israel and Egypt). Had the State Department acknowledged these political considerations in its report, the reasons for the discrepancy between the facts contained in the report and its less than forthright conclusions might have been more readily apparent to the reader.

United Kingdom/Hong Kong

For Hong Kong, 1995 will be remembered for the stark divergence between Hong Kong's evolving democratic institutions and the plans being put in place by the future sovereign. This was the year when China laid to rest any illusions about its intentions to incorporate Hong Kong into its own authoritarian system. It became clear that China intends largely to ignore or vitiate the requirements of the 1984 Sino-British Joint Declaration. The Joint Declaration's promise that the future Hong Kong Special Administrative Region (HKSAR) would have a high degree of autonomy, democracy and human rights, along with the promises of "one country, two systems" and "Hong Kong people ruling Hong Kong" became increasingly illusory. One pro-democracy leader was moved to reformulate the latter slogan to "Hong Kong people ruining Hong Kong," as China's Preliminary Working Committee (PWC), a select group of local pro-China supporters and mainlanders appointed by China to lay the groundwork for its future rule, set about systematically undermining the foundations of Hong Kong's fragile democratic system and human rights protections. Unfortunately, as in past years, the State Department's annual report on Hong Kong reflects very little of the turmoil and anxiety about human rights brought on by China's onslaught.

The most serious threats to human rights in Hong Kong derived from China's actions or threats. As Hong Kong's first fully elected Legislative Council (Legco) came into existence in September 1995, the PWC was already laying the groundwork for its demise. In its final plenary session in December 1995 the PWC declared, in accordance with earlier sub-group determinations, that the elected legislature should be dismissed on July 1, 1997 and replaced with an appointed provisional legislature, to be chosen by a Selection Committee made up of China's hand-picked Hong Kong supporters. At the same time, the PWC declared that certain key implementing provisions of the Hong Kong Bill of Rights Ordinance (BORO) would be eliminated and that six ordinances that had been reformed to conform to the BORO would be restored to their old draconian colonial character.

Critique 1995

The provisions to be deleted from the BORO related to its status as an implementing statute to fulfill Hong Kong obligations under the ICCPR; the BORO's override of previous ordinances; and the requirement that legislation enacted after the commencement date of the BORO, "to the extent it admits of such construction, be construed so as to be consistent with the ICCPR" (Art. 4). The ordinance reforms to be set aside related generally to free speech and association protections incorporated in several draconian ordinances, that the PWC now wants restored to their original form. (The amended ordinances include: the Societies (Amendment) Ordinance, 1992; Television Amendment Ordinance, 1993; Broadcast Authority Ordinance, 1993; Public Order Amendment Ordinance, 1995; and the Emergency Regulations Ordinance, 1995).

As if this twin attack on the pillars of Hong Kong's rule of law were not enough, the Chinese and British governments reached an agreement that provides that the Court of Final Appeal, required by the Joint Declaration, would not be created until the initiation of Chinese rule on July 1, 1997. While these developments are mentioned in the report, their significance is seriously understated.

The basic criticism of the State Department report in last year's edition of the *Critique* can be repeated verbatim in 1995: "While technically accurate with respect to those rights it addresses (especially respecting refugees, labor and women), [the report] seems reluctant to assess the importance of current developments and neglectful of China's role in events in Hong Kong." The persistence of this problem despite our repeated criticisms in recent years is of concern. Especially in view of the concomitant seriousness of the report on China, it appears that the State Department has made a conscious decision to pursue a "hands off" approach to Hong Kong and this has had a negative effect on the quality of its human rights reporting. With the transfer of sovereignty a year away, this cannot be reassuring to the people of Hong Kong.

The year 1995 saw the full implementation of Governor Chris Patten's proposals for greater democracy in Hong Kong, originally advanced three years earlier. Following direct elections to the District Boards in September 1994, similar elections were carried out for the

United Kingdom/Hong Kong

Urban and Regional Councils and the Legislative Council in March and September 1995. These included universal franchise for the district and regional bodies and direct election under a complex formula (20 directly elected/universal suffrage seats, 30 functional constituency seats, of which 10 were new broadly based constituencies, and 10 seats filled by an election committee made up from elected members from the other representative bodies) for Legco. It is noteworthy that, while China had formally opposed this rather conservative formula for being too liberal, China's official representatives in Hong Kong had actively supported pro-China candidates for all three levels of election. While contradictory, this support was evidence of interference in a local election in ways seemingly not contemplated by the "one country, two systems" formula.

Members of the Democratic Party and other independent pro-democracy candidates took the lion's share of the directly elected seats that were up for grabs in the September Legco elections. The Democrats took 12 of the 20 directly elected seats and seven indirectly elected seats, while independents and smaller party candidates closely aligned with the Democrats took 12 additional seats, giving the pro-democracy forces a possible majority in the 60-member Legco. After failing in its electoral efforts (the leading pro-China party took just two directly elected and four indirectly elected seats), these steps forward in democracy for Hong Kong were followed immediately by a large step backward, as China's PWC, in its final plenary session, formally voted to dismiss the elected legislature in 1997 and replace it with an appointed provisional legislature made up of supporters of Beijing.

In this regard, China's continued exclusion of pro-Hong Kong democracy supporters from all of its transitional bodies does not bode well for democratic rule after 1997. Not only have pro-democracy figures been excluded from various advisory bodies and the PWC, it also became clear that Democrats had been excluded from membership in the Preparatory Committee (PC). The PC is the formal body to replace the PWC (which was disbanded at the end of the year) designated to handle final transition matters, including the creation of the 400-member Selection Committee which is to choose the first Chief Executive, and, it now appears, to choose a Provisional Legislature. The actual announcement of the PC membership, made on December 29, is not mentioned in the State Department report. The list of 150 PC members includes 94 from Hong Kong and 56 from China. The local PC membership is stacked with business and professional leaders with strong records of support for China's positions. The PC included only one Democrat from a minor party and no one at all from the Democratic Party, which emerged from the September elections as the territory's dominant party. China continues to refuse all contact with leaders of the Democratic Party. (As China's leading spokesperson on Hong Kong, Lu Ping, recently threatened, even the one Democrat who was included in the PC may be excluded from the Selection Committee and the Provisional Legislature as a result of his opposition, in a formal PC vote in March 1996, to the planned creation of the Provisional Legislature.)

The report correctly notes the strong criticism of Hong Kong's existing electoral system by the U.N. Human Rights Committee in its November 1995 comment on the periodic report of the United Kingdom under the ICCPR. The committee, while noting Britain's reservations to the ICCPR with respect to universal suffrage in Hong Kong, argued that "once an elected Legislative Council is established its election must conform" to the ICCPR's call for direct popular election of all seats. As the State Department report correctly notes, the Human Rights Committee criticized the existing system of functional constituencies for giving "undue weight to the views of the business community" and for discriminating "on the basis of property and functions." The report also notes that the Hong Kong Court of Appeal ruled on November 24, 1995 against a challenge to the electoral system for these deficiencies. The report fails to emphasize, however, that China is set to perpetuate this discriminatory system and reacted very harshly to Governor Patten's attempts to expand the franchise. The Patten proposal would have dramatically enlarged the franchise for the 10 new functional constituencies, and this was among the primary grounds for China's decision to dismiss the existing Legislative Council.

It is against this backdrop of open and repeated Chinese hostility that human rights developments in Hong Kong in 1995 must be viewed. In this respect, the image of tranquility conveyed by the State Department report sorely misses the mark. As it mentions, China's hostility to Hong Kong's human rights protections was particularly directed against the BORO. This hostility seems unwarranted in that the BORO merely articulates the language of the ICCPR, to which the parties are bound. (While China is not a party to the ICCPR, it agreed in the Joint Declaration to the ICCPR's continued application to Hong Kong). At the same time, the PWC determined that six other ordinances, which were earlier reformed to conform to the Bill of Rights (especially in matters related to freedom of expression), should be restored to their former colonial character.

To make matters much worse, the Chief Justice of Hong Kong, Sir T. L. Yang (a frequently mentioned candidate for appointment as the future Chief Executive), entered the Bill of Rights dispute on the side of the Chinese government by endorsing plans to reduce the stature of the ordinance. The State Department report fails to mention this. Justice Yang was alleged by a top Chinese official to have made a remark that the Bill of Rights undermined the territory's legal system. When a furor erupted over this report, Justice Yang appeared to admit the remark and ultimately submitted a formal statement containing similar views to the executive branch of the government, thus further undermining confidence in both the rule of law and continued rights protection.

The PWC also set about its own review of all Hong Kong laws to have them conform to its interpretation of the Basic Law. As evident from the PWC's attack on the BORO, this non-judicial exercise of review power turned judicial review on its head — rather than aiming to protect human rights it aimed to insure that there was not excessive rights protection. At the same time, the rule of law came under attack on the institutional side by a Sino-British agreement that the new Hong Kong Court of Final Appeal will not actually be set up until July 1, 1997. This agreement included a provision limiting the courts jurisdiction over "acts of state" (a vaguely defined term for which the intended meaning seems much broader than the foreign affairs concerns usually implicated by the common law doctrine of acts of state), and limiting foreign judicial participation to only a single judge, a limitation that had previously met with widespread objections from Legco, the Law Society and the Bar

Association. There was no such limitation on foreign judges in either the Joint Declaration or the Basic Law and Hong Kong has had a long tradition of inviting qualified foreign common law judges to sit on its highest court. The democratic camp launched a serious challenge to this agreement but it was pushed through the partially appointed Legislative Council before the September election.

The report correctly points out growing community concern with the absence of an independent review of complaints against police. Complaints against police are rarely substantiated. Amidst growing public concern over police brutality, human rights groups such as the Hong Kong Human Rights Monitor and the private Hong Kong Human Rights Commission have called for further investigations into two cases of unexplained death while in police custody. Lee Shing-tat died 24 hours after claiming to be a victim of a police beating. After another prisoner, Lam Tin-ming died in police custody, an initial post-mortem showed broken ribs and a torn liver.

The State Department report also correctly notes criminal process-related reforms eliminating arrest and warrant powers previously granted to the Independent Commission Against Corruption (ICAC), as well as the persistent presumption that excessive unexplained assets held by civil servants are ill-gotten. However, the report makes no mention of the December recommendation by the Crime Wing of the Police Department to the Security Branch that the right to remain silent be watered down to allow juries to make adverse inference from the silence of an accused. As may be imagined, such issues, which are vitally important to the texture of the rule of law, are of great concern with only a year remaining before the transfer of sovereignty.

Closely related to concerns about law enforcement are the numerous problems in the immigration and refugee areas in Hong Kong, and these are addressed in the report. It notes that some 23,000 people remain in camps in Hong Kong, of whom 1,500 have been screened in as refugees. The report correctly notes that Hong Kong has never turned away Vietnamese boat people, although as problems with repatriation and resettlement have mounted, the community has had to employ harsher measures, including closed camps and voluntary (2,566 in 1995) and forced repatriation. Fifteen Vietnamese holding Taiwan passports, whom Vietnam refused to accept back, received a January 1995 High Court judgment in their favor in a lawsuit challenging their seven-year detention in closed camps. (After reversal at the Court of Appeal, this case ultimately resulted in a Privy Council ruling in their favor in April of 1996 and the immediate release by transfer to open camps of 207 detainees who were similarly situated). The report also notes that large numbers of illegal Chinese immigrants enter Hong Kong and are repatriated at the rate of 150 per day, although in rare cases temporary asylum is afforded. The most notorious case is that of Chinese independent labor activist Han Dongfang, who was expelled to Hong Kong and wants to return to China, but has been refused re-entry. The case of Han, as well as about 80 other cases of Chinese asylum seekers are of concern as 1997 approaches.

In a similar vein, the report completely ignores the continued concern of Hong Kong people, in particular minorities, about their future nationality status. Except for 50,000 heads of household and their families covered under the 1991 British Nationality Act, Britain continues to deny full British nationality to Hong Kong people. This has been of particular concern to Hong Kong minorities who fear becoming stateless after 1997. In offering glowing praise to Hong Kong concerning the right to travel, the report ignores the growing concern of Hong Kong people about their future freedom of travel and the international recognition of both their British National Overseas (BNO) and future Special Administrative Region passports. China has also failed to afford adequate assurances of the continued rights of residency of Hong Kong holders of foreign passports, or of future Chinese respect for the diplomatic protection allowed by such passports. This problem extends to the domestic front as well, as China has denied permits for entry for several Hong Kong political activists, sparking concern about a blacklist for exclusion based on political factors. Hong Kong people have understand-able anxieties about their right both to leave and return after 1997, and these issues deserve careful scrutiny in the 1996 State Department report.

The report offers substantial coverage of freedom of expression and of association. It appropriately notes the vibrant tradition of a free press in Hong Kong and the shadow that China now casts on that tradition. Among the most pressing tasks facing the current Hong Kong government is the effort, promoted by the Hong Kong Journalists Association, to update a number of overbearing colonial laws that limit press freedom. The colonial legal system formally allowed the government enormous powers over the press, especially in the interests of national security and in times of emergency, as well as to protect official secrecy. While the former powers were rarely exercised in Hong Kong, the principles of official secrecy have been applied. Concern that the Chinese authorities may apply these laws with a heavy hand after 1997 has encouraged a movement to reform and update these laws to conform to current actual or expected practices or to the norms set forth in the BORO.

Freedom of association is also a matter of concern. This goes beyond questions about the strict language currently contained in the Societies Ordinance, which the report mentions. There is growing concern that the provisions in the Basic Law banning foreign political organizations will be used to exclude such international organizations as Amnesty International, Human Rights Watch/Asia, Justice and Greenpeace, all of whom are currently permitted to operate in the territory. Furthermore, concern has arisen over those local organizations that Chinese officials have already criticized as "subversive." Membership in the allegedly subversive Alliance in Support of the Patriotic Democratic Movement in China has already been cited by Chinese officials as a basis for exclusion from the Legislative Council. Local human rights groups such as Hong Kong Human Rights Monitor or the Hong Kong Human Rights Commission could also come under attack. In considering issues related to freedom of association, the State Department report is excessively sanguine.

Whether the present Hong Kong government will take the task of reform to heart, in the face of strong Chinese opposition, must be in doubt. The government resisted a legislative proposal in 1995 for freedom of information legislation, offering an administrative code of access instead. In the face of Chinese opposition, plans to privatize the government-owned Radio Television Hong Kong (with the aim of insuring editorial independence) have apparently been abandoned. In October it was reported that China would be consulted over controversial radio and television reforms. As mentioned above, China's willingness to reverse the reforms already carried out under the Bill of Rights Ordinance offers little room for optimism in the development of progressive media laws. China has already become directly involved in censorship by attempting to control which Chinese films will be permitted to be shown in the annual Hong Kong film festival, even going so far as to withdraw its participation if the organizers do not agree.

More threatening than government censorship, at present, is the environment of self-censorship. This arises from Chinese intimidation of reporters covering the mainland, historical memory of blacklisting of newspapers (reported in previous editions of the *Critique*), favoritism and harassment of China's critics. As the report notes, the continued imprisonment under a 12-year sentence of Hong Kong *Ming Pao* reporter Xi Yang for reporting financial information China deemed secret continues to haunt the Hong Kong press and has stimulated demonstrations. The harassment of Hong Kong publisher Jimmy Lai has been equally vexing. After closing down his Beijing retail store in 1994 in response to an article critical of Premier Li Peng in his *Next* magazine, Chinese officials in 1995 took a dim view of his newly launched paper, *Apple Daily*, by refusing his reporters accreditation in China. China's continued exclusion from its Hong Kong consultative dialogue of local residents who supported the 1989 Beijing student movement under the banner of the Alliance in Support of the Patriotic Democratic Movement in China has also had a chilling effect on local freedoms of expression and association. It does not help that Hong Kong police are frequently observed to be filming demonstrators outside the offices of the Xinhua news agency, China's unofficial representation in Hong Kong.

Problems relating to the equal protection of residents has continued to vex Hong Kong. As noted above, China's main offense in this regard has been the exclusion of individuals from the country and from participation in its consultative processes, based on their political beliefs and activities. Under these circumstances of political favoritism, local civil servants have had reason to be concerned with the mainland government's recent request for their confidential files, a request which the current government has so far resisted. The present government has also confronted a range of issues in this regard. Most prominent have been challenges to its civil service localization policies, designed to insure that most top positions are occupied by qualified local Chinese, which the courts have largely rejected. Sex discrimination has also been a problem in Hong Kong. As the report highlights, the government did push through a limited anti-discrimination bill in 1995 banning discrimination based on sex and disability. However, this occurred after the government first refused to allow a more comprehensive bill to come before the Legislative Council in 1994, exercising its right of prior approval of members' bills requiring expenditure.

Discrimination takes many forms in Hong Kong. As the report notes, women face discrimination in employment, welfare and inheritance. Age discrimination is not prohibited by law and occurs openly. Treatment of the disabled, especially the mentally disabled, has been a problem, with communities opposing the location of facilities for the disabled in their neighborhoods. The report correctly points out that Filipino domestic workers, now totaling 140,000, have been the targets of reported mistreatment.   The employment laws sometimes work to their disadvantage, especially with respect to their right to remain in Hong Kong and seek employment. Such workers can be very vulnerable, as they face deportation if they lose their jobs. As the report notes, given China's huge labor supply, foreign domestic workers have some reason for concern about their continued right of abode after 1997.

It should be acknowledged that the report is especially thorough in other respects when reporting on worker rights. The most significant new development in 1995 was the election of several labor leaders to the Legislative Council. This can be expected to focus renewed attention on the range of problems noted in the report. The labor import scheme came under scrutiny almost immediately after the election. Local labor leaders, while opposing importation, to their credit, have also focused attention on abuse of foreign workers, especially several reported wage problems under sub-contracts in the mammoth new airport project. Labor leaders and other liberal political leaders have also sought to expand other social welfare benefits and the government's social welfare budget, especially for the elderly, seemed set at the end of the year for further modest expansion. Paradoxically, Communist leaders in China have harshly criticized Hong Kong's "runaway" social welfare spending.

In the face of worrisome human rights trends in Hong Kong, the U.N. Human Rights Committee and numerous local and international NGOs, including the Lawyers Committee, have expressed concern over China's expressed intention to discontinue the periodic human rights reports required under the ICCPR and the International Covenant on Economic, Social and Cultural Rights. In 1995 China indicated its intention to discontinue such reporting, despite its obligations to adhere to both covenants with respect to Hong Kong under both the Joint Declaration and the Basic Law. Disparate forces in the Legislative Council were even able to agree to send a delegation to the Human Rights Committee hearings on Hong Kong in October 1995 to lobby for support for continued reporting. In its November report the Committee concluded that China was bound to do so. In the same report, as a reflection of its continued interest in human rights developments in Hong Kong, and a demonstration of the importance of this international process, the Committee also voiced support for maintaining the status of the Bill of Rights Ordinance and for continued law reform under the Bill of Rights. It also expressed concern about the unfairness of the electoral system, the inadequacy of anti-discrimination legislation, the rights of Vietnamese boat people, the lack of an independent police complaints procedure, the lack of acceptable regulations concerning states of emergency and the limitations on jurisdiction over "acts of state" imposed by the Sino-British agreement to establish the new Court of Final Appeal. The Committee's concern over continued reporting was emphasized when it took the extraordinary measure of calling for an additional report from the United Kingdom in May 1996.

United Kingdom/Northern Ireland

The State Department report on Northern Ireland is more comprehensive than in previous years, providing a better picture of the range of human rights abuses which occurred in 1995. The report catalogues, albeit at a remove, dozens of allegations of state human rights abuses. The fact that the report refers to the possibility of the existence of such abuses is welcome. What is less fortunate is the manner chosen to acknowledge these and other serious concerns. The violations committed by the state are usually referred to as "allegations" or "complaints," which can be directly contrasted with the tone adopted when reporting violations of humanitarian law or other outrages carried out by paramilitaries. In the latter case, such violations are generally reported as real and proven, even where the allegations of state abuse are supported by as much, if not more, evidence. In one example the report states that paramilitary punishments such as exile are imposed for "sometimes even such acts as dating an IRA prisoner's girlfriend." This is worthy of contrast with the following: "There continued to be allegations that security forces . . . physically and psychologically abused detainees in holding centers." In fact there is clear and proven evidence of violations committed by both the state and by paramilitary organizations.

This difference in tone underlines the general bias endemic in the report, with different weight given to complaints of state human rights abuses on the one hand and to government claims that measures are being taken to improve matters on the other. The report frequently makes bald statements about government improvement or reform that conceal a reality entirely less favorable to the government of the United Kingdom. For example, the report states (correctly) that measures have been introduced to remedy the inadequate legal protection afforded to part-time workers. What it fails to report is that such legislative protection was forthcoming only after the European Court of Justice had found the UK in breach of its obligations under European Community law on the matter.

Such bias is perhaps most naked in the assertion that "The Government does not practice exile . . . but the terrorist organizations do." In fact *both* engage in practices which amount to exile, the government by way of exclusion orders under the Prevention of Terrorism Act (PTA), which are an administrative measure incapable of challenge either by way of judicial review or by appeal.

In an improvement over previous years, the report also contains a number of references to the pronouncements of international human rights bodies on matters of concern in Northern Ireland. It is particularly useful to see the references to the concerns of the U.N. Committee on Torture and the U.N. Human Rights Committee about human rights violations in Northern Ireland, as well as mention of the September 27 decision of the European Court of Human Rights in *Farrell et al v UK*, although no mention is made of the response to the judgment by the UK government, which asserted that it would ignore the ruling.

The contents of the report on Northern Ireland lend themselves to a number of themes, as well as a number of ancillary points. The report naturally makes reference to the existence throughout 1995 of the twin paramilitary ceasefires, although it does note, correctly, that there were apparent unacknowledged breaches of these ceasefires by both the IRA and Loyalist paramilitaries. In this respect the reporting is more accurate and less biased than in other areas. However the report contains one or two speculative remarks, such as the questionable assertion that the economy has improved in Northern Ireland since the ceasefires. Certainly, tourism improved dramatically, and business confidence improved, but unemployment remained more or less static.

The report also acknowledges the response by the UK government to the ceasefires, noting that emergency laws were nonetheless renewed, despite the call by the U.N. Human Rights Committee for the UK to end emergency law. Many have argued that the failure of the UK government to respond in a progressive, meaningful way to human rights concerns contributed in no small way to the ending of the ceasefires. Throughout 1995 a wide range of respected, independent NGOs in Britain and Ireland, including the Committee on the Administration of Justice (CAJ), Liberty, the Scottish Council for Civil Liberties, the Irish Council for Civil Liberties and British-Irish Rights Watch, argued that the failure to respond positively to the ceasefires was an obstacle to peace and reconciliation. They drew attention to the continuing emergency law regime, which had necessitated a UK derogation from both the ICCPR and the European Convention on Human Rights, a regime which itself drew the opprobrium of the U.N. Human Rights Committee. These groups also focused upon the failure of the UK government to move toward an earlier release of paramilitary prisoners, a situation compounded by the deterioration in the conditions in which such prisoners were held in Great Britain.

The report is right to note that many relatives of those killed by paramilitaries have not been told the truth of what happened and that the bodies of their relatives have not been returned to them by the paramilitaries. It does not, however, discuss the similar problems that continue for the many relatives of people killed or injured by the Royal Ulster Constabulary (RUC) or the Army. This is a difficult issue, but one that is being increasingly addressed in post-conflict societies and ought to have been addressed in this report.

The report notes, correctly, that the incidence of complaints of abuse in the holding centers has decreased. It summarizes accurately the available detention powers under the PTA, but its use of the term "judicial review" is confusing and somewhat misleading. Anyone arrested and detained under the PTA can be detained for an initial period of up to 48 hours, without charge. Access to a solicitor during this period can be denied, although the decision to deny a detainee access to his or her legal advisor may be challenged by way of judicial review. A detainee may also be denied the right to have anyone told of their whereabouts for these initial 48 hours. In order to detain someone without charge for more than 48 hours, the RUC must obtain the permission of the Secretary of State for Northern Ireland — not a judicial officer, but a politician. Such permission can only be used to detain the individual for a maximum of another five days, a total of seven in all. At no point in the proceedings is a court ordinarily involved in deciding whether a detention may continue. At the end of the initial 48 hours a person must be released, charged with a criminal offense or obtain the permission of the Secretary of State to extend the detention period. If someone is actually charged, then he or she may be brought before a court to decide the matter of bail. The report should have noted that this extensive detention power has been held to be in breach of the European Convention on Human Rights and has occasioned a derogation by the UK from the Convention.

While the PTA applies throughout the UK and one can be detained for up to seven days anywhere in the UK, the report correctly acknowledges that one's treatment if detained under the Act differs depending upon whether one is detained in Northern Ireland or in Great Britain. In the former, detention is governed by the Northern Ireland (Emergency Provisions) Act 1995 (EPA) and the situation as outlined above applies. In the latter, the provisions of the Police & Criminal Evidence Act 1984 (PACE) and the Codes of Practice issued thereunder apply, and one is entitled, among other things, to have one's lawyer present during questioning. The report leaves the impression that all criminal arrests and detentions in Northern Ireland are governed by emergency law, but in fact the law differentiates between "scheduled" and "non-scheduled" offenses and arrests, and detentions under the latter are governed by the Police & Criminal Evidence (NI) Order 1989, Northern Ireland's equivalent of PACE.

The manner in which the report deals with the issue of exclusion orders under the PTA is partial and inaccurate. Exclusion orders permit a member of the government — usually the Home Secretary, although a similar power is available to the Secretary of State for Northern Ireland — to make an administrative order excluding someone from either Great Britain or Northern Ireland. No evidence is required to sustain such an order nor can it be challenged in court. This the report acknowledges. However, it describes those who are the subject of exclusion orders as "suspected terrorists and supporters," when in fact evidence of such activity or support is neither supplied nor required for the making of an exclusion order.

The report also inaccurately characterizes the only form of review of such orders as an "appeal [which] may be made informally to an independent advisor." The process could not by any stretch of the imagination be described as an "independent appeal." Those who are the subject of an exclusion order can make representations to an adviser appointed by the Secretary of State, by way of a letter and possibly an interview. Finally, the report's failure to even acknowledge the trenchant criticism of this method of internal exile by a wide range of groups and political parties is a glaring omission.

The report should also have referred to the fact that the power of internment without trial remains on the statute books in Northern Ireland. This power has not been utilized since the mid-1970s, when its use drew widespread criticism, but it can be re-introduced by way of ministerial order, without recourse to Parliament or the courts. That such a power remained available throughout the ceasefires begs many questions about the government's approach to emergency law. The report should have acknowledged these concerns and the attempts made by NGOs to persuade the UK government to address them, not least because the U.N. Human Rights Committee, in its remarks on the inadequacies of the measures to protect human rights in the UK, reflected some of them.

The issue of policing is in many respects at the heart of the conflict in Northern Ireland, and the problems associated with it continue. One of the core difficulties is the matter of accountability, and many of the problems during the past year have revolved around this issue. Despite the government's apparent acknowledgment of the need for some reform of the operation of policing in Northern Ireland, little real change seems to have taken place. In this respect the report could have been a little more robust in acknowledging the developing debate, although it does helpfully report the views of the U.N. Human Rights Committee on the matter of the holding center at Castlereagh. The report's assertion that the police are "responsive to and under the *effective* control of civilian officials" (emphasis added) is questionable. Whether there is *de jure* control is debatable, but whether such control is effective in practice is highly dubious. Further, the manifest inadequacies of the complaints procedure mean that true accountability is a chimera. The report notes correctly that "watchdogs" appointed by the government have "no independent investigative powers," but does not refer to the actions taken in the civil courts by aggrieved individuals. While large sums of public monies are paid out each year in settlement of civil actions against the police and army, there are few successful disciplinary actions against errant officers and even fewer successful criminal actions. Dissatisfaction with the existing complaints system is widespread, but despite this no real change in the process is planned. This dissatisfaction is even expressed by the individuals appointed by the government to assess the system, something the report notes in a useful passage which quotes the statistics on substantiation of complaints.

Many of the complaints are about treatment in the holding centers, something that could in part be remedied by audio- and videotaping of the interviews there, which the UK government has, until now, sternly resisted, despite the plethora of opinion in favor of videotaping. Late last year the government finally succumbed to these arguments and announced that they would move toward the videotaping of interviews. The report notes the appointment of an Independent Commissioner for the Holding Centres, Sir Louis Blom-Cooper, but does not note the limited nature of his powers. For example, while he is empowered to make suggestions the government is not required to act on these. Thus, despite the fact that the commissioner (as well as the U.N. Human Rights Committee) has recommended the closure of the principal holding center at Castlereagh, it remains open. This is a familiar pattern in the field of supervision of emergency law: people are frequently appointed to investigate or supervise emergency law and their recommendations are either toothless or, when substantive, frequently ignored. This sort of process has resulted in a great deal of cynicism, to the extent that such "reviews" are often seen as a pointless exercise.

The report states that the commissioner has the power to make "unannounced" visits to the holding centers, but the evidence is that these visits are sometimes known about in advance. The commissioner also proposed changes in the way in which detainees would be legally represented which were widely criticized by NGOs including the Lawyers Committee and British-Irish Rights Watch, but which are not mentioned in the report.

The failure of the complaints process has led, as the report notes, to calls by human rights organizations for independent inquiries into a number of matters, not least the allegations of collusion between the security forces and Loyalist paramilitaries. The NGOs have been joined in this criticism of the process by the U.N. Human Rights Committee, which described the existing arrangements as "lacking sufficient credibility." The State Department report refers to perhaps the most notorious of these cases, that of the murder of Belfast lawyer Pat Finucane, and to the allegations that Brian Nelson, a Loyalist paramilitary and MI5 agent, had assisted in the murder. The report also usefully recounts the failure of the UK authorities to pursue prosecutions of members of the security forces.

The controversy surrounding the decision to release Private Lee Clegg, a soldier in the British Army who was convicted of murder, is also usefully documented in the report, although there are two omissions in its discussion of the case which require comment. First, the report notes that the decision to release then-Private Clegg (who has subsequently been promoted) was taken after recourse to the Northern Ireland Life Sentence Review Board, but fails to acknowledge that Northern Ireland's Chief Probation Officer, an ex officio member of the board, was so incensed by the process by which the decision was reached that she resigned and went public with her concerns. Second, the report claims that the decision was criticized by the "Nationalist Community," but does not note that it was also severely criticized by members of the Unionist community, as well as by many reputable human rights organizations. This leaves a partial impression which deserves correction.

Two other matters of concern are raised in the report. The first of these is the matter of allegations of harassment of members of the public by members of the RUC and the Armed Forces. These allegations range from those of being continually stopped and searched, to rudeness, offensive behavior, and the arbitrary use of arrest powers, to allegations of serious ill-treatment. The wording of the report in discussing these issues is unfortunate. It describes the areas from which most complaints of harassment stem as those "where support for terrorists is considered strong." A more accurate description would have been "rural and urban working-class areas." The report might also usefully have acknowledged the growing evidence that harassment is occurring not just in "nationalist" areas but in working-class Loyalist areas, as borne out by a CAJ study of the issue. The report might also have referred to the growing body of evidence that such harassment does indeed occur.

Second, the report valuably records the use of plastic bullets, which were deployed on a number of occasions in 1995. However, what is startling about the report is that there is no mention whatsoever of one of the most controversial issues of last year — the routing of Orange Lodge marches through nationalist areas and the police reaction to protests against them. This issue, perhaps more than any other, created contention and division in 1995. There is no mention in the report of any of the incidents in July and August which gave rise to serious allegations of abuse against the RUC, many of them supported by media coverage of the events.

In July an Orange Parade was scheduled to march down Belfast's Ormeau Road, to the consternation of the occupants of the lower part of that road, who are predominantly Catholic. After the Chief Constable refused to re-route the parade, which its organizers said was traditional, cultural and religious in character, local residents organized demonstrations against it. These were forcibly broken up by police. The police action was heavily criticized by the residents and television pictures tended to bear out some of their complaints. A similar debacle occurred in Derry on August 12 when residents of the mainly Catholic Bogside objected to a similar Apprentice Boys parade. This protest was also broken up by the RUC, in a heavy-handed and often violent fashion, which was documented by a local human rights organization. The failure of the report to mention either of these serious incidents is a major omission.

The report documents the continuing "punishment beatings" by members of paramilitary organizations — violent and horrific attacks on individuals whom they judge to have committed some form of crime. These attacks vary from exile of the individual under threat of death to sadistic and brutal beatings. There is no question that these attacks are wrong. What is interesting, however, is the tone in which the report records them, as compared with the way in which it details human rights abuses by the state. As discussed above, the former are presented as facts, the latter as allegations.

This tone operates throughout the report, as in, for example, the bald statement that "the judiciary is independent." This does not take into account the serious questions over the operation of the courts in Great Britain as well as Northern Ireland, and the many examples of questionable judicial balance, some of which are helpfully referred to in the report. Despite its assertion that "the law provides for fair trial," there are many areas in which it does not and many occasions where trials have later transpired to be manifestly unfair.

The passages on measures taken to secure equality are perhaps an improvement over previous reports, but still leave gaping holes of information. Here the report tends to regurgitate the official government line and frequently fails to examine the truth. Thus, it records that there is no legal bar on women holding public office, but fails to examine the huge under-representation of women in parliament or government. It claims that the government "respects all extant anti-discrimination laws" when the truth is that the government has been responsible for many breaches of such laws. Indeed, it reports that the government introduced legislation to extend employment rights to part-time workers, but fails to record that this was in response to a European Court of Justice judgment against the United Kingdom. The report states that the law "provides for equal opportunity between the sexes" — a questionable enough assertion in relation to the operation of the equal pay laws, but disguising the reality that the sex-discrimination measures apply only to employment and to the provision of goods, facilities and services. It does note, correctly, that new measures to deal with domestic violence are being introduced, although the legislation to prohibit race discrimination had not yet appeared at the end of the 1995 reporting period. (A draft Order in Council appeared in July 1996.) The latter omission is noteworthy.

In the field of religious discrimination, the report observes that "anti-Catholic discrimination persists in the private sector" as if there was none in the public sector, which is the largest employment sector in Northern Ireland. It acknowledges the efforts made by government, which are real, but does not record the criticisms of these as inadequate. The report records the gap in unemployment rates between Catholic and Protestant men, but does not mention the widening gap between Catholic and Protestant women. Finally, the report acknowledges the rise in applications by Catholics to join the RUC, but fails to record that few of those applications were successful. Nor does the report mention the review of the Fair Employment legislation which was undertaken by the government in 1995 and which is ongoing.

In summary, the 1995 report is most useful in its recitation of claims of human rights abuses in Northern Ireland as well as in the breadth of issues covered. The references to the findings of many distinguished international bodies is also a welcome improvement over previous years. Nonetheless, the tone of the report once again lacks balance and its drafters are again too quick to accept the government version of events as fact. It is especially unfortunate that in the face of much international criticism of the human rights status quo in Northern Ireland, the drafters of the report could only report these findings and not identify the U.S. State Department with them.

S ince 1978, the Lawyers Committee for Human Rights has worked to protect and promote fundamental human rights. Its work is impartial, holding each government to the standards affirmed in the International Bill of Human Rights, including

- the right to be free from torture, summary execution, abduction and "disappearance";

- the right to be free from arbitrary arrest, imprisonment without charge or trial, and indefinite incommunicado detention; and

- the right to due process and a fair trial before an independent judiciary

The Committee conducts fact-finding missions and publishes reports which serve as a starting point for sustained follow-up work within three areas: with locally-based human rights lawyers and activists; with policymakers involved in formulating U.S. foreign policy; and with intergovernmental organizations such as the United Nations, the Organization of American States, the Organization of African Unity and the World Bank.

The Committee's Refugee Project seeks to provide legal protection for refugees including the right to dignified treatment and a permanent home. It provides legal representation, without charge, to indigent refugees in the United States in flight from political persecution. With the assistance of hundreds of volunteer attorneys, the Project's staff also undertakes broader efforts — including participation in lawsuits of potential national significance — to protect the right to seek political asylum as guaranteed by U.S. and international law.

If you would like more information about the Lawyers Committee, write to us at:
Publications Department
Lawyers Committee for Human Rights
330 Seventh Avenue, 10th Floor
New York, NY 10001
USA

Tel: (212) 629-6170   E-mail: comm@lchr.org   Fax: (212) 967-0916